Dear Daddy,

Thank you for helpi~
dreams came true. Or
little house in the mountains &
a stimulating & challenging business
- both would not have been possible
without your generosity & advice.

I love you so much.
xoxo Lucy xoxo

THE
PATHFINDER

Dear Daddy,

What a special fathers day this
year all together, and what better
year for us to be able to celebrate
you and how wonderful, generous,
loving and kind you are. This year
we have all needed you more
than ever, and you have exceeded
all expectations. Thank you for being
you and for rescuing me + Isabelle
this year, we couldn't have done it without you
All our love,
from 2 of your Dorchester
ladies xxxx

THE
PATHFINDER

A.C. ANDERSON'S JOURNEYS IN THE WEST

Nancy Marguerite Anderson

VICTORIA | VANCOUVER | CALGARY

Heritage House Publishing Company Ltd.
www.heritagehouse.ca

LIBRARY AND ARCHIVES CANADA CATALOGUING IN PUBLICATION

Anderson, Nancy Marguerite
  The pathfinder: A.C. Anderson's journeys in the West / Nancy Marguerite Anderson.

Includes bibliographical references and index.
Issued also in electronic format.
ISBN 978-1-926936-82-6

  1. Anderson, Alexander Caulfield, 1814–1884. 2. Anderson, Alexander Caulfield, 1814–1884—Travel—Northwest, Canadian. 3. Hudson's Bay Company—Employees— Biography. 4. Fur traders—Northwest, Canadian—Biography. 5. Explorers—Northwest, Canadian—Biography. 6. British Columbia—Discovery and exploration. 7. Northwest, Canadian—Discovery and exploration. I. Title.

FC3212.1.A54A54 2011   971.1'02092   C2011-905023-4

Edited by Liesbeth Leatherbarrow
Proofread by Lesley Cameron
Cover and book design by Jacqui Thomas
Cover: Detail of map by Alexander Caulfield Anderson, BC Archives CM/F9; portrait of
    A.C. Anderson, BC Archives A-01076; trees by Peter Zelei/iStockphotocom
Frontispiece: Portrait of A.C. Anderson, BC Archives A-01075

This book was produced using FSC®-certified, acid-free paper, processed chlorine free and printed with vegetable-based inks.

Heritage House acknowledges the financial support for its publishing program from the Government of Canada through the Canada Book Fund (CBF), Canada Council for the Arts and the province of British Columbia through the British Columbia Arts Council and the Book Publishing Tax Credit.

Canadian   Patrimoine
Heritage   canadien   The Canada Council   Le Conseil des Arts
                             for the Arts   du Canada

BRITISH COLUMBIA
ARTS COUNCIL

15 14 13 12 11   1 2 3 4 5

Printed in Canada

This book is dedicated to Elton Alexander Anderson (1907–1975),
who introduced me to his grandfather Alexander Caulfield Anderson.

It is also dedicated to my friend Kenneth Crook (1960–2008),
who taught me how to write a better book.

CONTENTS

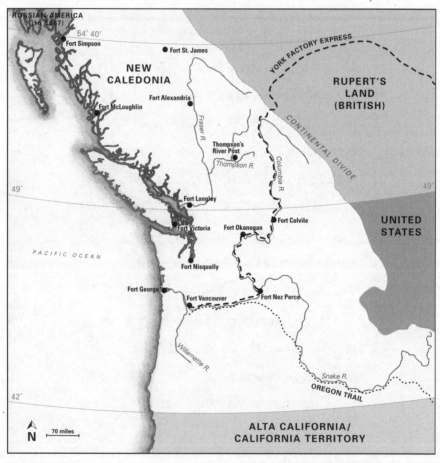

This map shows the HBC forts west of the mountains, as they existed about 1843. NWC partner Simon Fraser built the fort that later became Fort St. James in 1806; the men of the Pacific Fur Company built Fort George (Astoria) in 1811; and Donald McKenzie of the NWC constructed sturdy Fort Nez Perce in 1818. After the NWC's merger with the HBC in 1821, Fort Vancouver replaced Fort George as headquarters of the Company west of the Rocky Mountains.

MAP BY JACQUI THOMAS

INTRODUCTION:
A FISH OUT OF WATER

Two black-clad government officials stood in the charred ruins of the Native village they knew as Ko-omkootz (present-day Bella Coola) and listened to the story the old man was telling them. He talked of men who had explored the waters that reached deep into the mist-shrouded mountains of the coastline his people lived on. He described how his people had watched as the leader of these pale-skinned, ghostly figures stood quietly, with his goat-like face turned toward the sun, and he told how his people watched as this spirit-figure raised a shining instrument to the sun and held it still. Finally, the old man told the two officials how his people became frightened and paddled away to leave these spirit people in peace.

The two officials listened to the old man's story and understood it, because they knew the story was true. In the early summer of 1881, they knew that Ko-omkootz was the "Rascal's Village" mentioned in Alexander Mackenzie's published journals, and they recognized the pale-skinned, ghost-like figures the old man described as Alexander Mackenzie and his voyageurs, who had visited the area in 1793. The Nuxálk people of Ko-omkootz also knew this, and that is why they told their story to these government officials.

No one lived in Ko-omkootz now, and the platformed lodges that Mackenzie had described in his journals were ashes on the ground, destroyed a year or two earlier in a fierce conflagration. But Ko-omkootz was slowly coming back to life. Some of the village's former residents had returned, and .new cedar-plank lodges were rising from the ruins of their old houses.

Anderson visited Ko-omkootz (Bella Coola) in 1881. He wrote that the roofs of the cedar-plank lodges there were carefully made by the Nuxálk so that each board had two raised edges. The bottom layer of boards was placed with raised edges up; the spaces between the boards were covered by boards with raised edges down, making the roofs waterproof.

BC ARCHIVES E-03010 (PHOTOGRAPHER: EDWARD DOSSETTER)

The two men who listened to the Nuxálk man's story were Alexander Caulfield Anderson, the Dominion of Canada's inspector of fisheries, and Dr. Israel Wood Powell, the Dominion's superintendent of Indian reserves on the British Columbia coast. Both men knew the story of Mackenzie's exploration, but only one fully understood the story the Nuxálk man told them.

"The Indian tradition has been vividly preserved even to minute particulars," Alexander Caulfield Anderson wrote, "and it is interesting to note the different aspects which the same circumstances assume, when regarded from the opposite point of view."[1]

Alexander Caulfield Anderson was able to see both sides of the story, not because he was more intelligent than Dr. Powell, but because he had traded for furs from Native men in the territories that Mackenzie had passed through. Anderson had shared many of Mackenzie's experiences for, like Alexander Mackenzie, Alexander Caulfield Anderson had been a fur trader and an explorer.

Anderson had his own history in these waters and it was his fur-trade past that brought him back to Ko-omkootz in the early summer of 1881. Fifty years earlier, he and 40 other fur traders ventured into the same sound that Mackenzie explored in 1793, and on an island in its estuary they built a Hudson's Bay Company trading post, Fort McLoughlin. At this tiny outpost in the wilderness, Anderson had seen the eulachon spawn in a rushing flow of oily fish, and he had watched as the Natives harvested them for their valuable grease. A few years later, on the other side of the mountains that loomed behind Ko-omkootz, Anderson had paddled against the heavy flow of the Fraser River to its headwaters in the Rocky Mountains, and at Rearguard Falls, which finally blocked the canoe route upriver, he had watched the salmon die and drift downstream with the current. At other fur-trade posts in the interior of the territory that existed before British Columbia was a province, Anderson had studied the salmon that swam in scarlet-stained streams up the Fraser River to be caught by the thousands in the Natives' elaborate weirs. Sometimes, in the bright summer evenings, Anderson had carried his own scoop net to the banks of the Fraser and fished a few dozen salmon from its murky depths.

It was Anderson's experience in the fur trade that brought him his new career as Dominion inspector of fisheries, and it was his later career that brought him to Ko-omkootz. Anderson was here because of the fish he had studied for so many years as a fur trader. In the early summer of 1881, Alexander Caulfield Anderson was the perfect man in the perfect place.

It was unusual for him to fit well into the life he lived. Anderson had grown up a gentleman's son, and although he saw his father lose his fortune and grub for money to feed his family, Anderson had always understood that he was a gentleman, in the true sense of the word.

The fur trade was an unusual career choice for a young man of his genteel background. It was far more likely that young Scottish gentlemen of his time would choose careers in the British army or in India—arenas in which his cousins shone. But Anderson had envisioned the life of fur traders of the past, who paddled up wide prairie rivers and crossed mountain ranges to open up new territories in the west, just as Alexander Mackenzie had done.

The fur trade that Anderson found himself in was not the fur trade that had inspired him, and it was not the fur trade that Mackenzie had belonged to. Anderson's fur trade was a business micromanaged by powerful men who controlled all aspects of their territories from afar. Not only did Anderson not find the adventures he had dreamed of, but he never fitted well into the hierarchical and multicultural fur trade he discovered on his arrival. He was in the wrong fur trade.

If Anderson felt stifled by the business he worked in, he adjusted, but he was never content. Nor was he content with his life after he left the fur trade. Anderson built his family a home in the new Oregon Territory but found few prospects in that troubled district. When he moved his family to the British colony at Fort Victoria to seek opportunities among his fur-trade friends, Anderson discovered the new English immigrants who had come to make their fortunes looked down on him and other fur traders as colonials, scorning them for the Native women they married and the mixed-blood children they raised. The modern middle-class Englishman changed the culture of the colony, and not only was Anderson left behind by time—as all men eventually are—but he was also left behind by the changing culture of the place in which he lived.

On the 9th of May 1884
Our dear old Father breathed his
at Victoria B.C. about 3.30 PM
buried him beside our dear mother
South Saanich on Monday the 12th
The Rt Rev The Bishop of Colum
officiating.

[1] THE PROMISE OF
THE ANDERSON-SETON FAMILY

A lexander Caulfield Anderson's paternal grandfather was the eccentric and intellectual Dr. James Anderson, economist, self-trained agriculturist, inventor of the Scotch plough and editor of the magazines *The Bee* and *Recreations in Agriculture, Natural History, Arts and Miscellaneous Literature*. Born near Edinburgh in 1739, James Anderson took over his family's two farms after his parents' early death. This was a time when Scottish farmers studied agricultural science at local universities, and James Anderson attended lectures on agricultural chemistry. In 1760 he sold his family farms and took over the 1,300-acre Monkshill Farm near Old Meldrum, Aberdeenshire, quickly making it a profitable concern. Anderson wrote so many knowledge-able articles on farming and agriculture that the University of Aberdeen granted him the degree of Doctor of Law.[1]

In 1768 the 29-year-old farmer met Margaret Seton, heiress of the Seton family of Mounie, who lived nearby. Margaret was the daughter of George Seton of Mounie and granddaughter of the intellectual lawyer Sir Alexander Seton, Lord Pitmedden; she was descended from generations of noble Seton men who had served their Scottish kings. Margaret was a headstrong young woman. She could have chosen any nobleman in the country to be her husband, but instead she chose the tenant-farmer James Anderson.

Margaret gave birth to the couple's first children at Monkshill, and when she inherited the estates of Mounie in 1781, the family took residence in the turreted house for a short time. However, in 1783 Anderson

Margaret Seton, Anderson's paternal grandmother and the second daughter and heiress of George Seton, died in 1788, in Edinburgh, Scotland.

moved his family to a rundown farmhouse near Leith, Edinburgh's port city, to be closer to his intellectual friends.

Margaret faded and died within five years, and her children grew up in their father's indifferent care. James's affairs were always in a state of confusion, and money was short. One by one the children found their own path, but James Anderson's unloving and neglectful custody affected all of them in different ways. The children knew themselves to be gentlemen and gentlewomen, descended from the fine Seton family, but all were somehow cursed by their poverty-stricken upbringing and their father's emotional detachment. The Anderson-Seton family was difficult, argumentative and dysfunctional, producing many spectacular failures and, in spite of itself, a few great heroes.

The eldest son, Alexander, inherited Mounie, and as he was required to take on the Seton name to inherit, he changed his name by deed poll to avoid the confusion of having two surnames. Alexander Seton was an honorable and hard-working man who supported many of the younger members of his family through their difficulties. Although the business he was involved in had a reputation in London for integrity, it used slaves to harvest its West Indies sugar and the abolition of slavery severely affected the company's prosperity after 1830. A second blow to Seton's wealth came from a lawsuit resulting from actions the company had taken before he was a partner; despite Seton's innocence, his Scottish estate was attached and his personal fortune depleted.[2]

The third Anderson-Seton son, John, apprenticed as an engraver under the artist Thomas Bewick. John learned the trade quickly and showed great promise as an illustrator, but he refused to do his work well, if at all, and was fired from his apprenticeship. He then set up shop in London. His work received much acclaim, but his business fell into disarray and he escaped his debts by sailing to Australia. He abandoned his ship in South America and died in Africa in 1807.[3]

An Anderson daughter, Margaret, married the civil engineer Benjamin Outram. They had five children, but Outram died suddenly at age 41, leaving her no money with which to raise them. Margaret, an eccentric in her own right, accepted the legal help and money that Alexander Seton gave her. Although she received an allowance that supported her family for years and put her children through school, Margaret complained to her sons that Seton had entirely neglected her.[4]

The man who became Alexander Caulfield Anderson's father was Robert, the seventh son, who was born in 1781 at his father's farm at Monkshill. When he was 18, Robert Anderson sailed for India to join the East India Company's army, but jumped ship in Madras. A year later, Robert was acting-midshipman on a Calcutta-based trading vessel that sailed between India, China and Australia—a ship captained by his older brother, William. The sea did not suit Robert, however, and when William's ship arrived in Australia in 1800, Captain Anderson paid for Robert's commission as ensign in the New South Wales Corps of the British Army.

Robert served at Port Jackson on Norfolk Island, at that time a place of confinement for the worst criminals the British government exported to Australia. In 1804 he left Port Jackson for reassignment elsewhere, and by October was at Port Dalrymple, in northern Van Diemen's Land (Tasmania), where his commander sent him on a short expedition of exploration up a creek that later bore his name. Two months later, Anderson defended the impertinent behaviour of a female convict he called his woman. In doing so, he contradicted his superior officer, who sent him back to Port Jackson in disgrace. Ensign Anderson promptly sold his commission and, abandoning the woman, sailed for India.

By 1806, Robert was employed as an indigo manager. In 1809 he married Eliza Charlotte Simpson, daughter of a high-ranking East India Company civil servant who managed the Salsette Mint, near Bombay. A year later, Robert owned part of an indigo plantation near Ruttanpoor, north of Calcutta. He and his business partner, Alexander Gordon Caulfield, had already produced a great deal of indigo.

The demand for Bengal indigo varied, but after 1810 most indigo dye imported into England came from India rather than the West Indies. Anderson and Caulfield soon made their fortunes. In 1817, after an argument with his partner, Robert Anderson quit the indigo business and brought his wife and three sons home to London. Alexander Caulfield Anderson, then three years old, had been born on March 10, 1814, on his father's plantation.

For a few years, Robert avoided the Anderson curse. He settled his family into a house in West Ham, an area of London inhabited by the gentry. The three boys—Henry, James and Alexander—attended Rokeby Academy, where they received a "liberal education," reading books written by great thinkers of the past and focusing on culture and cultivation of the mind. James's education gave him a passion for poetry; Alexander took pleasure in reading Latin.

But Robert Anderson was not satisfied with the wealth he had attained so easily in India; he wanted more. He invested his money in a rope-manufacturing concern and over the next few years lost everything. The older boys were forced to abandon their schooling and find employment to help support the children of the now impoverished family. Thirteen-year-old Alexander became a clerk in the Leadenhall Street offices of Redman & Co., traders to China, and worked there for more than two years.

At that time, young gentlemen generally chose careers in the army of the East India Company or obtained cadetships in the British Army. Indeed, Alexander considered a career in the Far East. But at a London party, he and his older brother James met two veteran fur traders who filled the boys' heads with exciting tales of adventure in the fur trade. The men had worked for the now-defunct North West Company, so they likely told stories of far-travelling explorers such as David Thompson, Simon Fraser and his clerk John Stuart, and Alexander Mackenzie. The call of the West proved strong, and both boys expressed their desire to join the fur trade.

Once again, the boys' uncle, Alexander Seton, stepped forward to help his relatives. Seton was a businessman and justice of the peace who, by 1830, was one of two partners of Colvile and Co., West Indies rum

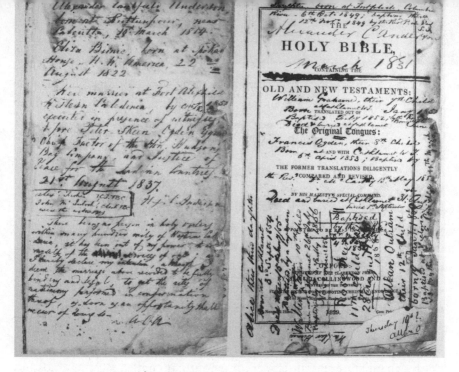

Anderson used this small red-covered Bible until May 28, 1871, when he transferred the family information into his new three-volume Bible. BC ARCHIVES #MAN31A

and sugar importers. Seton's business partner, Andrew Colvile, had long been an influential member of the board of directors of the Company of Adventurers of England Trading into Hudson's Bay—the Hudson's Bay Company (HBC). Through Alexander Seton's 20-year-long partnership with Andrew Colvile, the two boys obtained positions as apprentice-clerks in the Company.

Alexander signed his contract of service on March 23, 1831, only three weeks after his 17th birthday. He purchased a fine gun, a Bible and other essential items, and in early April boarded the ship *British Sovereign* for Montreal. Anderson described the vessel that carried him across the Atlantic Ocean as a "clumsy merchantman, loaded to the gunwales with a ponderous cargo."[5]

Two months after Alexander Anderson said goodbye to his parents in London, his brother James sailed for Moose Factory on the shores of James Bay. In the same year, their impoverished father emigrated to Upper Canada with his family. With the exception of the oldest boy, Henry, now at sea aboard the East India Company's ship *Eden*, the entire Anderson family began new lives in North America.

James Anderson's portrait shows a blue-eyed, brown-haired man. There is no such portrait of Alexander Anderson, but later photographs show a lean, long-legged man who towered above his companions. Like his brother, Alexander had blue eyes, and in his youth his wavy hair might have been the same dark brown.

⇒ ⇐

In 1668 Pierre-Esprit Radisson and Médard Chouart, Sieur des Groseilliers, spent a winter on the shores of Hudson Bay, collecting furs for the Company of Adventurers of England. They returned to London with a rich cargo of furs, and by 1670 Charles II of England had granted the Company of Adventurers exclusive rights to trade in the lands surrounding Hudson Bay. For years the Hudson's Bay Company's fur traders perched in their forts at the edge of the bay, demanding that the Natives of the interior journey east with their furs to trade with them.

Independent Scottish traders in Montreal challenged the Hudson's Bay Company's hold on the fur trade by venturing farther into the interior to trade directly with the Natives, and the HBC followed their lead. In the 1780s the Montreal fur traders merged under the name of the North West Company (NWC), and competition between the NWC and the HBC heated up. Even though the forts were often built side by side for protection, the two companies competed aggressively for the Natives' furs.

On the Saskatchewan River and in the Athabasca district, the rivalry resulted in kidnappings, beatings and murders. Eventually, the expenses of the running battles they had begun became too much for the Nor'Westers. In 1821 the North West Company and Hudson's Bay Company merged under the name of the HBC.

The governor of the new HBC was a short, red-headed man named George Simpson, born about 1792 in Scotland. Around age 16, Simpson had taken an apprenticeship in London at his uncle's sugar brokerage. In 1812 the brokerage merged with Wedderburn, Colvile and Company— the same West Indies rum and sugar importer in which Alexander Seton was a partner, and which would later become Colvile and Company. At Wedderburn, Colvile and Company, Simpson, then about 21 years old, met Andrew Colvile. Colvile encouraged the HBC's board of governors in London to send George Simpson to the Company's trading post at

York Factory as substitute governor, ready to take command of the company should the current governor-in-chief be placed under arrest by the North West Company.

George Simpson took charge of the Athabasca district in 1820. Instead of wasting his time in battles with the NWC, Simpson ran his district so efficiently that he came to the notice of the officers of his own company. When the NWC finally merged with the HBC, George Simpson became governor of the Northern department—the massive territory stretching west from Hudson Bay to the Pacific Ocean.

Immediately Simpson reorganized the fur trade, amalgamating duplicate posts belonging to the two companies, cutting excess staff and reducing the voyageurs' wages. He was a ruthless administrator, rewarding the more pliant gentlemen and encouraging troublesome fur traders to retire. He was decisive and matter-of-fact, a smooth talker who quieted complaints but who nevertheless got his own way. His goals were to cut costs, reduce waste and improve efficiency and shareholders' profits. Gradually, the fur traders realized that fewer highly paid chief factors and more lower-paid chief traders were employed in Simpson's fur trade.

This was the still-evolving world Alexander Anderson entered when he arrived in Montreal in 1831.

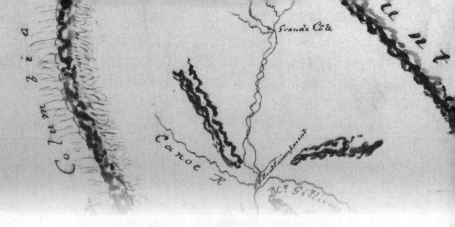

[2] FROM LACHINE HOUSE
TO FORT VANCOUVER, 1831-32

I n the summer of 1831, Alexander Anderson disembarked in Montreal and clambered into a lumbering, two-wheeled, horse-drawn cart—called a calèche—for the nine-mile trek west to Lachine. The post stood at the head of the Lachine rapids, which blocked marine traffic on the St. Lawrence River west of Montreal. As headquarters of the North West Company, Lachine House had once been the busiest place on the continent, its stone warehouse bulging with rich furs from the interior. But the HBC's headquarters was now at York Factory, on Hudson Bay, and Anderson soon realized that his dreams of adventure in Indian country would never occur at this quiet post.

Anderson was employed in copying ancient documents filled with English legal terms and scraps of French, under the charge of Chief Factor James Keith. Now 50 years old, Keith had served the NWC in the Columbia district. To his apprentice-clerks he was a stiff and formal man who resembled a dried spider. After their long workday, Keith and his bored clerks sat down to a glass of Madeira with their soup and port with the pudding. A quick rubber of whist completed the day, and the boys were sent to bed.

When the brigades came down from the Ottawa River posts bearing their furs, however, Lachine burst into life. The French-Canadian voyageurs in their brightly coloured ribbons and sashes pulled their birchbark canoes onto the landing in front of the fort, and everyone rushed down to the waterfront to greet them. Chaos reigned as the voyageurs drank their regale of rum and fought, danced and filled the air with their ribald songs. In the main house, the servants prepared a feast and the guests flooded in from Montreal. "Staid and decorous was the outset of these occasional symposia," Anderson wrote, "but soon the ice would melt, the flood of fun which underlay the host's hard exterior would be loosened, and as if by magic a change ensued, by contrast the most amusing."[1]

Simon Fraser, the NWC explorer who had opened up the New Caledonia district west of the Rocky Mountains 25 years earlier, attended the parties at Lachine in 1831. So, too, did David Thompson, an explorer who had constructed three forts in the NWC's fur-rich Kootenai district. Another celebrator at Lachine was Chief Factor William Connolly, who had come from his post in New Caledonia to enjoy a year's furlough in Montreal. These fur traders, young and old, recounted stories of their past, and the 17-year-old Anderson listened, enthralled.

Barbarous sounds, the names of native chiefs or of remote localities, which if since familiar were at that time strange to me, broke on the ear with almost mysterious significance & then when the cloth was removed songs succeeded: the wild choruses of the Franco-Canadian voyageurs, some of especial adaptation, others the relics of La Vieille France imported by the ancient immigrants, and at last, if the fun did not grow exactly "fast and furious," it presented at least a very warm contrast with the wonted frigidity of our every day's existence.[2]

In spring 1832, the governor and council of the Hudson's Bay Company assigned Anderson to the Columbia district, where Chief Factor John McLoughlin would put him to good use. In April, two flotillas of canoes paddled away from Lachine. The express boats travelled light and fast with papers and accounts for the annual meeting of the Company at Norway House. Behind them came the slower canoes of the brigade, heavily laden with the outgoing provisions and passengers for the interior. One of these brigade canoes carried Anderson away from Lachine House.

From Lachine House, the canoe route followed the traditional river road used for hundreds of years by the coureurs de bois (early French fur traders), and more recently by the voyageurs of the NWC. David Thompson had travelled this route many times, as had Simon Fraser and Alexander Mackenzie. Now 18-year-old Anderson followed the same

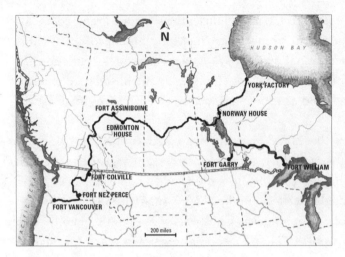

The brigaders left Lachine House, near Montreal, in April and arrived in York Factory, via Fort William, nine weeks later. Then they travelled from York Factory to Fort Vancouver, a distance of 2,000 miles, arriving at their destination in early November, six months after they had left Lachine House.
MAP BY JACQUI THOMAS

route his predecessors had travelled, westward into the territory they had opened to the fur trade.

The brigade travelled in 40-foot Montreal canoes made of white or silver birch, with seams tightly sewn with spruce fibres called *wapete*, and waterproofed with many applications of spruce gum. Despite their delicate birchbark skins, these were tough, strong canoes, ideally suited for the rough river passage, and they carried four tons of freight and passengers.

The brigade leader was an experienced voyageur who chose the camping spots and announced the rests, when the men fired up their pipes to enjoy a leisurely smoke. Each canoe carried a bowsman and steersman—veterans who wielded their enormous paddles to steer their canoes around the many hazards that littered the river routes—and middlemen, who paddled or poled for 18 hours a day. These voyageurs were muscular men, physically suited to paddling 300-pound canoes upriver and carrying freight over the many portages on the route. They dressed in multicoloured sashes and red shirts with decorations of ribbons and ostrich feathers, and sang their chansons to a fierce rhythm of 40 to 50 paddle strokes a minute. The language they spoke was a French patois that included more epithets than the average person was comfortable hearing.

A sharp delineation existed between the French-Canadian voyageurs and the Scottish or English gentlemen who ran the HBC posts. Chief traders and chief factors were, of course, gentlemen, but clerks, no matter how lowly and inexperienced, were also considered gentlemen in the fur trade, and even though voyageurs and gentlemen worked and travelled side by side, in the Hudson's Bay Company the two levels did not mix. At a fur-trade post, the voyageurs never ate at the same table as the gentlemen, nor did they share the same quarters. On a brigade, voyageurs paddled the canoes while gentlemen conversed; voyageurs carried the loads over portages while the chief trader climbed the hill to admire the view and the junior clerks stood guard over the packages. The voyageur erected the gentlemen's tents and prepared the food, but when night fell he rolled up in a blanket and slept beneath his overturned canoe. In this fur trade, a voyageur rarely hoped to become a gentleman, and a gentleman would never be allowed to do the work of a voyageur.

From Lachine, the voyageurs paddled their canoes across Lac St. Louis to St. Anne's convent, where they paused to put in a few coins and receive a blessing. A quick paddle across the Lake of Two Mountains brought them to the mouth of the Ottawa River, which would carry the brigaders north to a point where they could cross the height of land by the Mattawa River and paddle through a series of lakes to the French River and a rushing downriver tumble into Lake Huron. It would take the brigade three to four weeks to make the journey from Lachine to Lake Huron, and another week before they reached Fort William on Lake Superior. This was only the first leg of Anderson's journey to the territories west of the Rocky Mountains, and he would not reach Fort Vancouver before late October or early November.

At the mouth of the Ottawa River, the brigade made its first camp. The voyageurs cooked supper in pots over the fires on the beach and erected the gentlemen's leather tents. When their work was done, the gentleman in charge handed the voyageurs their traditional pint of rum.

The next morning the brigaders began their journey up the Ottawa River, almost immediately tackling the Long Sault, 12 miles of rapids in three fierce sets. The voyageurs "lined"[3] their canoes upriver, while the gentlemen sat quietly in the boats or walked up the riverbanks. Sixty miles later, the brigade reached Chaudière Falls where the water at the bottom of the falls boiled as if in a kettle. The voyageurs brought the canoes ashore below the falls, and as the gentlemen kept an eye on the freight at the head and foot of the trail, the voyageurs carried 90-pound bundles, two at a time, at a dogtrot over the rough trail, so close to the riverbank they were sprayed with the windblown water. Finally they brought the canoes over the portage on their shoulders, and the gentlemen followed them over the trail.

From the launching place north of Chaudière Falls, the voyageurs paddled across Lac Duschênes and portaged around three more sets of rapids and two sets of falls. At Fort Coulonge, the largest and oldest fort on the Ottawa River, the brigade rested briefly and re-provisioned. To the north were more rapids, and the granite cliffs of the Canadian Shield closed in and towered over both men and boats. When at last the cliffs opened up again, the voyageurs set up camp on a sandy point of land on the west shore. Across the river from their camp loomed a black-stained cliff, a special place for the Natives, who tied tobacco to the arrows they shot at the cliff face as an offering.

This was a special place for the voyageurs, too. New voyageurs were baptized in the river off the sandy point, and gentlemen who crossed this height of land for the first time also took part in the ceremony. Almost certainly, Alexander Anderson received a splash of water in his face from a branch dipped in the river, along with a playful request that he never kiss a voyageur's wife without her permission. When the mock baptism was finished, the voyageurs celebrated by firing their guns in the air. The fur trade was a mixture of cultures, and while the mock baptism mimicked the religious practices of the Roman Catholic voyageurs, the firing of guns into the air was a Native tradition.

At last the brigaders portaged around the final set of rapids and pushed up the rock-bound Mattawa River through lush undergrowth that brushed the men's shoulders as they passed. At another height of land, the voyageurs reached the end of their long upriver push and, throwing away their poles, took up their paddles. A portage over rock ridges brought them into narrow creeks they followed to Lake Nipissing, and they paddled along the lake's sheltered shoreline to another portage that carried them into the French River. Once there, the brigaders enjoyed an exhilarating day's journey down the river and into Lake Huron. At this point, the brigade was 430 miles from Lachine House.

On the Great Lakes, the voyageurs often travelled early in the morning and made camp when the dangerous afternoon winds blew. They followed Lake Huron's north shore to Sault Ste. Marie, where they paddled through a narrow canal built many years earlier by the men of the NWC. Their next major stop would be at Fort William, on the north shore of Lake Superior, a few hundred miles to the west.

The chief trader in charge at Fort William (present-day Thunder Bay, Ontario) kept concise records of weather, arrivals and departures, and other important events at his post. In the middle of May 1832 he recorded weather much colder and cloudier than normal. On May 21 a fierce gale blew through, followed a few days later by rain, hail and another storm. On May 29 the Montreal express arrived while the wind was blowing fresh and cold from the north. In early June the weather cleared, and on June 6 the Montreal brigade paddled into Fort William, six weeks after leaving Lachine.[4]

At this post, the brigade men clambered into five North canoes. Smaller and lighter than the vessels they had been travelling in to this point, these were the only canoes that could be used on the small rivers and difficult portages north of Lake Superior. Their next destination was Lake Winnipeg, hundreds of miles to the northwest, and their

These voyageurs are probably carrying their North canoes over one of 26 portages around falls or rapids on the wild and beautiful Winnipeg River, just like Anderson and his men would have, travelling to the forts in the west. BC ARCHIVES PDP00046 (ARTIST: SIR HENRY JAMES WARRE)

immediate route led them through Dog Lake and along many marshy rivers and lakes to wild and beautiful Rainy Lake. After a quick stop for reprovisioning at the Rainy Lake fort, the voyageurs paddled down Rainy River and crossed Lake of the Woods by the Grand Traverse. At Rat Portage they entered the spectacular Winnipeg River and followed its course through winding rock channels to Lake Winnipeg. At the south end of Lake Winnipeg lay Red River and Fort Garry.

At that time, the original Fort Garry, which had been flooded out so many times the wooden buildings were rotten, was in the process of being replaced by a stone fort closer to Lake Winnipeg. The new fort was only half finished, but the brigaders stopped here to pick up the Red River fur returns, which they were to carry north to York Factory. At Fort Garry, the chief factor arranged for Anderson to travel by canoe ahead of the brigade so he could catch up to the boats from the Saskatchewan District to the west as they passed through Norway House, at the north end of Lake Winnipeg, on their way to York Factory.

Anderson arrived at Norway House on the morning of June 27, and by five o'clock that evening he was travelling east toward York Factory with the men from Edmonton House and the Columbia District.[5] The Fort Vancouver men had crossed the Rocky Mountains in the early spring, carrying the papers and records of the Columbia district east to the annual meeting of the Company at Norway House. While the chief factors attended the meeting, the men of the Columbia express continued on to York Factory to help the Saskatchewan men off-load their furs for shipment to England, and pick up the thousands of pounds of supplies and trade goods to be carried back to Edmonton House. As Anderson had been assigned to the Columbia District, he would now travel with the Columbia express wherever it went—first east to York Factory; then west to Edmonton House and beyond.

The Saskatchewan boats crossed Playgreen Lake, at the north end of Lake Winnipeg, and entered the Nelson River, a rough waterway that carried the combined flow of the Saskatchewan, Red and Winnipeg rivers north to Hudson Bay. "The descent for a certain distance from Lake Winnipeg towards the sea," Anderson learned, "by a series of lakes terminating in Split Lake, is necessarily very gradual; thence consequently to its mouth the Nelson rushes with great impetuosity."[6] The brigaders soon left the boisterous river for a tiny stream so blocked by beaver lodges that it was little more than a series of still ponds that carried the boats into the calmer Hayes River, at a place called Painted Stone Portage. The men paddled quickly downriver and within a day or two arrived at the Company's headquarters on Hudson Bay.

York Factory stood on a muddy peninsula covered with scrub willow and saw grass; its docks lay at the far end of three miles of boardwalks across flooding bogs. The officers' store sold goods that came straight from London via the Company ships that anchored offshore. There were flannel and gingham shirts, trousers, shawls, hose, tobacco, clay pipes by the dozen, finger rings, breast pins and beaver hats. Anderson bought a few items he had missed on the journey north—an enamel wash basin, soap, cotton suspenders and a fur cap. He played with the idea of purchasing a sextant but decided against it. Then the wide selection of candies tempted him, and he bought Scotch caraways, candied sugar and almonds. He was only 18 years old.[7]

On Sunday, August 5, Anderson was back at Norway House. He now travelled in a Hudson's Bay York boat—a plank boat, pointed at both ends, that was bigger and heavier than a canoe and rowed by men with oars instead of paddles. These were the boats that had carried the Saskatchewan men all the way from Edmonton House in the spring, and these boats would carry them the thousand miles home. The eight boats of the Saskatchewan brigade set off early the next day, and the Norway House journals report that it rained heavily on the morning of their departure.[8]

The brigade route lay across the top of Lake Winnipeg, where dangerous winds from the south could push the boats into the limestone cliffs that lined the shore of the lake. A gentleman later reported that "much risk was run in the crossing of Lake Winnipeg."[9] In spite of the hazards presented by winds and waves, the brigaders made their way safely to the Saskatchewan River and portaged around the Grand Rapids that blocked its mouth. Anderson described the country the brigade travelled through:

Hence to Edmonton on the Saskatchewan there are no impediments to the navigation of any moment, save the Coles' Rapids, near the confluence of the north and south branches, some twelve miles in length, which are navigable with care and skill, and the Grand Rapid near the mouth, where the river bursts through the ridge of limestone which forms the north-western boundary of Lake Winnipeg.[10]

They worked their way upriver past marshy sandbanks and islands, and later high riverbanks blocked their view of the plains that surrounded them. In mid-August they arrived at Cumberland House. The trader-in-charge gave them a hearty meal and sent them quickly on their way—they still had 600 miles to travel before they reached Edmonton House.[11]

Their next stop was Carlton House, which stood on a fertile plain on the North Saskatchewan River, 1,000 miles from York Factory. On September 2, the post's chief trader noted in his journals that the weather had been unsettled for the previous month. The next day the skies cleared, and the first of the boats arrived with "Chief Traders [Francis] Heron and [Robert] Cowie, Clerks Mr. [Francis] Annance and Anderson."[12] The Saskatchewan boats had left Norway House on August 6; on September 6 they poled away from Carlton House.[13]

To the west was La Montée, where the gentlemen left the slow-moving boats in the hands of the voyageurs and mounted Carlton House horses to hunt the buffalo that roamed in vast numbers over the plains. Anderson had purchased the best gun he could afford when he entered the fur trade, and here he shot a buffalo. At last, after a long and boring year at Lachine House and a difficult journey halfway across the continent, Anderson's dreams of action and adventure in the far west appeared to be coming to fruition.

For a few days the gentlemen returned every night to the voyageurs' camp on the riverbank, keeping the men supplied with fresh meat from their hunt. But when they came closer to Edmonton House, the senior gentlemen rode their horses straight across the plains to the fort, leaving the lowly apprentice-clerks behind with the slow-moving boats. This fur trade was proving to be a far less interesting business than Anderson had anticipated, and once again he was forced to sit quietly while the voyageurs worked the boats upriver.

Edmonton House perched on the top of a high bank that looked south over the broad valley of the curving North Saskatchewan River. The brigade journey from Norway House took six weeks, and Anderson arrived with the second batch of boats on the evening of September 20. The fort employees unloaded the boats and carried the goods into the warehouses to be dried and sorted. In the kitchen, the cooks prepared a huge meal that was served in the dining room, and the feast was followed by a country dance, which everyone at the fort attended.

Work began again the next morning, and the brigaders hurried over a rough trail cut through the forests to Fort Assiniboine, on the banks of the Athabasca River. The express-men had to cross the Rocky Mountains before deep snow fell: there was no time to waste. The Edmonton House post journal described the Columbia express's departure:

> *The Columbia party consisting of thirty one men, besides the following Gentlemen viz. Chief Traders Heron & Cowie, and Messrs. [William] Kittson, Annance & Anderson left this about eleven o'clock for Fort Assiniboine from which place they are to proceed on their voyage in Canoes. They have twenty four horses loaded with baggage, provisions & vegetables in good store, besides ten riding horses for passengers. The party is under the immediate charge of C.T. Heron.[14]*

At Fort Assiniboine, the voyageurs gummed the seams of the boats that had carried them downriver earlier in the year and loaded them with provisions. Then they poled and lined the canoes 250 miles west against the strong current of the rapid-filled Athabasca River toward Jasper's House, on the eastern edge of the Rocky Mountains.

> *Thus on ascending the Athabasca, on reaching what is called the "Vue de la Montagne," where the first grand outline of the Rocky Mountains bursts upon the view, the snow suddenly ceases along the river, and the banks continue bare as far as Jasper's House, a distance of fifty miles.[15]*

Two trails led from Jasper's House into the territories west of the Rocky Mountains. The northern route followed a shallow valley through the mountains to the headwaters of the Fraser River, continuing down that river to the fur-trade posts established by the NWC explorers Simon Fraser and John Stuart between 1805 and 1808. The southern trail led southwest from Jasper's House, reached the Columbia River at Boat Encampment, and followed the river south and west to the Columbia District's headquarters at Fort Vancouver.

Boat Encampment stood on the point of land between the Canoe River, falling in from the north (centre), and the Wood River flowing west from the Rocky Mountains (right). This historic piece of land is buried under today's Kinbasket Lake. BC ARCHIVES A-05428

After a brief provisioning stop at Jasper's House, the men of the Columbia express mounted horses and rode toward the high pass that led through the mountains to the banks of the Columbia River. They followed a boulder-strewn track past a lake they named the Committee's Punch Bowl, for its resemblance to the punch bowl that decorated the table at the Company's annual meetings. From the lake, the steep mountain trail led upward to Athabasca Pass, where snowshoes were always needed. The men crossed this height of land and plunged down the mountains' western slopes, following the steep trail through the waist-deep waters of Pacific and Jeffrey creeks to the banks of the Wood River. Surprisingly quickly, they found themselves on the point of land called Boat Encampment, on the Columbia River between the Wood and Canoe rivers.

It was now October. Anderson had left Lachine in late April. It had taken him six months to cross the continent by canoe and boat, on foot and on horseback, and finally enter the territory west of the Rocky Mountains. It had been a long, strange journey for this young gentleman who had come straight from the cultured society of London to this mostly unexplored land. Anderson's boyish dreams of adventure had been intensified by the stories told by the two Nor'Westers in London, and reinforced by the veteran fur traders who attended the Lachine House banquets. He now stood in the territory where his dreams had led him, but had enjoyed no adventure of note. A long river voyage still lay ahead of him. Fort Vancouver stood hundreds of miles to the southwest.

The gentlemen waited as the voyageurs gummed the rough clinker boats to make them watertight. Soon the boats were afloat, and the gentlemen doused their fire and clambered in. It was late in the year, and as usual the river was low, offering safe but fast travel. Often two or three boats drifted downstream together, needing only a little help from the paddle to keep them on course.

The first Columbia River post reached by the incoming Columbia express was comfortable Fort Colvile, which stood in a pretty valley surrounded by impressive snow-topped hills. After a hearty meal and a renewal of provisions, the express-men continued their downriver journey toward Fort Vancouver, 600 miles away. They stopped briefly at the next small post at the mouth of the Okanogan River (spelled Okanagan in Canada), and Anderson learned to spell the name of this place, "Okinagan," and pronounce it "O-kee-na-gan." South of Fort Okanogan the landscape changed from wooded hills to dry and rocky desert covered with sagebrush, bunchgrass, prickly pear cactus and wild onions. The express-men portaged around the vicious Priest's Rapids with the help of the local Natives. A hundred miles downriver, and still in desert country, they reached Fort Nez Perce, a small, square post built of driftwood fished out of the Columbia River. The fort stood on the north banks of the Walla Walla River, which gave its name to the surrounding district and sometimes to the fort itself.

Eighteen miles past Fort Nez Perce, the Columbia River turned sharply westward and forced its way through a narrow canyon with perpendicular walls. The rapids that blocked this canyon were followed closely by another set of rapids at the Big Island. With those disruptions behind them, the voyageurs guided their boats down the fast-flowing river until at last they reached the foot of the Cascade Mountains, 100 miles east of Fort Vancouver.

This was the most dangerous stretch of the Columbia River. The mountains forced the Columbia through a rocky passage only 150 paces wide, and the river fell 20 feet almost immediately and continued to tumble down rocky rapids, known as The Chutes, as it carved its way to the sea. The voyageurs partially avoided the hazards of The Chutes by beaching their boats and carrying their loads over the narrow trail along the riverbanks. The boats themselves they ran downriver over the three sections of Celilo Falls and into the rapids of The Dalles, where the river continued its downhill tumble between perpendicular walls of basalt for four rough miles. At the two-mile mark of The Dalles, however, the men and supplies waited on a sheltered beach for the boats, for in the low waters of autumn the remaining rapids were a passable, but exciting, ride.

Below The Chutes and The Dalles came the Cascades, a foaming chain of rapids that rushed around a sharp bend in the river and was avoided by the use of a narrow, slippery, four-mile portage along the bank of the Columbia. There were no rattlesnakes here, as there had been on the other portages, for between The Dalles and the Cascades the desert faded away as if a line had been drawn in the sand and the lush green growth of the coast flourished.

Once the difficulties of the Cascades were behind them, the voyageurs paddled their boats down the smoothly flowing river toward Fort Vancouver. They paused on the riverbank near the fort's sawmill to don their colourful clothes before paddling quickly downriver, their voices raised in song. Soon the headquarters loomed above them on the grassy slopes, and HBC employees crowded the banks to greet the new arrivals. Eager for their regale, the voyageurs raised their red-painted paddles in a noisy salute, while the guns of the ships anchored in the river boomed a welcome.

Fort Vancouver stood back 400 feet from the north bank of the river, overlooking Sauvé Island where the Company had its dairy. Forests of pine and cedar covered the surrounding hills, and to the east loomed tri-angular Mount Hood. Inside the tall palisades that surrounded the fort's quadrangle clustered the many buildings needed to keep the district running, among them a bakery, a blacksmith's shop, an Indian trading store and warehouses that stored two years' worth of trading goods. The Big House, or chief factor's residence, was an imposing one-storey building draped at the front with a grapevine, and two old-fashioned muzzle-loading cannons stood prominently on its front steps. Inside the Big House was the gentlemen's mess hall, where Chief Factor John McLoughlin steered his visitors to their places at the table, with chief traders seated near the head and clerks at the foot. The table itself was graced with good cut glass and decanters from England, and its tableware was Wedgewood's best Queen's Ware. Dinner consisted of roast pork or beef, baked salmon and boiled ham, and the vegetables came fresh from the gardens outside the fort walls. Bread baked in the bakeshop was made with wheat grown in the fields and ground in the fort's gristmill. After dinner, the gentlemen retired to the lounge, where they enjoyed good wine, pipe tobacco and lively discussions.

Anderson was assigned a bed in the bachelors' hall, which, though comfortable, was much more austere. He was immediately put to work in the fort office under Head Clerk James Douglas. In the comfort of the Fort Vancouver office, Anderson and Douglas, son-in-law of William Connolly who had befriended Anderson at Lachine, began a friendship that lasted many years.

Fort Vancouver was a fur-trade post, but it employed many more people in agriculture than in any other activity. Fields of grain grew on the fertile grounds around the fort, and herds of cattle, horses, sheep and hogs grazed on the plains. The farm grew bushels of potatoes, peas and turnips, and melons by the thousands. Outside the fort's back gate, the first fruit trees west of the mountains were already producing apples. "The river is huge & navigable for 100 miles from its mouth," Anderson wrote to his uncle Alexander Seton in February 1833. "Salmon are in immense quantity as well as the moose. I have killed only one Buffalo & one deer since I have been in this country and a great many ducks, geese, partridges, etc."[16]

Anderson arrived at Fort Vancouver on November 4, 1832. In early February 1833, he was assigned to help build a new fort at a place called Milbanke Sound, on the northwest coast. On the morning of March 14, the gentlemen boarded the brig *Dryad* at Fort George (Astoria), at the mouth of the Columbia River.[17]

[3] HOSTILITIES ON THE
NORTHWEST COAST, 1833-34

The Hudson's Bay men aboard the *Dryad* were to build a new Company fort in an area of the northwest coast where one of many grease trails connected the coastal Natives with the Dakelh, or Ta-Cully, tribes of New Caledonia. The coastal Nuxálk carried their valuable eulachon oil (the "grease") up the trail, which wound through the coastal mountains to lakes where the Dakelh fished and feasted, and then returned to their villages with the dark, rich furs the Dakelh people trapped. The HBC men knew that this grease trail was the route that the North West Company explorer Alexander Mackenzie had followed to the ocean in 1793.

Mackenzie's reason for his early attempt to find an easy route to the Pacific Ocean differed markedly from that of the HBC. The NWC had once sold sea-otter pelts in China for fabulous prices, and the Company's explorers had searched, unsuccessfully, for a more direct route to that valuable Pacific market. The HBC on the coast had little interest in the China trade, but was intent on preventing valuable New Caledonia furs from falling into the hands of the American ship captains who traded up and down this coast.

The *Dryad* sailed downriver from Fort George toward the entrance of the Columbia River on March 14, 1833. Breakers thundered over the treacherous sandbars that almost entirely blocked the narrow mouth of the river, and the captain dropped anchor in sheltered Baker's Bay to await fair weather. A long delay was not unexpected here. In bad weather, the westerly winds pushing against the heavy flow of the Columbia turned

HBC clerk James Birnie was the father of Anderson's wife, Betsy Birnie. In his Character Book, Governor Simpson described Birnie as a loose-talking liar, possibly because Birnie spoke in a broad Scottish brogue that reminded the governor of his illegitimate birth and unhappy childhood in Scotland.
BC ARCHIVES A-01089

the river's mouth into a mass of boisterous breakers that sometimes broke 100 feet into the air and prevented ships from crossing for weeks at a time.

The 36-year-old clerk Donald Manson was in charge of the expedition. Manson was a red-headed, hot-tempered giant, tall, muscular and energetic. Anderson acted as Manson's second-in-command, and James Birnie, a chubby, 40-year-old Scottish clerk, accompanied them north to Fort Simpson with his Métis wife and numerous daughters. In this exposed and windy bay just inside the entrance of the Columbia River, Anderson met the chestnut-haired child who would eventually become his wife. At the time, Betsy Birnie was only 11 years old, and as the daughter of a Scotsman and a woman who had a French-Canadian father and a Cree mother, she was one of the whitest women in the territory.

After four weeks of heavy weather and squalls, the seas at last quieted and the fine north winds allowed the *Dryad* to slip across a smooth bar and sail westward into the open ocean. Once clear of the hazards presented by land, she tacked north, and two weeks later sailed into the wide estuary of the Nass River between rugged, tree-covered mountains topped with snow. In Nass Bay, where Fort Simpson stood, the captain fired a five-gun salute and dropped his anchor.

On May 1, the *Dryad* and the brig *Lama* weighed anchor and made all clear for the last leg of the journey to Milbanke Sound, halfway down the empty coast between Fort Simpson and Fort Langley on the Fraser River. Eight days after leaving Fort Simpson, the ships rounded

Point Day and sailed with the wind into the massive collection of islands and channels the Hudson's Bay men called Milbanke Sound. The two ships tacked northeast around an island and anchored in Active's Bay (Kynumpt Harbour), at the north end of Campbell Island.

Over the next week, various parties explored the area, but none found a good location for the new fort. At last the ships pulled anchor and swept to a bay 10 miles distant, where the men quickly located a good site with enough wood to build a sturdy post for the trade. The French Canadians chopped down trees and bushes, and five days later had cleared enough land for the cargo to be off-loaded from the *Dryad*. By June 4, the captain of the *Lama* felt it was safe for him to leave the *Dryad* alone to protect the building crew with her guns, and he sailed for Fort Vancouver.

Fort construction was extremely hard and heavy work, and there was no rest for the officers or for the French Canadians who did most of the heavy labour. By late September the men had finished the fort's walls and built several substantial houses inside. The new fort, named Fort McLoughlin, stood about 120 feet square with palisades 18 feet tall and 2 feet in diameter. A gallery ran around the interior of the walls, allowing the Company men a good view over the palisades. In each of the two bastions stood an array of nine-pound guns.

The Heiltsuk (Bella Bella) and Nuxálk (Bella Coola) people quickly discovered the fur traders' presence and brought in their furs to trade. By early October, Fort McLoughlin was secure enough to allow the *Dryad* to sail for Fort Vancouver, and the Company men wondered if this territory was as dangerous as previous visitors had warned them.

On Thursday, October 10, a French Canadian named Joseph Richard was nowhere to be found inside the fort. Richard had been spotted earlier signalling across the palisades to a Native, and Manson suspected he had escaped to live among the Heiltsuk—a foolish choice, as Richard would have little chance of survival.[1]

When the chief, Kyeet, entered the fort to trade, Manson offered a reward for the return of the deserter. On Kyeet's second visit, Manson renewed his offer, but the chief now denied any knowledge of Richard's whereabouts. Manson did not believe him and immediately detained Kyeet as a hostage, placing him under guard in the fort's kitchen. Manson explained to Kyeet's men why he had detained their chief, then ushered them quickly out of the fort and locked the gate behind them.

The startled Heiltsuk assembled outside the palisades and called for Kyeet's release. Eventually they dispersed. A suspicious quiet fell, so Manson ordered his men to keep a close lookout. Manson showed Kyeet around the fort, ensuring he saw the bastions with their big guns. However, Kyeet showed no signs of fear, in spite of being a hostage, and impressed the Company men with his calm demeanour.

Anderson wrote of the occurrences of the following few days:

Tyeet [Kyeet], the chief in question, was a well disposed Indian, as we supposed, and we found it difficult to reconcile the contradictory statements that we induced at various periods of our enquiry, yet nothing further could be done save to retain him until some intelligence of our missing man should transpire. Everything remained quiet and undisturbed for a few days, yet I could not but suspect the untoward tranquility that reigned around. It was a Sunday and not a soul was to be seen outside the fort, save only a solitary Indian seated by a small fire on the opposite side of the Bay. Evening came on, and the men asked permission to go outside for water. Reluctant to do so at that late hour, I declined to give the keys without the sanction of my superior; which being given, the men went out leaving two only within the fort who were appointed to guard our hostage; and one who guarded the wicket. I myself went out, having my pistols upon me, and leaving my other arms where they were easily accessible, for I had my misgivings, and they were very shortly realized.

I advanced to the edge of the bank and was looking around when suddenly, within a few paces of me, I saw darting through the bushes a host of armed Indians. I turned at once, gave the alarm, and retreating to the fort was speedily prepared to defend the entrance.[2]

From the gallery, Manson alerted the men. Anderson stood at the fort gates and fired upon the attackers, keeping the space around the wicket gate clear until the French Canadians could return to safety. The attackers cornered two French Canadians, but one, Fabian Malois, grabbed an axe from his opponent and defended himself with it. As Malois ran for the safety of the wicket gate, Anderson shot and killed the Heiltsuk man who threatened Malois's life.

One by one the remaining French Canadians made it to the safety of the fort, and the gate slammed shut behind them. Only one man, Pascal Caille, was missing and presumed dead. The attackers at last withdrew, but the Company men kept a nervous watch from the gallery. Late that evening, a faint cry rose from the darkness outside the fort's walls, calling Manson's name. The captive, Caille, told Manson the Heiltsuk wanted to trade him for their chief, Kyeet; if the trade was refused, they would kill him.

Manson refused to make the trade, but he brought Kyeet to the gallery to tell his tribesmen he would be released when both their prisoner, Caille, and the deserter, Richard, were back in the hands of the Company men. Kyeet assured the Heiltsuk he was safe, and they returned to their village with their frightened prisoner. In the morning the Natives returned to continue negotiations, and Caille finally convinced Manson the Heiltsuk did not know what had happened to Richard. The two sides agreed that Kyeet would be traded for Caille and two lesser tribal chiefs, who would be held as security for the return of Richard sometime in the future. The frightened Caille came into the fort, weak from his wounds, and Kyeet returned to his men, carrying gifts of blankets and tobacco.

For a while the fort gate remained firmly closed, though Kyeet's men fetched water for the Company men, who rewarded them with gifts of tobacco. Eventually the Heiltsuk returned to their villages. Anderson may have considered the scuffle a normal though exciting part of the fur trade, but his superiors did not. As the Natives had seen Anderson shoot one of their men, Chief Factor McLoughlin decided he should return to Fort Vancouver.

Anderson's replacement, Doctor William Fraser Tolmie, arrived with the *Cadboro* a few days before Christmas. Tolmie and Anderson immediately struck up a friendship, with Dr. Tolmie describing his new friend as "a frank and openhearted young man, well educated and of good abilities."[3] The two men explored the beaches around the fort, skated on the pond nearby and went shooting, and Tolmie reported that Anderson was an excellent shot. "We have unbosomed a good deal to each other," Tolmie wrote in his journal. "A[nderson] intends he says to espouse the daughter of Mr. Birnie's at Nasse (with a halfbreed woman) as soon as she is marriageable . . ."[4]

On New Year's Eve, the men of the fort celebrated while Anderson stood watch on the gallery. The next morning Tolmie and Anderson said

Weighing only 70 tons, the schooner *Cadboro* was 56 feet long with a 17-foot beam and a hold only 8 feet deep. Many Native canoes were longer and higher out of the water than the *Cadboro*, yet this little ship sailed everywhere. BC ARCHIVES A-00278

their goodbyes before Anderson sailed away from Fort McLoughlin on the *Cadboro*.

The HBC fur traders were always interested in the stories of the NWC explorers who had come before them. At Fort McLoughlin they would have discussed the location of the rock, supposedly 25 miles east of Fort McLoughlin, where in 1793 Alexander Mackenzie took a sextant reading. A copy of Mackenzie's "Voyages from Montreal"—a published account of his exploration west of the Rockies, drawn from his journals—had been available for reading at Fort McLoughlin. On his way down the coast in the *Cadboro*, Anderson wrote a memorandum that quoted directly from Mackenzie's journal, comparing Mackenzie's vocabulary with the vocabulary of the Natives around Fort McLoughlin. Anderson would not have realized that Mackenzie had learned vocabulary from the Nuxálk people of Bella Coola, an offshoot of the Salish tribes of the southern Fraser River and Vancouver's Island, whereas Anderson had collected vocabulary of the coastal Heiltsuk, Kwakwaka'wakw and Tsms'yen tribes who traded at Fort McLoughlin.

> *On comparing Mr. McKenzie's (Sir Alexr.) vocabulary with the Millbank words corresponding in meaning, I find two which are the same in his vocabulary as in the Millbank language, viz. Couloun—Beaver Skin and Wattse—a dog—the former of these words he spells as I do, in the other he omits the "e"—making it watts—none of the other words in his vocabulary correspond with the Millbank language . . .[5]*

After spending the winter of 1833–34 at Fort Vancouver, Anderson once again boarded the brig *Dryad*, along with 40 other men, on May 1, 1834. At Fort George, Chief Trader Peter Skene Ogden joined the party, and the ship continued its journey downstream to the river's mouth. Once there, the captain found the breezes too light to carry the ship safely across the bar, and the *Dryad* anchored in Baker's Bay.

Sometime during the eight days of forced inactivity at Baker's Bay, Queen Sally, a Cathlamet Native who lived near the mouth of the Columbia River, boarded the vessel and told the story of a shipwreck. Anderson wrote of this encounter:

> *In 1834, at Cape Disappointment, on our way to the northwest coast, Indians boarded our vessel and produced a map with some writing in Japanese characters, a string of the perforated copper coins of that country; and other convincing proofs of a shipwreck.[6]*

The Hudson's Bay gentlemen examined the drawing and admired the coins, but as they were unable to take any actions, Ogden sent the woman to Fort Vancouver with her message. McLoughlin dispatched Captain William H. McNeill to locate the site of the shipwreck, and the *Lama* eventually returned to Fort Vancouver with three Japanese sailors who had been enslaved by the Natives.

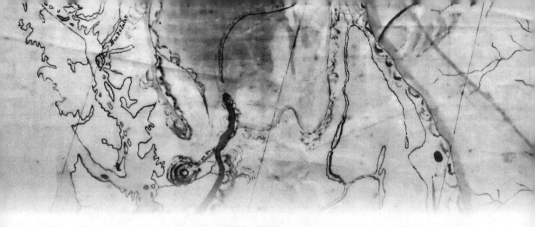

[4] THE WRECK OF
THE *HOJUNMARU*, 1833-34

On an early November morning in 1832, a Japanese junk, the *Hojunmaru*, sailed from the tiny seaport of Tobu, bound for the city of Edo (Tokyo) to the east. The 150-ton *Hojunmaru*, with its crew of 14 sailors, bore fine porcelain pieces intended as gifts for the shogun (emperor).

One day after the *Hojunmaru* left the safety of Tobu, a typhoon struck the Japanese coast. The skies turned black, violent winds battered the boat and fierce ocean waves swept across its deck and snapped the delicate rudder. To save the junk from floundering, the crew desperately chopped down the mast with its tangled sails and lines.

The ship rode out the storm in safety. But when the winds slowed and the waves died down, the crew faced a larger problem. With no rudder and no mast, the *Hojunmaru* drifted helplessly with the northward-flowing Kuroshio Current, the Great Black River that carried the ship into the frigid North Pacific Ocean.

There was only rice to eat once the sailors ran out of fresh food, and one barrel of drinking water stood on the deck. The desperate sailors made fresh water by boiling seawater over fires stoked by wood hacked from their vessel. Weeks turned into months, and dehydration, starvation and scurvy took their toll. Finally, after 13 long months at sea, the ship drifted close to land. Only three crew members—14-year-old Otokichi, 16-year-old Kyuchi and 28-year-old Iwakichi—remained alive. They saw a heavily forested land and gravel beaches lined with curious Natives, the Makah, dressed in robes of cedar.

The Makah boarded the vessel and took the three frightened crewmen captive. However, the sailors were not as far from help as they supposed. News of the shipwreck passed through the Native tribes to Fort Nisqually, where the chief trader sent an employee to verify the story. "Late in the evening Ouvre returned," the chief trader wrote, "and reported that the story about the shipwreck is a mere fabrication . . ."[1]

But the Makah did not give up. A message of some sort was fashioned for the HBC men at Fort Vancouver, perhaps by the Japanese captives themselves. A piece of wood from the vessel accompanied the message, along with the string of pierced Oriental coins. This crude message passed down the coast from tribe to tribe until it eventually reached the hands of Queen Sally.

After they were rescued by Captain McNeill, Otokichi, Kyuchi and Iwakichi attended school and studied English and religion under the missionary schoolteacher. In November 1834 McLoughlin put them on the London ship. John McLoughlin, who had worked for the NWC before 1821, still held the goals of his old Company close to his heart, and hoped that the boys' safe delivery to Japan by the HBC might finally open up that closed country for trade. But the HBC's London directors had long ago given up any idea of establishing trade with China and Japan—the shoguns of Japan, in particular, enforced rules that isolated their island nation from trade with any country but China and the far-travelling Dutch traders. In the end, the three sailors from the *Hojunmaru* were off-loaded in Macao, a Portuguese colony off the coast of China.

⇒ ⇐

"Strong breezes and heavy swell" prevented the *Dryad* from crossing the Columbia River sandbar on May 18, but the next morning the breakers subsided and Captain Kipling ran his ship across the bar. After a short visit at Fort McLoughlin, where Dr. Tolmie joined them, the *Dryad* swept with the wind and tide up the silted Nass estuary and, on June 9, dropped anchor in front of Fort Simpson. The gentlemen abandoned the cramped vessel and took up temporary residence in the fort, and Anderson re-established his friendship with James Birnie and his daughter Betsy.

Six days later the fur traders reboarded the cramped vessel and set off with the small crew—6 gentlemen including Tolmie, James Birnie and his wife and children, and 11 French Canadians—who were to build a new fort on the Stikine River, 200 miles north of Fort Simpson. Chief Trader

Peter Skene Ogden was in charge of the expedition.

The Stikine River flowed west through rugged coastal mountains and a narrow strip of land claimed by Russian fur traders. In 1833, Ogden had visited the river mouth, where he heard stories of the rich bounty of furs that travelled down the Stikine from the Interior. According to the 1825 Treaty of St. Petersburg between the Russian and British governments, the HBC had the right to use rivers that passed through Russian territory to reach their own territory inland, so Ogden planned to build a fur-trade post 30 miles up the Stikine River in British territory.

The men aboard the *Dryad* enjoyed a comfortable journey north, and a few of them noted that the coast appeared less rugged and the mountains lower than those to the south. But the impression of the Stikine as a friendly place did not last long. On June 18 Ogden stood on the ship's deck and stared in astonishment at the collection of rough log buildings huddling on a grassy point at the mouth of the river. Baron Ferdinand von Wrangel, governor of the Russian-American Company at Sitka, had heard of Ogden's earlier visit, and ordered that a post be built at the mouth of the Stikine River to establish a Russian presence.

The HBC men watched as a whaleboat left the new post and pulled alongside the *Dryad*. The four stout men on the oars carefully showed off the swivel gun mounted at the boat's bow. A Russian officer boarded the *Dryad* and presented Ogden with a document stating the British were forbidden from trading anywhere in the vicinity, and ordering them to leave immediately. Ogden paid no attention. In his return note, he expressed his determination to proceed as planned up the Stikine River.

The *Dryad* dropped anchor five miles from the Russian post, and almost immediately another boat pulled alongside. The Company men politely ushered a well-dressed Russian officer into their cabin and served him drinks, and the gentlemen sat down to negotiate. However, there was no negotiation, only a reinforcement of the original threat. The Russian knew no English, but as he toasted his British competitors with numerous glasses of the Company's best brandy, he conveyed the message that if the *Dryad* attempted to ascend the river, the Russian fort would "boxum" them. His unusual word resembled the blast of a big gun, and the HBC men had little trouble understanding the Russian's threat.

The Russian officer had barely left the *Dryad* when the whaleboat returned with another officer and a Spanish-speaking sailor who indicated that the Russians were sending a boat to Sitka to ask von Wrangel for instructions. They invited Ogden to visit their fort, and Ogden chose the two most smartly dressed men—Captain Kipling and Dr. Tolmie—to represent him to the Russians. As the two men approached the point of land, Tolmie saw that the supposed fort was little more than a log house with a false front but, to his astonishment, he spotted a well-armed vessel, its rigging hung with greenery as camouflage, lying at anchor in front of the post.

The Russian officer welcomed his visitors aboard the ship and served them wine, but again impressed upon them that he would not allow them to proceed upriver. When Tolmie returned to the *Dryad*, he described the brawny, well-armed Russian sailors he had seen, and the 12 cannons and 4 swivel guns prominently displayed on the deck of the Russian ship. But his story was interrupted by the arrival of two Tlingit chiefs who boarded the *Dryad* and fiercely told Ogden that he would not pass by their village.

By this time the Company men were thoroughly intimidated, and Ogden no longer reiterated that he would make his way upriver. He took the only feasible course of action and waited for the return of the boat from Sitka. But when the boat returned to the Russian post a week later, it brought the news that Baron von Wrangel was absent from Sitka until the end of August, and no permission could be granted in his absence.

Aboard the *Dryad*, Ogden and his men decided that the combined resistance of the Russians and Natives made it too dangerous to proceed upriver. Reluctantly, Ogden gave orders to return to Fort Simpson.

In his journals Tolmie described one of the Tlingit chiefs. There was no reason why Anderson would stand out among the fur traders unless the young clerk carried himself with the erect bearing of a Seton gentleman whose long family history gave him a dignity equal to that of the hereditary Native chief. But in describing the Tlingit chief, Tolmie compared the Native man to his friend Anderson:

> *He is a tall well formed Indian, rather corpulent but that adds to his dignity of deportment—countenance on the Grecian model, encircled by flowing locks of jet black hair, bushy whiskers, mustachios and beard of the same hue—his dress a fox skin robe—he looks somewhat like Colonel Anderson, but his features are larger—is forward and presuming.*[2]

[5] RELOCATING
OLD FORT SIMPSON, 1834

Ogden sailed away from the Stikine River with a plan. The current Fort Simpson was located in an isolated bay that lay far up the estuary of the Nass River. When Ogden had built the fort in the summer of 1831, he had thought it was a good location, close to Native fisheries and at the end of a second grease trail that brought rich interior furs to the coast. However, in every season but summer the north winds whistled around the walls of the fort and turned its harbour into a dangerous anchorage. Ogden had a shipload of men and supplies to build a fur-trade fort, so he decided to rebuild Fort Simpson in a better location.

On July 19, 1834, the *Dryad* dropped its anchor in a five-mile-wide bay in the outer estuary of the Nass River. Immediately the gentlemen began looking for a good site for the new post—they needed fresh water, level ground and good timber with which to build the palisades. Within a few days they identified two suitable locations, and Ogden chose the first for its better anchorage. Birnie, an experienced fort builder, supervised the construction of the new post, and Anderson and Tolmie acted as his assistants. With little delay, the French Canadians began a vigorous attack on the bushes and trees, and by evening they had cleared a large area, which they surrounded with a barricade of fallen trees. Inside this enclosure the gentlemen set up their tents, and the French Canadians built rough shelters out of branches.

Early the next morning, Ogden set off in the *Dryad* for Fort Simpson, where he ordered Donald Manson to begin dismantling the fort. By July 24, Manson's men had taken apart two buildings and stored them in pieces aboard the ship. The *Dryad* immediately set sail for the new fort.

On his arrival at the fledgling fort, Ogden viewed the progress made by the hard-working builders, who already had 333 pickets lying on the ground. Ogden handed Tolmie a dictionary of the local Native languages and promoted him to Indian trader, in charge of the goods and store. The French Canadians laid foundation logs for the new store and erected the frame of the old building upon them. The new fort was being constructed in Tsms'yen territory, and the Natives were already setting up their lodges outside the barricade of fallen trees that encircled the front of the building.

By the end of July the men had cut, peeled and squared 1,050 log pickets, enough to enclose an area of 155 feet square. In early August the fort builders took a day off and played a bowling game with rocks. Birnie, Anderson and Tolmie first challenged each other to the longest throw. Then the French Canadians joined in the game. A Scotsman from the Isle of Lewis won the prize of a fathom of tobacco offered to the best thrower, but it was the tall, long-legged Anderson who excelled at "throwing a large melle Boule."[1] Considering that the description of this game was written by Tolmie, a Scotsman who may have been unfamiliar with French spelling, this phrase might translate as "free-for-all boules"— boules being a popular French game that involved throwing steel balls to land as close as possible to a small wooden ball, knocking opponents' balls out of the way.

At old Fort Simpson, the men dismantled the remaining buildings and loaded them in pieces aboard the *Dryad*. In the three years the post had stood on this rocky point, the Nisga'a people had not been troublesome or dishonest, though the Company men knew them to be some of the most treacherous on the coast. Now, however, the Nisga'a understood the fort was moving out of their territory, and they showed their displeasure by gathering outside the pickets. A dozen Natives with muskets stood on the hill behind the fort, where they threatened to take potshots through the now flimsy barricade. Closer to the fort wall, armed Nisga'a gathered at a place where they could mount the remaining pickets.

The fur traders may not have realized they were abandoning Nisga'a territory and moving to Tsms'yen territory. Another complication to the removal of the old fort was the fact that, because of fierce competition from American trading vessels in the area, the Company had recently begun to sell liquor to the Natives, and a few were very intoxicated. Two Nisga'a men came to blows when they were given a last chance to trade, and the alarmed Company men decided to abandon the remainder of their product and make their way to the safety of the *Dryad*. Ogden invited two Nisga'a chiefs aboard the *Dryad* and held them hostage to ensure the safety of his men still on land. Inside the fort, the remaining Company men disabled the last of the muskets and left the fort in a group, with one man remaining at the gate. When he abandoned his position, the Nisga'a swarmed into the fort to pillage it.

Ogden released the hostages, and the *Dryad* remained at anchor offshore from the old fort all night. The Hudson's Bay men listened to the discharge of firearms, the yells of celebration and the ripping and hammering of the timbers as the Nisga'a dismantled the fort for its nails. At last, when the sun rose and the northeastern wind picked up, the *Dryad* abandoned the anchorage for the last time, and sailed for new Fort Simpson.

By early September, the new fort was almost complete, 200 feet square with bastions in each corner. The massive wooden gates were six or seven inches thick and studded with large nails, and a small door cut into the gate admitted one person at a time. Three coffins that had been disinterred from the grounds of the abandoned post were carried off the *Dryad* and reburied outside the new fort.

In mid-September, Ogden sailed north to Sitka, where the Russian governor entertained him graciously but remained firm in his decision to prevent the Company men from building a post on the Stikine River. Disappointed, Ogden arrived back at Fort Simpson in mid-October. Three days later the men raised the fort's flag for the first time and saluted the *Dryad* with five guns. The ship returned the salute, and all hands celebrated the occasion with a dram. A few days later, 22 men, including Anderson, boarded the *Dryad* for Fort McLoughlin, leaving behind a staff of 30 men at the new Fort Simpson.

Wind delayed the *Dryad* in the anchorage, and the voyage was plagued by foul weather. On different days the ship's log reported "strong breezes and thick rain," "hard gale, thick rain, heavy sea" and fierce southeast winds, gales and squalls. A journey that normally took eight days turned into a three-week marathon. There was plenty of time for conversation, and almost certainly Anderson approached Ogden to discuss family. He would have noticed Ogden's middle name, as two members of Anderson's direct family had married into the Skene family of Aberdeenshire. Peter Skene Ogden was not a Skene, however, but Ogden's father had been close friends with members of the Skene family of New York, and a member of that family had acted as Peter Skene Ogden's godfather. Though Ogden and Anderson were complete opposites in almost every way, knowledge of their shared family connections might partly explain why Peter Skene Ogden took an early interest in the then 21-year-old Anderson.

Peter Skene Ogden has been described as either stocky or obese, with almost no neck and a high-pitched voice that amused the Natives. The 44-year-old Ogden was lively but dignified, a cheerful jokester who laughed in the face of danger and a natural leader of men. Before 1821, Ogden had worked for the NWC on the Saskatchewan River. As a result of Ogden's active role in the battles between the NWC and HBC, Governor George Simpson had assigned Ogden the worst jobs the new Company had to offer. After the merger, Ogden spent six long years trapping the deserts of the Snake River district until Simpson finally rewarded him with better positions.

John Mix Stanley captured Chief Trader Peter Skene Ogden's mischievous nature perfectly in this portrait, painted in 1847 when Ogden was in charge at Fort Vancouver.

BC ARCHIVES A-01813

(ARTIST: JOHN MIX STANLEY)

Anderson also discussed with Ogden his plans to marry James Birnie's daughter, 14-year-old Betsy. Though Anderson and Betsy had spent time together in the cramped quarters aboard ship and in crowded Fort Simpson, where Betsy lived with her parents, it is probable that Anderson's romance was little more than a friendship that included discussions of marriage with Betsy's father, and the promise of a future together.

≡ ≡

The *Dryad* reached the mouth of the Columbia River on November 27, 1834. A heavy coastal fog prevented a good view of the bar, but the men could hear the violent crash of the breakers. The fog blew away the next day, but a heavy swell rose from the west and the breakers again pounded on the bar. Aboard the *Dryad*, a severe shortage of fresh water and provisions made the men's situation uncomfortable. When a hard gale blew in a week later, the *Dryad* sailed out to sea for safety. She finally crossed the bar in five fathoms of smooth water on the morning of December 12, with all sails out, and reached Fort George on Sunday, December 14.[2]

In the spring of 1835, Peter Skene Ogden was made chief factor and placed in charge of New Caledonia, which had its headquarters at Stuart's Lake. On June 25, when the voyageurs paddled the 9 or 10 New Caledonia boats away from Fort Vancouver, Anderson travelled with them.

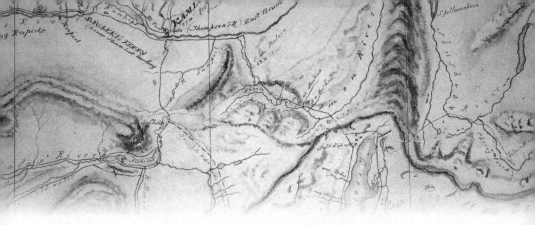

[6] THE PROMISE
OF THE FUR TRADE, 1835-36

The New Caledonia brigade travelled east against the heavy flow of the Columbia River, following as far as Fort Okanogan along the same route that Anderson had seen when he entered the territory in 1832. But Anderson had never travelled this river with the brigade, a much larger and noisier affair than the fast-travelling express. The 60 or more voyageurs and their gentlemen passengers left Fort Vancouver and stopped for the night five miles upriver, where Ogden distributed regale. The hard work began the next morning, when the voyageurs paddled or rowed against the heavy current of the Columbia, choosing a route close to the banks where many eddies made the paddling easier. Once at the Cascades, some men emptied the boats and tracked them upriver with lines; others carried the cargo on their backs over the three portages. That evening, the brigaders feasted on fresh salmon traded from the Natives at Celilo Falls.

The long hours of summer allowed for early starts and 18-hour working days. The brigade began moving at three o'clock in the morning and stopped for a breakfast of dried salmon five hours later. After a second pause in the early afternoon, the men worked their way upriver without stopping until evening, when they set up camp before darkness fell.

In early July, the men pulled their boats onto the beach in front of Fort Nez Perce, where the gentlemen attended the horse races at the Native village outside the fort. A horse cost a blanket, and as there was always a shortage of horses, Ogden traded for as many as he could afford. Then, while the voyageurs worked their way upriver in the boats, the gentlemen herded the unbroken horses up the east bank of the Columbia River.

The horse trail between Fort Nez Perce and Fort Okanogan passed Priest's Rapids and entered red-rocked Grand Coulee, "an extraordinary ravine, the origin of which has been a matter of much speculation," Anderson wrote. "The bottom of this ravine is very smooth, and affords excellent traveling; good encampments are found at regular intervals. After following it for about sixty miles, the trail strokes off for the Columbia, at a point a few miles beyond a small lake, called by the voyageurs Le Lac à L'Eau Bleue."[1] Once out of the coulee, the Company men took a northwest route, swimming their horses across the Columbia River and arriving at Fort Okanogan a few days before the boats.

The Fort Colvile men continued upriver in their boats, but the Thompson's River and New Caledonia brigades left Fort Okanogan on horseback. At Okanogan, the new horses were gelded, and the packhorses that had carried the brigades south in May were captured and hobbled. On the morning of departure, the voyageurs loaded the 200 horses of the brigade, broken and unbroken alike.

As was usual for the gentleman in charge of the brigade, Ogden rode at the head of the column. Immediately behind him rode the employee assigned the job of maintaining communications between Ogden and the various brigades that followed. Following the cluster of gentlemen and horses at the head of the column trotted the packhorses carrying camp provisions and leather tents, in the care of two men. On arrival at camp, these men quickly unloaded the goods and turned their horses loose to graze. Then, with flint and steel—matches were used only to impress the Natives with the power of the white trader—they lit the fires and put supper on to cook.

Behind the provisioning brigade trotted the individual brigades of heavily loaded horses. Each string of seven to nine horses was under the care of two men responsible for the horses and their loads. Loading the packhorses began at four o'clock in the morning and was not usually completed before nine o'clock. The brigade travelled about 15 miles a day, and the pack day, or hitching, ended before dusk so the men could set up camp in daylight. Travel in an HBC brigade was a dusty and noisy affair with the neighs of horses, the colourful oaths of the men, the jingle of the pack bells and the constant rattle of hooves.

The trail led up the east bank of the Okanogan River. North of its junction with the Similkameen, the brigade crossed to the west bank of the Okanogan at a place where a Native fishery flourished. Anderson learned that it was "good policy to supply the chiefs with a little tobacco, to smoke with his followers. Good will is thus cheaply secured."[2]

The brigade followed the trail through open grasslands that provided good feed for the horses. When they reached the western shoreline of Okanagan Lake, they entered a rocky terrain where many creeks tumbled down hillsides and across their path. At the north end of the 70-mile lake, the men passed Lac Ronde and climbed Monte Hills, following Monte Creek to the Thompson's River post. Here the chief trader entertained the gentlemen while the voyageurs released their tired horses and captured fresh animals from the herds that roamed the plains outside the fort.

The brigaders had more than 200 miles of rough ground to cover before they reached Fort Alexandria. Within a day or two they set off up the North Thompson River on the most difficult leg of their journey. The east bank of the North Thompson River was rough and rocky in places, and occasionally a horse tumbled down the cliffs into the river. The men would rescue the valuable packs if they could, but many horses did not survive the falls.

The Traverse (Little Fort), or Crossing Plains, was 40 miles north of the Thompson's River post. Here the brigaders used a 35-foot canoe to carry their baggage across the river, while the horses swam. From the Traverse, the brigaders followed the edges of the hills until they mounted the Big Hill, a rock-bound and heavily wooded plateau west of the river. On the plateau, a swamp, the Grand Muskeg, lay across their trail. Beyond that their path led along the north shores of a series of lakes hidden among the trees—Lac des Rochers, Lac Tranquil, Salt Lake and Drowned Horse Lake. By the time they reached Lac la Hache and Fish Lake (Williams Lake), the brigade was following meandering streams through open valleys that led them west toward the Fraser River. They eventually cut north and west to reach the banks of the Fraser River at the Atnah Rapids (Soda Creek Rapids), jogged around White Mud Lake (McLeese Lake) and followed the east bank of the Fraser north until they reached Fort Alexandria.

The gentlemen enjoyed a few days' rest at the fort but there was no break for the voyageurs. The men unpacked and sorted the goods, doctored the injured horses and released the remainder at the horse guard.

Then they hauled out the canoes that had carried them downriver in the early spring and prepared them for the journey north. Within days the cluster of New Caledonia canoes headed up the Fraser River toward Fort George and the district headquarters at Stuart's Lake. Two weeks later, the brigade paddled into Fort George, which stood at the junction of the Fraser and Nechako rivers.

At Fort George, Anderson left the brigade. Ogden had placed him in charge of eight men and two canoes, and he was to travel across this unfamiliar land to the base of the Rocky Mountains and pick up the supply of leather that was being shipped this year through Tête Jaune Pass (also known as Yellowhead or Leather Pass).[3] They expected this to be a short trip up and down the Fraser River.

⇒ ⇐

Anderson's eight voyageurs paddled their birchbark canoes against the heavy flow of the twisting Fraser River north and east toward Grand Rapids, two narrow canyons that foamed with ferocious waves. The voyageurs quickly portaged around these canyons and followed the meandering river along its forested alluvial valley. It took Anderson and his men 12 days to reach Tête Jaune Cache from Fort George.

For these fur traders, a cache was usually a log platform suspended from tree trunks, high enough from the ground to protect the stores from wild animals. But Tête Jaune Cache was an actual building, constructed years earlier by a trapper who used it to stash his furs and still used by the Company men to store goods that were being shipped across the mountains.

When Anderson's men opened the door of the cache in October 1835, they found it empty. Anderson and a few men began walking toward Jasper's House, 150 miles away on the other side of Tête Jaune Pass. At the foot of Rearguard Falls, Anderson viewed with amazement the myriad salmon spawning there, and the bears that feasted on the carcasses.

The once brilliant salmon . . . may be here seen, the function of spawning completed, almost torpid from exhaustion; its nose in many instances worn to the bone, its tail and fins in tatters, nay its very flesh in a state of half-animated decay, either helplessly floating in the eddies, or with momentary exertion still struggling to ascend.[4]

From Rearguard Falls the men climbed the sparsely wooded ridges to the summit of the pass and followed the Miette River through clear pastureland to Jasper's House, on the Snake Indian River. It was early October, and the express boats had not yet come from Edmonton House. Because the post was already short of provisions, the New Caledonia men set up camp at the lake southwest of Jasper's House and fished for their suppers.

Ten days passed before the express boats finally arrived with 60 packs of leather and five adult passengers bound for New Caledonia—including clerks Archibald McKinlay and John McIntosh, who was accompanied by his wife and children. As the son of an HBC chief trader, 32-year-old McIntosh had 14 years' experience in the fur trade and was the senior member of the party.

The Jasper's House men provided packhorses for the leather and riding horses for the passengers, but deep snow now obstructed the pass and made travelling difficult. It took the party 11 days to cross the mountains, and by the time they reached Tête Jaune Cache they were already short of provisions. At the cache, the men unpacked the snow-soaked leathers and dried the valuable skins over the fire to prevent rot. Then the voyageurs loaded the packs into the canoes and the Jasper's House men returned home with their horses. The first snow of winter lay on the ground, and ice formed on the edges of the Fraser River. Still, severe winter weather did not normally arrive before the middle of November, and the fur traders expected to reach Fort George in safety.

But severe cold descended, and 15 miles below the cache, thick river ice stopped the party in its tracks. For the second time the men lit fires to dry the soaked leather, and McIntosh complained that much time was being lost unnecessarily. When they set off again, they had to portage the canoes and loads around huge chunks of ice that blocked their passage downriver. They were further delayed when an accident wrecked McIntosh's canoe. At last Anderson decided they must cache as much leather as they could and go forward without it. The men made one final attempt to reach Fort George, but on October 22 their canoes froze into the river ice. They were in serious straits. The riverbanks were relatively free of snow but the river itself was frozen solid. It was 15 days' travel to Fort George by land and 15 days to Jasper's House, and they only had food enough for 3 or 4 days' travel. Some men "yielded to despair."[5]

As leader of the party, Anderson considered his options. The Dakelh Native who was their guide wanted to continue on to Fort George, but Ogden had earlier warned Anderson the man was unreliable.[6] Anderson decided it would be better to return to Jasper's House, and most agreed with him. Anderson described their journey:

After a few days our provisions were entirely exhausted. We expected when we encamped to go to bed supperless, and with no provisions for the morning, but no sooner had the illumination of our newly lit fire spread through the valley, when a neighing was heard, and a fine fat unbroken horse which had strayed from the return party, galloped fearlessly into camp, apparently delighted to meet again with human beings. With much compunction, for it seemed a heartless act, we sacrificed the beast, and the supply thus obtained enabled us to go on for two or three days longer. Then suddenly, we fell in with a herd of reindeer, only one of which we shot, and thus from hand to mouth we at length reached Jasper's, under the light of a full moon at midnight, about a fortnight after turning back.[7]

They found warmth but little food at Jasper's House, and realized they must continue their retreat to Edmonton House, 400 miles to the east. It was the first week of November, and Anderson took McIntosh aside to ask that he remain at Jasper's House with his wife and children. Unwilling to spend the rest of the winter trapped in the tiny outpost, McIntosh insisted on returning to Edmonton House with the rest of the party.

The Jasper's House men provided the party with snowshoes and loaned them dogs and sleds for the journey. Anderson sent hunters ahead to shoot animals for food, and at that evening's camp a hot smoky fire cured the meat of six elk overnight. But on the east side of the mountains the temperature dropped to 40 degrees below zero. No one had clothes enough for the cold, and everyone suffered.

Their route lay over the frozen Athabasca River to Fort Assiniboine, but the party split up when Anderson and some hardier members attempted the rough crossing due east to Edmonton House by a direct route, rarely used because of the many burned trees that blocked the trail. This alternative proved too difficult, and when the men reached the McLeod River they abandoned their cross-country attempt and walked the river's frozen surface north to the Athabasca River. Both parties finally reached the safety of Fort Assiniboine.

Anderson and some of his men crossed the frozen portage to reach Edmonton House in late November, in deplorable condition. Chief Factor John Rowand greeted them and arranged that the McIntosh family remain at Edmonton House until spring. In early December, Anderson and a few men retraced their steps toward Fort Assiniboine and Jasper's House, this time with seven sledges, drawn by three dogs apiece, that carried 300 pounds of pemmican. Anderson described their journey:

> *Three of us passed in advance in order to trace the road, while the sledge drivers followed in the rear upon the track thus beaten. Of course, all were provided with large snow-shoes. . . . On such occasions we usually started about two o'clock in the morning, and continued till near sunset, with the solid delay of an hour for breakfast. The dogs used for transport in this part of the country are ordinary curs; the sole requisites being that they combine hardiness under severe cold with a certain degree of strength, activity, and endurance. The sledges used are merely flat planks of Birch half an inch thick, turned up in front, about sixteen inches broad and nine feet of length for load. The load is protected by a parchment envelope which is laced over all with a stout cord passing through a succession of loops fastened along either side of the sledge.*[8]

In six days, Anderson's party crossed the portage to Fort Assiniboine. Two weeks later they reached Jasper's House, where they celebrated their Christmas early and had a day's rest.

Snow fell on the surrounding mountaintops as they travelled westward up the rain-soaked valley, and fresh snow lay eight feet deep at the summit of the pass and down the west side of the mountains. Eight days after they left Jasper's House, they reached Tête Jaune Cache. The men loaded the sledges with leather packs from their cache and walked through a heavy rainfall down the clear river ice, donning their snowshoes 40 miles downstream when the rain turned to snow. Twelve days later they saw their first sign of life when, shortly before they reached Fort George, they met the men who had been sent out to find them.

Anderson and McKinlay continued their journey north to Ogden's headquarters at Stuart's Lake and arrived there in early 1836. From

Sir George Simpson was governor of the Hudson's Bay Company territories after 1821, and governor-in-chief after 1839. His fur-trade employees called him "the Little Emperor," a name he lived up to. Simpson died in harness at Lachine, in September 1860.

BC ARCHIVES PDP02186

Edmonton House, Rowand casually reported Anderson's retreat to Edmonton House in a letter to Governor Simpson, but John McIntosh was not so unconcerned. In spring the clerk wrote to Simpson, complaining about the many unnecessary delays and Anderson's refusal to follow the instructions of his guide. Anderson learnt of McIntosh's complaint, but he did not know that Simpson's immediate response to McIntosh was a letter of reprimand in which he stated that he "could discover no good reason for your return to Edmonton, as you might and ought to have remained at Jasper's House."[9] Simpson then told McIntosh not to expect a raise in pay.

In spring 1836, the traders of New Caledonia heard news of McIntosh's actions after Anderson had left him at Edmonton House. The clerk had been dispatched to hunt for meat with a few other men. At their camp, some distance from the fort, they had discovered a party of Assiniboine hunters prowling around their horses. The men captured eight Natives and brought them into their camp, where they held a mock court martial and executed them on the spot. The news of this atrocity caused "a thrill of shame and indignation throughout the country."[10]

[7] THE TRADITIONAL FUR TRADE, 1836

The Stuart's Lake post (soon to be renamed Fort St. James), headquarters of the Company in New Caledonia, stood on the southeastern shore of a long, narrow lake surrounded by sharp-edged mountains. To the west was Fraser's Lake post. Fort Kilmaur lay to the north on Babine Lake, McLeod's Lake was to the east and the post at Connolly's Lake was far to the north. To the south stood the two posts on the Fraser River, Fort George (Prince George) and Fort Alexandria.

The original forts in this territory still bore the names of the North West Company explorers who had opened up New Caledonia to the fur trade in the early 1800s. Both Fraser's Lake post and the Fraser River itself were named for Simon Fraser, and Stuart's Lake honoured Fraser's clerk, John Stuart. Anderson could not know their stories firsthand, as Simon Fraser's journal remained unpublished, but he had met Simon Fraser at Lachine House, and he would have heard the many stories related by other fur traders. Now Anderson had the opportunity to build his own fur-trade career in the same territory that Fraser and Stuart had opened to the fur trade.

In February 1836, Anderson took charge of the post at Fraser's Lake. This compact and palisaded fort stood in a wide, green valley, open to the southwest and sheltered from the cold northeast winds by a range of hills, close to the place where the Nechako River flowed out of Fraser's Lake. Winter seldom came before December, and in May the ice disappeared and the frost left the ground.

Isolation was a constant worry in New Caledonia, where miles of unbroken forest, rocky ridges and rushing rivers separated the posts. Starvation always threatened: the salmon runs often failed, there were no large animals to hunt, deer were small and hard to find and moose never ventured into this heavily forested land. Over the summer of 1835, few salmon had reached the New Caledonia posts, and that winter fur traders and Natives had starved. Because of the shortage of food, Anderson took an immediate interest in the many rainbow and cutthroat trout the Natives caught at Fraser's Lake.

In early spring the natives catch them by making holes in the ice and roofing them over with pine-boughs so as to exclude the surface-light. In this way the fish, attracted by a lure, is readily detected and speared . . . This device, it may be noticed, is merely a modification of the Norwegian water-telescope; and shows how readily Man, in exigency, arrives through different processes at a common end.[1]

The shortage of food in the Company forts was the first of many problems that Ogden addressed, and he advised the Company men to encourage the Natives to trade their salmon. "At the post of Fraser's Lake," Anderson later reported, "in 1836, 36,000 dried salmon were purchased and stored for use; and at other Posts proportionate quantities were likewise secured out of the superabundant provision made by the natives. The year in question, it is true, was one of great abundance."[2]

Ogden also urged the men to grow more of their own food. The soil at most New Caledonia forts was good enough to grow potatoes and root vegetables and little else, but there had long been a thriving garden at Fraser's Lake, and the fertile soil here produced potatoes, turnips, tomatoes, onions, carrots, beets, parsnips and Indian corn. Rich grasslands surrounded the fort, and cows provided milk and butter. When he had joined the fur trade five years earlier, Anderson had anticipated he would enjoy adventures such as those experienced by the explorers of the NWC—to his surprise, he found himself organizing agricultural work on the farmlands that surrounded the fort, and trading for furs with Natives who were a "peaceful race, well disposed towards their white traders; yet . . . subject to violent though transitory outbursts of passion."[3]

The Dakelh people who populated New Caledonia still bore the names given them by the early fur traders—the Carriers, or Ta-Cully. At Fraser's Lake, Anderson traded with Dakelh men he called the Nâtléhotin (Nadleh Whut'en), the Nechaotin (Nazko) and the Stellâ from the village at the west end of Fraser's Lake (Stellat'en). Over the years, earlier fur traders had created a troublesome debt system that Ogden now changed. The Dakelh hunters received their guns, ammunition and tobacco on credit each fall and were expected to repay their debt over the winter months with the furs they brought in. There were many problems with this plan. Though any excess in the value of the furs over the debt was paid to the Natives in goods, the hunters refused to bring in their furs when they knew they would not receive any goods for them. Moreover, the Dakelh were close enough to the coast that they could easily trade their furs with the coastal Natives for trinkets and eulachon oil.

Under Ogden's new system, the traders forced the hunters to trade furs for their supplies for the coming trapping season, and to gradually pay off debts accumulated under the old system. The Dakelh hunters who traded at Fraser's Lake, and the T'silhquot'in people who surrounded the Chilcotin Post south of Fort Alexandria, had a reputation for being difficult, and this year they caused so much trouble that Ogden ordered the temporary closure of the Chilcotin post.[4] It took four years for Ogden's traders to completely change the old system, and the Natives' dissatisfaction had an immediate effect on the fur trade. In the year before Anderson arrived at Fraser's Lake, the New Caledonia brigade had delivered 4,800 large and 2,200 small beaver skins to Fort Vancouver, well up to par for the district. In Outfit 1835—the months from June 1835 to May 1836— fewer beaver skins came into the posts: only 3,800 large and 1,400 small pelts. Other furs were traded at much lower levels as well. In the winter of 1836–37 the numbers bounced back, and the Native hunters delivered 4,100 large and 1,650 small beaver skins, which may have included furs they had refused to trade the year before.[5]

Anderson quickly learned the rhythm of the Fraser's Lake post. In spring the rivers opened and the men shook out the year's take in furs before packing them for transport by boat to Fort Vancouver. Beaver was still plentiful, but the Dakelh also brought in the furs of the river and sea otter, black bear, silver fox, mink and wolf. The fur trade was a smelly business, and hot weather caused any fat left on the pelts to go rancid. In addition, many of these animals had anal glands that gave off a musky odour. The marten gave off a peculiar aroma that differed from the mild-smelling mink and otter. Bear skins had a faint smell, but fisher skins often had a pungent odour. Wolf skins stank, beaver and fox had almost no scent at all and the stench of skunk skins hung in the air even though their scent glands had been removed.[6]

The outgoing 1836 brigade set off from Stuart's Lake as soon as the rivers opened. Ogden left his post on April 22, travelling by the overland trail to Fraser's Lake, where the brigaders prepared the boats for their journey to Fort Alexandria. Anderson did not travel out with the brigade, but remained behind to take charge of the agricultural work.

In early July, Anderson saw the salmon the Natives called the *Kase* (chinook) leave the Nechako River to flood up the short Nautley River to spawn. The smaller *Ta-lo* (sockeye) arrived a few weeks later and swam through the lake to continue their journey upriver. The Natives manned their weirs, and the fur traders caught fresh fish in the lakes to eat. At summer's end, while the Company men harvested crops and made preparations for the winter, the Natives abandoned their salmon fisheries and prepared for trapping season. They brought in the last of the previous

Anderson was amazed to learn that Natives who fished at the salmon weir on Fraser's Lake, shown here, also killed fish by submerging the barrel of a flintlock gun up to the breach in the water and pulling the trigger. The resulting explosion stunned the fish, which floated to the surface, and the gun never burst as it would have done if only the muzzle was submerged. BC ARCHIVES G-03743

winter's furs to be inspected by the trader. Natives everywhere negotiated with great deliberation and ceremony, and many pipes were smoked by both hunter and trader while the discussion went on. Eventually the trader accepted the Native's furs and gave him the guns, traps and ammunition he needed to catch his winter supply of food and furs.

Not all of Anderson's time at Fraser's Lake was spent at work. Especially in the dead of winter, the gentlemen had a good deal of free time and entertained themselves by visiting between posts, arguing politics or religion and playing music or singing songs. They read books delivered up the brigade trail from the circulating library at Fort Vancouver and shared newspapers that were a year old by the time they arrived in the territory. They wrote letters, business and personal, though it would be months before their letters crossed the mountains and a year or more before they arrived at their destination.

It is probable that Anderson addressed one of his personal letters to James Birnie, finalizing his plans to marry Betsy. His proposal would have left Fraser's Lake with the outgoing 1836 brigade, reaching Fort Vancouver in midsummer. But James Birnie was at Fort Simpson on the northwest coast, and would not have received Anderson's letter before the brigade left Fort Vancouver. However the two men communicated, Anderson understood that Betsy had accepted his proposal and would travel into New Caledonia with the 1837 brigade.

Anderson also filled his quiet time by writing down the stories he had heard from other fur traders. At Fort McLoughlin, he had kept notes on the weather and began a Native language dictionary. Now he wrote for publication in London, collecting the stories he had heard in Lachine and Fort Vancouver and putting them together in a manuscript. When his work was completed, he forwarded the document to his uncle Alexander Seton, who received the manuscript in late 1837 and presented it to a publisher for consideration.

At this time, the HBC faced constant criticism in London, and the directors wanted no attention drawn to themselves. A Company director spoke privately to Seton, asking him to withdraw his nephew's manuscript. By this time Seton had also heard from the publisher. There were problems with Anderson's writing style, in the "constant calling in of adventitious ornament, poetical allusions and inflated departure from plainness and simplicity." Anderson did not receive his uncle's letter until late summer 1839, and it was some time before he absorbed the rest of Seton's message: "A fault of this kind is very natural to a person of your age, and I am sure that a little more experience and reading will induce you to see it and to avoid it."[7]

In a later essay Anderson included a sample of his early writing, which might have come from his 1837 manuscript:

Bye the bye: what be your notion of a Beaver-lodge? The question seems so simple that one feels almost disposed to apologize while putting it. Judging, however, from my own misconceptions of some years back, and again from the marvelous accounts one sees constantly blazoned to the World in print, it may not be amiss to dwell awhile on the subject. For instance, I very recently saw in a work, professedly for the instruction of youth, a plate, supposed to represent a group of Beaver-lodges. Nice little mud cottages with neatly rounded roofs, and accurately vaulted doors, seated on a pretty eminence and shared by palms and other trees of tropical vegetation. The following revelation accompanies the print. "This vignette represents the Beaver, with several huts of three stories high, built on the edge of a clear stream, supported and shaded (!) by tall trees and brambles. The huts have usually two doors, one to the water, and one to the land." And to complete the picture a veritable beaver, perhaps intended to represent the "oldest inhabitant," is gravely promenading in the foreground! What can our old and esteemed friend, the worthy Mr. Wombwell, say after this?[8]—His vocation's gone, Hal, depend on't, the philosophers have usurped it.[9]

Caledonia, 21st August 1837.

1 — Eliza Charlotte, their first child, born at Fort St. James, Stuarts Lake, March 10th 18[?] Baptised at Fort Vancouver by the Revd Daniel Lee — July 1840.

2. Robert James, born at Ft Nisqually, Puget Sound, N.W. Coast of Amerca, 19th June 1841. Baptised by the Revd J. P. Richmond August 1841.

3 — Henry born at Fort Alexandria, Wint[?]

[8] THE FRASER'S LAKE POST, 1837-41

Life at Fraser's Lake continued peacefully, and in 1837 the Company increased Anderson's annual pay to £75. Anderson had already asked for Betsy Birnie's hand in marriage; this year he arranged that Peter Skene Ogden bring 15-year-old Betsy north with him in the New Caledonia brigade.

At Fort Vancouver, Ogden asked the newly arrived Anglican chaplain, Herbert Beaver, to baptize Betsy. But Reverend Beaver had brought his old-country values with him to this new country; he despised the Natives to whom he was a missionary and was disgusted by the gentlemen of the fort who lived with Native women. Beaver was horrified by Ogden's request and refused. He declared that Betsy was a young woman "being consigned to a state of concubinage"[1] who had not seen her future husband in four years. Beaver also argued she was not "acquainted with the principles of religion."[2]

Ogden knew that the last accusation was as true for Betsy as it was for every person born in the territory. He stated he would have Betsy baptized by the missionaries at Fort Nez Perce, and that he, a justice of the peace, would perform the marriage ceremony. This enraged Reverend Beaver. He wrote a letter of protest to Anderson and delivered it to Ogden before the brigade left Fort Vancouver. In it, Beaver wrote:

> As when, I am told, you expressed a desire, that a daughter of Mr. Birnie should accompany the Brigade on its return, you was probably not aware of the appointment of a Chaplain by the

Honorable Company, and of his arrival in this country, I consider it to be a part of my public duty in that capacity, to state, for the information of those whom it may concern, that all such unions, as that apparently contemplated are, now regular marriage may be had, both irreligious and illegal.[3]

Anderson met the incoming brigade at Fort Alexandria, and Ogden performed the marriage service on August 21, 1837. The marriage was probably celebrated with a dram of rum handed out to all the men, and a dance that lasted until morning. Three days later the new bride and groom travelled north with the men and boats of the New Caledonia brigade, and at Fraser's Lake they began their married life together.

At her marriage, Betsy exchanged her childhood name for the more formal Eliza, a name far better suited for the wife of a gentleman. But the new name would not stick, and Betsy never became the gentlewoman that Anderson wanted her to be. In fact, Betsy probably fit in more smoothly at Fraser's Lake than her young husband did, and she had far more experience in the fur trade than Anderson.

Betsy had been born at the North West Company's Fort Spokane in 1822 and was a toddler at Fort Okanogan. When she was five years old, Birnie brought his family to the crowded headquarters at Fort Vancouver, and Betsy grew used to its noisy bustle. Two years later she was living in

Betsy Birnie's very much younger sister, Victoria, was born in 1838 and considered herself the plainest of all the Birnie girls. In 1835, Betsy might have resembled her younger, supposedly plainer, sister.

BC ARCHIVES I-68766

the isolated post that her father manned at The Dalles of the Columbia River, and when she was 10 or 11 she travelled north with her parents to Fort Simpson on the northwest coast. By the summer of 1837 the Birnie family was at Fort George, at the mouth of the Columbia River—a post almost as lonely as Fort Simpson had been.

As a child of the fur trade, Betsy dressed in the simple handmade dresses, leggings and leather moccasins that every girl and woman at the trading posts wore. These practical but unfashionable garments were a mixture of Native dress and English clothing—long-sleeved, high-waisted gowns with shapeless gathered skirts that drooped to the ankles, worn over leggings of red or blue cloth and moccasins that she sewed herself. Before her marriage, the bodice of Betsy's dress would have been modestly high, but when she became a wife and mother, her dress would be cut low over her breasts to enable easy breastfeeding, with the neckline filled in with crossed scarves. Like other women of her time and place, Betsy braided her chestnut hair in a single thick braid that hung down her back, and in public she covered her dress with a blanket thrown over her shoulders. Like every other man, woman and child at these fur-trade posts, she probably smoked tobacco in the elegant, long-stemmed pipes readily available by the dozen in the post stores.

Betsy's life and work at Fraser's Lake would differ little from what her mother knew at Fort Simpson. Though far from Fort Vancouver, the New Caledonia posts carried the same English woollens and the British-India cottons and calicos. Fabrics, ribbons and lace, along with awls and needles for working with leather and cloth, were delivered with the trade goods by boat and packhorse up the brigade trail. Everyone in the fur-trade posts had work to do, and girls learned their needlework from their mothers at an early age. The women sewed their own clothes and their husband's as well; they made hundreds of pairs of moccasins from leather and sewed the caps, mittens and leggings worn by everyone inside the fort and sold in the fort's store.

Women's work did not stop at needlework. They preserved the salmon, gathered berries and dried them, snared small game such as rabbits and martens, and caught fish for the table and for storage in the ice house. Women weeded and maintained the Company's gardens, planted and harvested the potatoes that grew outside the walls of every fort west of the mountains and planted their own vegetables near the house. They also scrubbed and washed the post every spring.

However, when visitors arrived, Betsy did not play an active role in their entertainment. For the most part, these Métis women were self-effacing and almost invisible. They never sat at the table with their husbands when there was anyone to see them and they never joined in the gentlemen's conversations except to take part in a dance. Like other women of her time, Betsy followed the long-established traditions of her Native and fur-trade culture. She remained in the background, walking behind her husband in public rather than taking his arm as an Englishwoman would have done. Although the fur traders did not parade their Métis wives, they were not ashamed of them. These women were not subservient but were strong workers who contributed a great deal to the business of the fur trade.

Most important, the women broke the monotony of the fur traders' lives when no one else was around and provided companionship for the gentlemen, who could not befriend their employees for fear of losing authority over them. Betsy was not a well-educated woman; she was unfamiliar with the world outside the fur trade and could not understand it. But there were many other entertainments she and her husband could enjoy together. When their children arrived, Anderson had the time and the interest to give them the education he felt they needed.

In November 1837, Anderson visited the Stuart's Lake post where, with Ogden's help, he drew up a simple will that left all his money to his new wife. Ogden was a justice of the peace who had trained as a lawyer before entering the fur trade and he assured Anderson that, even in Canada and Britain where chaplains were readily available, a justice of the peace could perform a legal marriage. Fully armed with the facts, Anderson wrote a letter to Reverend Beaver. His seven-page epistle was written in the ornamental style he had not yet abandoned, but he easily demolished Reverend Beaver's arguments.

> *You state that "all such unions as that apparently contemplated are, now regular marriage is to be had, both irreligious and illegal"; I on the other hand, deny, indignantly deny, that the union then contemplated in my case, and now accordingly effected, is either irreligious, illegal, or indeed in any manner censorable. . . . Marriage according to the established usage, has always been in a degree available to the denizens of the Indian country. England*

and Canada, where clerical assistance could be procured, have at
all times been accessible. That assistance, once so far removed, is
now rendered somewhat more available by your arrival at Fort
Vancouver; but to those resident in the interior, circumstanced
as I find myself, Fort Vancouver is scarcely more convenient of
access than, prior to your coming, were the more distance places
of resort which I have mentioned.[4]

━ ━

In March 1839 Betsy gave birth to the couple's first child at the Stuart's Lake post where Ogden's wife acted as midwife. Following Scottish tradition, Anderson named the girl for her two grandmothers—Eliza Charlotte. Soon afterward, Anderson learned he would be reassigned to the Columbia district the following spring, and in December, Ogden told Anderson he was now a "Clerk of the 1st class" with an annual salary of £100. Anderson received Ogden's letter at Fort George, where he was making preparations for his second journey to Tête Jaune Cache. Another man was sent in his place, and Anderson travelled with his wife to Stuart's Lake so he could deliver the Fort Alexandria and Fort George accounts to Ogden.

On the last day of January 1840, Ogden reported in the post journal that "Anderson arrived from Fort George today. He did not come by Nantlais [Natleh or Fraser Lake] but by Nakasley [Na'kaztli or Stuart] River, a far shorter route, and one we shall in future follow—a great saving of time and provisions."[5] Until this time, the HBC men had fallen into the habit of travelling via the Nechako River to Fraser's Lake, then taking the overland trail to Stuart's Lake. While Stuart River flowed out of Stuart's Lake and joined the Nechako River near the Native village of Chinlac, two sets of rapids on the river might have discouraged travel. It does not appear that Anderson discussed re-exploring the river to open a direct route to Stuart's Lake, but Ogden's obvious surprise at Anderson's route reinforces the fact that the HBC men had forgotten many of the routes that had once been well known to the NWC explorers. After Anderson reintroduced the new route in 1840, the brigades from Stuart's Lake and Fraser's Lake travelled south by separate river routes, meeting near Chinlac and travelling together to Fort George.

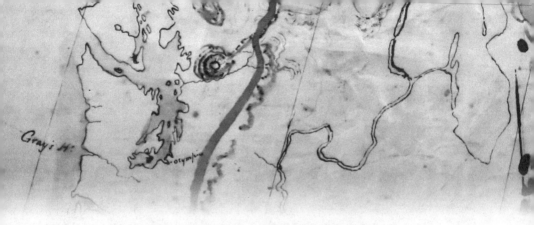

[9] COWLITZ FARM
AND FORT NISQUALLY, 1840-42

In spring 1840 the Anderson family left Stuart's Lake with the outgoing New Caledonia brigade and reached Fort Vancouver in late June. A few days later, Anderson travelled with Chief Factor John McLoughlin to the Company's newly established farm at Cowlitz Prairie, northwest of Fort Vancouver on the grasslands that surrounded the headwaters of Cowlitz River. Anderson was to take charge of the Cowlitz Farm for two months over the busy harvest season, assisting the manager and superintending the men but not interfering with any orders.

Cowlitz Farm formed part of the newly created Puget Sound Agricultural Company. As a result of the negotiations between the Russian and British governments after Ogden's failure to establish a post up the Stikine River in 1835, the HBC had won lucrative contracts to supply the Russian posts with fresh foods. Anderson's abilities as a farmer at Fraser's Lake had impressed Governor Simpson, who moved him south to take part in the important new industry.

At Cowlitz Farm, experienced farm managers using modern farm equipment had already brought 1,500 acres under cultivation. In spring the farm employees had planted crops of wheat, oats and barley in numbered fields that were rotated, fertilized with manure and drained by an extensive system of ditches. Now, under Anderson's direction, more than 60 men worked the fields during the busy harvest season, bringing in the crops and thrashing the wheat in an expensive mill of English manufacture.[1]

McLoughlin then sent Anderson north to take charge of Fort Nisqually, which stood at the southeast end of Puget Sound, half a mile

The original Fort Nisqually, sketched by artist Joseph Samuel Whiting, was established in 1833. Though some of the original buildings remained, Whiting drew this image almost 100 years after the fort was built and long after it was moved from its original location.

BC ARCHIVES F-01282 (ARTIST: J. S. WHITING)

from the abrupt 200-foot cliffs that tumbled to the beach. The aging post's rotting palisades offered little protection for the cramped collection of buildings: storage sheds for crops and farm equipment, the Indian hall and the half-dozen houses built of logs and roofed with bark. Four corner bastions looked out over peaceful grassy plains, and groves of pine, arbutus and cedar provided a green and sheltering backdrop. East of the shabby fort loomed the snow-covered peaks of the Cascade Range. On the fort's north side stood the mission buildings and residence of the American missionary Dr. John P. Richmond.

Anderson soon saw that the farming practices at Fort Nisqually were sloppy and disorganized. He directed the farmers to pen flocks of sheep and cattle in the fields overnight, shifting the animals as the ground became enriched with their droppings. Large herds of cattle grazed on the natural grasslands that surrounded the fort; some were milked so butter and cheese could be produced in the dairy five miles away. English farmhands brought valuable imported rams to be bred with sheep recently brought up from California, and shepherds resided among the flocks in moveable huts on wheels. Potatoes, turnips and other vegetables grew here, as did spring and fall wheat, barley, pease and oats.[2]

Over the previous 10 years, farming had become an important part of the fur trade west of the mountains. Before the merger in 1821, the North West Company had imported much of its food from the Sandwich (Hawaiian) Islands, an expensive proposition for the NWC. In 1824 Governor Simpson stopped such wasteful extravagances and ordered each fort to grow its own food. During his 1828 visit, Simpson initiated the export of salmon and lumber to markets in the Sandwich Islands and California, and five years later the Company set up an agency in the Sandwich Islands, where it sold country produce from the Columbia district.

Agriculture had been well established in the Sandwich Islands for many years, and coffee and sugar cane were already important crops. The latter especially might have piqued Anderson's interest. His uncle Alexander Seton was still heavily involved in Colvile and Company, which imported sugar to England from the West Indies, and Anderson could have seen this connection as an entrée into the business. He believed the Sandwich Islands were well situated for trade, sitting on what he thought might be the future shipping lanes between New York and Australia or Asia.[3] Perhaps for these reasons, Anderson seriously considered a move to the Sandwich Islands. He may even have received an offer from someone who had a business there. When he reported to Governor Simpson the miserably low fur-trade returns from Fort Nisqually in 1840, he also mentioned that he wanted to move to the Sandwich Islands, requesting passage for himself and his family.[4]

In the late spring of 1841, the men at Fort Nisqually received word of some unexpected visitors when a small boat pulled onto the beach below the fort. The ships of the United States Exploring Squadron, under the command of Lieutenant Charles Wilkes, lay at anchor farther up the sound, and Wilkes requested guidance to their fort.

In August 1838, the six magnificent vessels of the Exploring Squadron had set off from Norfolk, Virginia, on an ambitious voyage of discovery. The squadron's goal was to explore and survey all the unknown islands of the Atlantic and Pacific oceans. It had visited the Azores and touched the shores of the Antarctic, before exploring the islands of the South Pacific. From the Sandwich Islands, Wilkes set sail for the Oregon Territory.

In 1841 the boundary line between British territory and the United States extended west as far as the east side of the Rocky Mountains, and the governments of Britain and the United States jointly owned the

Oregon Territory. The American government instructed the Exploring Squadron to explore the territory that the HBC men occupied, and Wilkes sailed north with this purpose in mind. At the mouth of the Columbia River he watched as the massive waves broke across the bar and gave orders to sail for Puget Sound. On Tuesday, May 11, 1841, the crews of the *Porpoise* and *Vincennes* dropped anchor in the water below Fort Nisqually, and Anderson and William H. McNeill, now captain of the Company's steamer *Beaver*, boarded Wilkes's ship to welcome the American explorers. The Company men offered the Americans all the assistance in their power, and Wilkes was soon surprised by their generosity. But the help was not free, and not without conditions, for the Americans were sternly warned not to interfere with the fur trade.

Wilkes asked for permission to establish an "observatory" onshore, and on May 12 the Americans constructed a rough building at the top of the hill where the *Beaver*'s crew cut firewood. The geologists set up their telescopes and pendulum clocks within its shelter and affixed their transit instruments to sawn-off stumps. Other scientists—map-makers, artists, conchologists and botanists—swarmed over the post, visiting the store and gardens and noting the sights they saw in their various journals. One scientist included a good description of Anderson in his journal:

> *I found Mr. Anderson busily employed in trading for a few skins just brought in by the natives; though the value of the whole could have been only 10 or 15 dollars much time was occupied and many pipes smoked before the bargain was concluded. I was informed that furs of all kinds were every year becoming more scarce and that the prices were also slightly increasing.*[5]

The Americans were astonished that the fort was situated almost a mile from its source of water; one scientist noted it could never withstand a siege. However, the visitors soon came to understand the peaceful qualities of the Natives who flocked aboard their ships to trade moccasins and baskets for red paint and looking glasses. So many American trinkets fell into Native hands that Anderson knew they would have little need to trade their furs at his post. The fur trade, he told Governor Simpson, would be affected for some time after the Americans' visit.

The first American landing party set out on horseback to Cowlitz and Fort Vancouver on May 18. The *Porpoise* sailed away to survey Admiralty

Inlet, and smaller boats explored the bays and landmarks in the area of Hood's Canal. Soon all the American visitors were away from the fort. In the quiet of early summer, Betsy gave birth to a second child, a boy they named James Robert.

At the end of June, Lieutenant Wilkes returned to Fort Nisqually and decided to throw an Independence Day party, on July 5 instead of July 4. The Americans had no fireworks, so at sunrise they fired 26 shots from their brass howitzers—one boom for each state of the union—and laughed as the alarmed fur traders rushed from their fort to investigate the noise. To the music of their pipes and drums, the sailors paraded from the observatory, saluting the fort with loud cheers before marching on to the picnic grounds set up near the American missionary's house. Wilkes invited the fur traders to games of football and baseball, and a seaman played his fiddle while sailors danced on a door laid on the ground. At last, everyone sat down to a meal of roasted ox and fresh-baked bread on rough tables set up in the meadows. The speechmaking began after dinner, and the American missionary, who had set up his mission with the considerable support of the HBC, gave a rousing speech that celebrated the region's future in American hands.

The Americans left Fort Nisqually in the middle of July but continued their survey of the area. They named many bays and landmarks around the fort for the Hudson's Bay men, including Anderson Island, where the Nisqually men dug the clay for building their chimneys, and McNeil Island (a misspelled tribute to Captain William McNeill).

Governor George Simpson arrived at Fort Nisqually from Fort Vancouver on September 5, 1841. Anderson was not at the fort at the time of Simpson's visit, and the governor left him a note stating that for "a variety of reasons which it may not be necessary to detail at present, I think a change of management here is likely to be advantageous in several points of view."[6]

Anderson had previously expressed dissatisfaction with his career at Fort Nisqually, and with reason. Under Peter Skene Ogden, Anderson had enjoyed his independence, but in the Columbia District McLoughlin ruled with an iron fist. The chief factor was a "man of great force of character, somewhat domineering and of strong opinions."[7] Anderson was not used to blindly obeying orders, and it was hard for him to receive McLoughlin's many politely worded but terse, detailed letters of instructions—instructions Anderson did not always follow to the letter. On one occasion when McLoughlin wrote to inquire why Anderson had deviated from his orders, Anderson responded with a hot-tempered letter of his own. James Douglas immediately rebuked Anderson for his "warm expostulatory style, which I regret is neither proper nor respectful." McLoughlin had intended to punish Anderson, but Douglas had intervened, arguing that Anderson's error was one of manner and not of intent. Douglas finished his note with a stern warning, "You have got to learn at this hour, that obedience is the very first and most important of our duties."[8]

Douglas had warned Anderson that "it has been said within the circle of Batchelor's Hall that you are unpopular with the Indians of Nisqually."[9] Captain McNeill had also reported to McLoughlin that "very little fur makes its appearance at this place however I have seen some Beaver brought here and taken away again."[10] It appears that Anderson was too severe with the Native hunters, who chose to stay away from the fort. He was probably using the trading practices he had learned in New Caledonia, where Ogden and his fur traders had to forcibly change the old debt system. But that debt system had never existed at Fort Nisqually, and the Natives resented Anderson for the hard bargains he thought he had to drive.

Chief Factor John McLoughlin was described by Anderson's son James as "the Big Doctor" who could argue with anyone and be friends again within 48 hours. BC ARCHIVES A-01637

Another incident forced the decision to remove Anderson from Nisqually. Anderson had quarrelled with a French-Canadian employee, Sauveur St. Martin, because the man had not carried out his orders promptly and cheerfully; now St. Martin refused to remain at Fort Nisqually. James Douglas, John McLoughlin and Captain McNeill all felt that Anderson's "recent conduct in reference to St. Martin has been exceeding improper."[11] It is possible that Anderson struck the man—a punishment common in New Caledonia but one of which Chief Factor McLoughlin strongly disapproved.

After receiving Simpson's note, Anderson packed up his belongings and rode away from Fort Nisqually. He spent the winter at Fort Vancouver under McLoughlin's disapproving eye and in the spring led the annual express up the Columbia River toward York Factory.

The ships at anchor in front of the fort fired noisy salutes as the 20 or so voyageurs paddled away from Fort Vancouver. It would be early November before they returned, and Anderson would not be with them. He had been reassigned to New Caledonia, the Siberia of the fur trade.

[10] THE YORK FACTORY EXPRESS, 1842

The express boats arrived at Fort Colvile on April 17, 1842, and after installing his family in their room in the fort, where they would remain until his return in the fall, Anderson began preparations for the long journey across the continent to York Factory. The closing of the year's business delayed the express's departure until April 24, and when it finally got underway, there were further delays. Rain caused the Columbia River to flood between the Upper Arrow Lakes and the vicious rapids called Les Dalles des Morts. Anderson later reported that the Hudson's Bay express boats generally reached Boat Encampment in 10 days. "In 1842 I . . . reached the mountains only on the twelfth day, though my boats were unusually well manned with Canadian and other voyageurs, and the most expert Iroquois conductors."[1]

From Boat Encampment, the voyageurs led the outgoing passengers over the steep trail that climbed the west side of the Rocky Mountains. From Jasper's House, the express party travelled by boat down the rapid-filled Athabasca River to Fort Assiniboine, and then on horseback across the portage to Edmonton House. Once at Edmonton House, Anderson traded two dressed skins for a cotton handkerchief, white duffle and strouds.[2] Both Belgian-made duffle and English strouds were coarse, thick, woollen materials used for making the coats the fur traders wore. Now 28 years old, Anderson no longer spent his money on candies and almonds as he had the first year he crossed the country.

This year, all 21 boats of the combined York Factory express and the Saskatchewan brigade arrived at Norway House on the morning of June 20.

Anderson remained behind to attend the annual governor and council meeting, while the Saskatchewan boats continued their journey to York Factory. On July 1 Anderson also left Norway House in a light canoe, travelling toward York Factory.[3]

The gentlemen arrived at York Factory on July 7, five days after the Saskatchewan boats.[4] On the raw, cold morning of July 16, Anderson left the Factory, travelling upriver through rain and fog in one of the 10 Saskatchewan boats and arriving at Norway House on July 31. Three days later, he set off on the next stage of his long journey west on a sultry day with a light south breeze running up the lake.[5]

Some months after Anderson left York Factory, the chief factor's wife wrote a gossipy letter that included a tidbit of information about Anderson:

The gentlemen here are too apt to thrash and indeed point their guns at their men and Mr. Anderson, who came across from Vancouver last year was so detested that they confessed that if he had fallen into the river, not one would have held out a stick to him.[6]

At first glance it is hard to understand why Anderson was so detested by the voyageurs. In 1842 he was a relative stranger to them and none knew him personally. But while no one now knows the details of the incident that caused Anderson's removal from Fort Nisqually, they would have been familiar to the Columbia district voyageurs he travelled with, and Anderson's offence—his argument with St. Martin—was likely so severe that nothing could have made them like him.

Moreover, the descriptions of Anderson that survive suggest he was not an easy man to know or like. The voyageurs loved Peter Skene Ogden because he was an open, friendly man who liked practical jokes—they called him M'Sieu Pete. But Anderson would have rejected the familiarity that Ogden encouraged. Though William Tolmie described Anderson as a frank and open young man in 1833, fur traders of later years had quite a different impression of him. One of the best depictions of Anderson as leader of a brigade or express comes from his son James, who accompanied his father on a later brigade:

In spite of the fact that the horses are hobbled, it sometimes happens owing perhaps to scarcity of feed or an extraordinary pestilence of flies and mosquitos, that they will wander far afield and before they can be rounded up, perhaps half a day is lost. The impatience of the gentleman in charge under such circumstances can better be imagined than described; as he would glance every few minutes at his watch and impotently pace the camp ground probably thinking unutterable things. The esprit de corps amongst the officers of the company was remarkable, loyalty to the general interests and the determination not to be out-done in the success and expedition in the discharge of their duties was the invariable characteristic of every officer. It can therefore, be readily realized that such circumstances as I relate, although utterly beyond his control, had the effect of considerably destroying the equanimity of mind of the officer in charge.[7]

The hard-working voyageurs would not have been tolerant of Anderson's impatience during the difficult 1842 passage up the rain-flooded Columbia River, especially if he expressed his frustration by constantly checking his watch. And this was not the only habit that might have upset the voyageurs; he might also have offended by not responding to their jokes or sallies, or by keeping his distance from them. In later years, another fur trader described Anderson as "one of the most intelligent and efficient officers in the area. I at first thought him rather proud, and restrained, but he is not so, excepting with people who assume too much."[8]

Chief Factor McLoughlin may have given Anderson the job of taking the 1842 express to York Factory to teach him the value of treating his employees well. If so, it was a lesson that Anderson learned. In later years, his employees remained loyal to the Company in spite of the many temptations vying for their attention in those times, which drew employees away from other posts in the district.

⇒ ⇐

Anderson returned to Fort Colvile with the express boats at the end of October. He and his family left the fort on horseback, riding in front of four men new to the territory and some heavily laden brigade horses. Their path led them north and west along the Kettle River, past Rock Creek and over the strip of gravel that crossed Osoyoos Lake.[9] On November 3, Anderson's party arrived at the old Thompson's River post, where Chief Trader John Tod was newly installed. Already Tod's men were constructing a new post on the northwest corner of the river junction opposite the old fort.[10]

On November 5 Anderson's group began their journey to Fort Alexandria, 200 miles to the northwest. One of the two men who accompanied Anderson was Michel Ogden, Peter Skene Ogden's son, now a clerk in the fur trade. Ogden and the other Thompson's River man guided Anderson toward Fort Alexandria by a Native trail that appeared, in part, on the maps of that time. This trail was seen as a possible alternative to the trail over the Thompson plateau, and Anderson may have been asked to decide whether it should become the Company's brigade trail.

The route led west from the Thompson's River fort to the mouth of Copper Creek, which flowed into the north side of Kamloops Lake. The party followed Copper Creek north, crossing several ridges to Criss Creek and eventually fording Rivière du Défunt (Deadman's River) at its upper end. From there they followed the trails north and west, passing by the east end of Loon Lake and the west end of Green Lake. At Bridge Creek they joined the old brigade trail west of Drowned Horse Lake, and followed it past Lac la Hache and Fish Lake. On November 13, Anderson and his men arrived at Fort Alexandria in intensely cold weather.

Now called Death Rapids, Les Dalles des Morts earned its name when, in 1817, seven Nor'Westers drowned here on their return from Boat Encampment.

BC ARCHIVES PDP00057 (ARTIST: SIR HENRY JAMES WARRE, 1846)

[11] THE SIBERIA
OF THE FUR TRADE, 1842-43

Fort Alexandria had been named for Alexander Mackenzie. In 1793 the North West Company explorer had paused on the banks of the Fraser River, near where the fort later stood, and listened while the Natives told him of a river trail that led westward to the sea. Mackenzie had taken the Natives' advice to avoid the dangerous rapids of the lower Fraser, but before he returned north to find his West Road River (Blackwater River), he carved his name and the date into a nearby tree trunk. Whether the NWC men who built Fort Alexandria ever found the tree is unknown, but Anderson never mentioned it.

Fort Alexandria originally stood on the east bank of the river but had been rebuilt on a low flat on the Fraser's west bank. From the fort gates, the Fort Alexandria men looked across the river at the fine open plains rising in gentle steps through scattered groves of fir and poplar, and meadows of long grass and wildflowers. None of the other northern posts boasted such fine agricultural land, and Fort Alexandria was valuable as a place to pasture many of the horses used in the HBC brigades.

Donald McLean, the fort's red-headed clerk, welcomed Anderson to Fort Alexandria, and Anderson's family settled into the crowded dwelling house. Reverend Modeste Demers, the first missionary to penetrate into New Caledonia, was a temporary resident of Fort Alexandria's gentleman's house. He had travelled north with Ogden's brigade in the summer, and when he passed through Fort Alexandria he had encouraged the Dakelh people of the area to build their own church outside the walls of the fort. Now Demers was back at the fort, and the Natives' rough building of worship stood almost complete.

On November 17 the men squared timbers for an addition to the gentleman's house. The following day Anderson took charge of the fort, and McLean set off for the Chilcotin post to the south. Winter arrived early and hard, and Anderson sent men to find firewood upriver. Some employees hauled timbers while another searched for a missing horse, a necessary task that Anderson would find wasted much time at this place. Michel Ogden and a Native boy secured the barley safe from rats while the carpenter cleaned his shop. "I'm out of breath with this long enumeration," Anderson wrote in the post journal, "and shall in future confine my remarks to general topics!"[1]

There was good reason to limit the number and length of entries in the post journals. Everything imported into this isolated district was carried 1,000 miles by boat and horseback from the warehouses of Fort Vancouver, including the ledgers used to keep track of company business, the paper and the ink cakes. Journal entries were often written with watered-down ink as the trader preserved what little remained at the post, and there were times when he could make no journal entries at all because his ink was used up.

The chief of the Dakelh village near the fort was Anderson's first official visitor, and Anderson presented him with the annual gift of tobacco. When he learned that the chief was preparing for a hunting trip with his men, he encouraged them to trap the small fur-bearing animals. Under Peter Skene Ogden, it had become policy to encourage Native hunters to trap marten and similar furs rather than concentrating on the beaver, which, even here, was becoming scarce.

As at Fraser's Lake, the Dakelh or Ta-Cully Natives lived in the area immediately around Fort Alexandria. According to Anderson, the northern boundary of their territory was at the mouth of Quesnel's River, while the southern lay at White Mud Lake. South of White Mud Lake was "Shewhapmuch" (Secwepemc) territory. It made little difference to the Hudson's Bay men what the Secwepemc people called themselves—at Fort Alexandria they were known only by the Dakelh word for "stranger": Atnah.

Work continued as usual at Fort Alexandria, and when snow fell in late November, replacing the rotting fort timbers became a priority. Some men cut wood or hauled timbers, while others sawed logs to build a boat, or dug a hole for the new "necessary," or outhouse. One man camped at the horse guard across the river, where he tended the horses and maintained the fenced pens. On a warm and thawing Christmas Eve day, Anderson gave his employees a half-day off and handed out their regale of pork and horse meat.

Work continued on the gentleman's house after Christmas, and Anderson moved his family into their new private quarters at the end of December. On New Year's Eve the men celebrated another holiday, and Anderson set up a shooting contest between the Dakelh men and the employees of the fort. A set of leggings was the prize for the best shot, but almost everyone shot poorly because of the extreme cold. For the most part, the French Canadians made better shots than the Natives, but a Dakelh man named Grand Corps carried off Anderson's prize for the best shot made that day.

There were many fantastic names at Fort Alexandria. The voyageurs gave French names to all the horses and to all the Natives they dealt with, and few of the names were complimentary. An old man named Tout-Laid (All Ugly) worked at the fort and often cared for the Anderson children. Another man with a rotund shape was Gros Ventre (Large Belly), and they called an old man suspected of cannibalism Mangeur de Monde (Eater of the World). The horses carried names such as Patte Croche (Trip-up) and Cendre Wapiti (Grey Elk), and an untameable horse with a vicious temper was called Misère du Monde (Poverty of the World). Anderson's son James rode a strawberry roan that bore the name Petite Cendre (Little Cinder).

In January, Reverend Demers left Fort Alexandria to visit the Secwepemc, and the men built doors for the new houses and cut firewood. Snow fell. Anderson sent two men to bring horses across the river, which was beginning to freeze over. The men crossed at a spot where the ice was too thin, and a valuable mare plunged through and was drowned. Eventually an employee herded the remaining horses safely across the river on solid ice, during a snowstorm.

Anderson discovered that the fort's returns had declined drastically in the previous few years. He was able to increase the trade of furs, mostly by encouraging the Natives to trap marten and other small fur-bearing animals. "Yet," he wrote to Governor Simpson, "upon the whole the result is deplorable."[2] Even the Natives agreed that the beaver was over-hunted.

Anderson knew that beaver thrived in places far from the Company's posts; on his journey to Leather Pass in 1835 he had seen many bear and beaver. He was never shy about making suggestions to Governor Simpson and in his January 1843 report he recommended that a small outpost be built 100 miles west of Tête Jaune Cache to encourage the Sekani Natives from McLeod's Lake region to hunt those beaver-rich lands. Anderson also suggested that the Chilcotin post be closed down and a new post built at Thleuz-cuz (Kluskoil) Lake, on the Blackwater River. The Thleuz-cuz post would cut off the anticipated flow of furs to the coast now that Fort McLoughlin was closing, and, unlike the T'silhquot'ins, the Natives who lived around Thleuz-cuz Lake were both friendly and industrious.

If Anderson and Ogden had worked for Alexander Mackenzie's now defunct North West Company, they could have acted quickly and efficiently to improve their trade by opening a post at the lake that Mackenzie had passed by 50 years earlier on his way to the Pacific coast. But they worked for the Hudson's Bay Company, and though the Company called itself the "Company of Adventurers," its governors were anything but adventurous. HBC fur traders had to ask permission to make even relatively minor changes in their trade, and the man who gave permission, Governor Simpson, lived on the far side of the continent. Anderson's letter was set aside to await the outgoing express. As was usual with all correspondence, it was months before Simpson read this report and a year or more before Anderson received the Governor's response.

＝＝

When Peter Skene Ogden led his outgoing Fort Colvile express into Fort Alexandria in February 1843, he brought news that the man in charge of the Babine Lake post had been murdered by a Native. Ogden planned to return from Fort Colvile, meeting the outgoing New Caledonia brigade somewhere south of Kamloops and leading them to Fort Vancouver and back. Because of his anticipated summer-long absence from New Caledonia, Ogden sent Anderson north to Fort St. James to deal with any problems that might occur at Babine Lake, and to organize the brigade's departure.

Anderson travelled north with the voyageurs who had brought Ogden south with the express, and arrived at Fort St. James on March 1, 1843. By that time the murderer had been tempted from cover, then shot and killed by a fort employee. The Natives, angry at the HBC men's betrayal, demanded restitution for their relative's death, and Anderson instructed the man in charge of the post to pay the dead man's relatives to avert ill will. "In this we compromise none of our standing with the natives," he wrote, "seeing that we were the aggressors in this affair."[3]

Anderson's most important job at Fort St. James was to supervise the construction of six new boats for the brigade. When Ogden entered New Caledonia in 1835, he had given his men instructions to replace the birchbark canoes used in this region with wooden boats similar to those used on the Columbia River. Birchbark was not easily obtained on the west side of the Rocky Mountains, and boats were sturdier and carried heavier loads than canoes. The sickness of two employees delayed the work, and in early March the weather was still too cold to bend the ribs, though three men prepared the keels for two boats and one man made rivets with a lathe. By March 15 the weather moderated and the employees bent the ribs with the aid of a steam box; within three days they had bent enough wood to complete six boats, and on March 22 the first boat was ready for planking. By April 4 they had planked and finished three boats, but they had not cut enough wood to complete more than four boats, and little time remained to obtain more supplies.

Little changed in New Caledonia in the 50 years after Anderson left the area, and Frank Swannell's photographs show images, such as this one of a Hudson's Bay boat at Fort St. James, that were familiar to all the fur traders. BC ARCHIVES I-33272 (PHOTOGRAPHER: FRANK SWANNELL)

In the meantime, Anderson was dealing with demands for salmon from the trader at McLeod's Lake (he dispatched four dog-trains to the fort with 800 dried fish) and with the Babine post clerk's news that the salmon cache at the end of the portage had collapsed, crushing a Native to death. There was good news, too. The first swans had flown north, and on March 14 Anderson noted: "Rooks are said to have made their appearance this morning. These black coated gentry are usually the fore-runners of fine weather."[4] What Anderson called a rook was actually New Caledonia's crow—a bird both sleeker and darker than the untidy English rook, and one that wandered south in winter.

In preparation for the brigade's departure, the French Canadians shook out the furs and stacked them in the fur press to be pressed into 90-pound bundles and wrapped in leather. Only 34 packs of mixed furs and 8 packs of martens were now ready, but by the end of the month, two men had packed 56 bales of salmon and 3 packs of leather. On April 17 Anderson named the members of the brigade crews, and one day later the men gummed the boats for the journey south. All was ready for a Friday departure, but Anderson reported, "The Canadians have a superstitious reluctance to starting on a Friday, which it is customary and prudent to humour, where there is no probability of eradicating it."[5]

The brigade left Fort St. James on Saturday, April 22, and arrived at Fort Alexandria four days later. By May 1, 1843, all was ready for the brigade's overland journey to the Thompson's River post. For the first time, the 24 men of the New Caledonia brigade travelled south to Thompson's River by the new brigade trail, which Anderson had followed north the previous winter. Anderson revelled in the beauty of the countryside:

Beautiful prairies, bordered by lofty hills sparsely scattered with timber, stretch around. The massive fronds of the Pinus Ponderosa replace the elegant leaflets of the Cedar, no longer found save rarely, perchance, in some deep dell moistened by a purling streamlet. Groves of aspen appear here and there. The Balsam Poplar shows itself at intervals only, along the streams. The white racemes of the Service-berry flower, and the chaste flowers (blossoms) of the Mock Orange, load the air with their fragrance. Every copse re-echoes with the low drumming of the Ruffed Grouse; the trees resound with the muffled booming of the Cock of the Woods. The "Pheasant" whirrs past; the scrannel-pipe of the larger Crane—an ever watchful sentinel—grates harshly on the ear; and the shrill whistle of the Curlew as it soars aloft aides the general concert of the re-opined year. I speak still of Spring; for the impressions of that jocum season are ever the most vivid, and naturally recur with the greatest force in after years.[6]

The brigade arrived at Thompson's River on May 11 and departed the next day with John Tod in charge. Anderson accompanied the New Caledonia portion of the brigade for a few more days, but when Ogden rode in from Fort Colvile to meet them at Prairie de Nicholas, Anderson returned to Fort Alexandria.[7]

[12] AGRICULTURE AT
FORT ALEXANDRIA, 1843-44

I n spring, the work of the fur trade faded away and the work of the farm took its place. The men planted wheat, barley and oats soon after the ground was prepared, usually by mid-April. In 1843 they had received a poor-quality seed from Fort Colvile, and it had to be sown extra thick to ensure a rich growth. Vegetable crops followed the grains, and the men planted potatoes, swede turnips (rutabaga), cabbage and carrots in great quantities.

June came in with unsettled weather, and the river rose and fell. The men herded a flock of sheep close to the fort, and a few employees pulled down the old chimney in Anderson's room and built a new one. Turkey hens sat on eggs, and the barley crop grew and quickly matured.

The fur-trade posts of New Caledonia were always quiet over the summer. Half the male population of the territory travelled with the brigade, and the few remaining men were scattered around the vicinity of the fort. One man camped at the horse guard to protect the horses from theft; another camped next to the potato fields for the same reason. The Dakelh were busy fishing for their winter food and stayed away from the fort. At the height of the summer, Anderson expressed his boredom in his post journal:

Saturday [July] 22nd—very sultry. Nothing of any kind occurring worthy of being jotted down in this notable tablet of commonplaces.[1]

In early August the wheat towered six feet tall in places where there was good earth, though the oats ripened slowly. The men mowed the natural grasslands around the fort, putting up hay for winter, and they constructed a thatched roof of grass over the boat shed. On August 15 they received word that the incoming brigade had arrived at Thompson's River, and Anderson, Michel Ogden and the Native employees of the fort set off with fresh horses to help the returning voyageurs over the last few miles.

The brigade arrived at Fort Alexandria on August 16, and the men unpacked and distributed the loads. One boat had been wrecked on the way upriver; a number of 90-pound packs had been lost and two voyageurs drowned. On August 29 the men from Fort St. James continued their journey, while the employees of Fort Alexandria harvested their wheat. Soon 800 sheaves of wheat and 500 sheaves of barley were housed in the barn, and the boathouse was completely filled with the overflow of grain. Already this was a good harvest, and the oats and red wheat were still to come.

By mid-September all the crops were in and the men began work on the cavereau—a pit or shed, lined with blocks of ice taken from the river, where meat was preserved over the winter. Even though few fish had come up the Fraser River that year, the HBC men knew they would not suffer from a shortage of food. From the poor seed planted in the spring, they had harvested 500 bushels of excellent wheat, enough for their own general use in the territory with some left over to take out with the brigade in 1844. There were also 40 cartloads of barley, 12 cartloads of oats, 660 bushels of potatoes and 300 kegs of turnips.

≡ ≡

New Caledonia was a large territory which, from its beginnings, suffered periods of starvation. Peter Skene Ogden commented that in some years there was more fasting than feasting. Farming was now an important part of the fur trade in a region where barley and root vegetables grew well, but wheat did not. When Anderson arrived at Fort Alexandria in 1842, wheat was sown on a limited scale. Under Anderson's charge, the land around Fort Alexandria began to produce as much as 40 bushels of wheat per acre, and with this abundance the men at the fort were able to supply flour to all the nearby posts. Although there is no mention in the 1843 journals of a mill arriving at the fort, the incoming brigade must have carried the millstones north. The first mention of a Fort Alexandria mill occurred in April 1844, when Anderson wrote in the post journal:

"Unluckily our mill is out of trim at present, and cannot grind until it undergoes substantial repair."[2] Twenty years later, Anderson wrote an excellent description of the Fort Alexandria mill:

> To grind our wheat we had a small portable mill, with stones two feet in diameter. This mill of American manufacture was bought at Fort Vancouver on the Columbia, taken up the Columbia by water to Okinagan and thence packed on horse back piece-meal, to its destination. The mill itself was well made and efficient, but the driving gear, constructed at Alexandria, was a marvelous piece of workmanship. In those days of make-shifts, and dove tailing of means and appliances, to turn a Canadian voyageur into a millwright was nothing. Hence our mill, of which by the way we were very proud, rumbled round in a most eccentric manner. It did its work, though, but with a wondrous strain upon the poor horses who tugged the unwieldy machine around. The flour thus produced was of excellent quality; and tasted all the sweeter, I doubt not, as being the result of our own exertions.[3]

The Company men would not starve this winter, but it was a different story for the Natives. Michel Ogden went to the Chilcotin River barrière to trade for 3,000 salmon, but he returned from a second expedition to the Chutes of the Fraser River with none.[4] In a report to Governor Simpson, Anderson wrote that "the general dearth of salmon has not . . . been attended with an inconvenience, owing to the successful issue of our farming operations at Alexandria during the past season: the product of which . . . has enabled me to assist the starving natives materially."[5]

In April 1844, the agricultural work of the fort began again. The men harrowed and rolled the last of the wheat seed while others planted potatoes. Some men packed the winter furs for the brigade. The brigade boats arrived from Fort St. James on April 24, bringing Fort Alexandria's leather supplies for the year. Unfortunately, the brigaders had left behind their supply of dried fish from Babine Lake's ever-reliable salmon run, so there was not enough food to carry the men to Thompson's River. To replace the fish, Anderson dug into the fort supplies for the little flour that remained and sent off the horses and men under Donald McLean.

May came in with hard frosts, and a violent storm damaged the oats so badly they were resown. To Anderson, it appeared the year was going backwards. Summer seemed further away all the time. However, the warm weather eventually returned, and the furs trickled into the fort. The river rose rapidly, and one of the Natives, Scoolay, borrowed an axe to split wood for his verveau, or fish weir, in preparation for the summer flood of salmon.[6] With the brigade's return in late summer, Anderson finally received instructions from Governor George Simpson.

One year after Anderson recommended that the troublesome Chilcotin post be closed down and replaced with a post at Thleuz-cuz Lake, Ogden sent word that Simpson had approved the suggestion. In May 1844 Anderson set out on the difficult cross-country journey to the isolated cluster of lakes along Mackenzie's West Road River, to choose the place where the new trading post should be constructed.

For a few miles Anderson's party followed a company pack trail that climbed the hills west of the fort and eventually led to Fraser's Lake. Thleuz-cuz was to the west, however, and the trading party left the HBC trail to follow a Dakelh footpath that took them over many wooded ridges and along the shorelines of several small lakes. As the Dakelh people travelled great distances on foot, the fur traders found that riding horses over their uncleared footpaths was slow and tiring work.

After five days the trading party reached the banks of the Blackwater River, named for its tea-coloured waters. A short time later they arrived at the meeting place on the lake the Dakelh called Thleuz-uz-cuz. There they found a large number of Natives gathered for a feast.

The Dakelh assembled at Thleuz-cuz Lake for their fisheries every summer and were usually joined by Nuxálk men who carried precious fish oil up one of many grease trails that wound through the mountains that separated the lake from the coast. The Nuxálk rendered this whitish, lard-like oil from the eulachon, a smelt or herring that spawned every summer in such numbers they turned the tidal rivers black. At Thleuz-cuz and other traditional trading places, the Nuxálk traded their oil for furs from the Interior.

Although the Dakelh were accustomed to being visited by the derouine parties[7] from the Chilcotin post, they were delighted when Anderson said he planned to set up a post at Thleuz-cuz. They traded as many furs as they could, but made it clear to Anderson that if he did not set up a post here, their furs would continue to find their way to the coast via the Native grease trail. This confirmed Anderson's decision to establish a new post at the lake. He chose the location for the new post, but left the actual post building until a later date. In a report to Governor Simpson, Anderson wrote of his visit to Thleuz-cuz:

> *The post of Thleuz-cuz was established in September; and I am happy to inform you, is doing extremely well. I visited the place in June in order to make the necessary preliminary arrangements, and met there a large concourse of Indians from different posts in the vicinity. Among them were some of my quondam friends of Fort McLoughlin, who after a while recognized me.*[8]

[13] LANDSLIDES AND
SALMON RUNS, 1844-45

The normal work at Fort Alexandria continued. In mid-June 1844 the men hauled pickets to replace those in the rotting front wall of the fort. Two weeks later they dismantled a second wall and replaced its pickets. A refreshing rain fell after months of drought, and the men rolled and harrowed turnips and potatoes, while the Dakelh gathered for their summer fisheries and a feast of eggs and eulachon oil.

Because of the importance of the farm crops, the possibility of drought in this region worried the fur traders every summer. But the fisheries were also vital to the success of the fur trade, as Natives and fur traders alike depended on the thousands of salmon that flooded up the Fraser River every summer. Without a good summer fishery, the Dakelh starved over the winter and their hunts suffered.

The Fraser salmon fishery lasted only a few months of the year. The Dakelh spent the winter in roomy huts of thickly interwoven pine boughs, but they built temporary houses every June at points on the river where the fish were abundant and easily caught. The airy summer houses had substantial bark roofs supported by posts, with walls filled in with neatly peeled pine boughs. The salmon dried in the smoke of the fires that kept the residents warm in the evening.

After building their houses, the Dakelh men chopped wood for their weirs, which they set up in the murky waters of the Fraser. The first salmon to swim past the fort in early July were the *Sa-qui* (now known as chinook or spring salmon). Anderson preferred these fish, which were stronger and richer than the later catch, equal in size and quality to the salmon of his native Scotland. The second rush of salmon, which arrived in mid-July, was the *Suck-kai,* a name later transformed into the fish's modern name, sockeye. These smaller salmon swam in enormous numbers up the Fraser and Chilcotin rivers; by the end of July they had almost caught up to the larger chinook at Fraser and Stuart lakes.

There were many methods of fishing for salmon on the Fraser River. Downriver, the Natives used drift or scoop nets to catch salmon from wooden platforms suspended over the rapids. On many of the smaller rivers, and at Fraser and Stuart lakes, the Dakelh constructed weirs and fish traps that almost blocked the river. At Fort Alexandria, where the Fraser River was so wide it could not be blocked, they trapped their fish in wooden weirs. Anderson described these ingenious traps:

> A close fence of light hurdles, supported by strong stakes driven into the bottom, is projected some forty or fifty feet into the stream, where the current is swift, and the bottom gradually shelving. Another fence is run downstream; then at a right angle six feet or so towards the bank, and again upwards nearly to the first transverse fence. The ascending fish thus intercepted in their progress by the upper fence seek in vain to round the obstacles, and after a while enter a large cylindrical basket which is sunk at the angle where the descending fence is formed with slender rods converging inwards, like the entrance of a wire mouse-trap. Great numbers are thus caught.[1]

The Dakelh traded some of their catch to the HBC men and dried the rest for themselves. It was tradition for the chiefs to present the trader with a fish, and in 1843, Anderson received his gifts on July 17:

> Kasetan this morning gave me . . . a fine Salmon of the smaller kind—this being the first fruits of the fishery, he was liberally compensated, according to the good old custom in N. Caledonia. In the evening Koneltalh and Telhpah brought each a fine Kase for which they get a piece of tobo. gratis & some ammunition in payment.[2]

Early that summer, Anderson recorded that "salmon are pretty abundant & the natives are day by day adding to their stock, besides supplying us abundantly for daily consumption."[3] By mid-August, however, the river waters were falling and salmon had become scarce. Though the run recovered, Anderson worried that he might not have enough salmon for winter storage. Moreover, John Tod at Kamloops reported having few fish to spare, and Ogden arrived from Fort St. James with the news that very few salmon had reached there. Anderson's men had been able to trade for thousands of salmon at the Native fisheries on the Chilcotin River, but in spite of that, in autumn 1843 the fort had only 4,000 fish in storage to feed the men over the winter. The numbers were very low; in 1836, Anderson had seen 36,000 salmon stored at Fraser's Lake.

Everyone hoped that 1844 would be a better year, but when the Dakelh assembled at their fisheries in mid-June, the river waters remained so high they could not install their weirs. The waters finally subsided at the end of June. A month later, Anderson picked up his goose-quill pen to report that the long-rumoured arrival of the salmon was not to be; no fish had made their appearance at Fort Alexandria.

Rain fell in September, the river level rose and the Dakelh fishermen removed their weirs before they could be carried away by the river's fierce current. Though the salmon fisheries at Fort Alexandria had failed, Michel Ogden returned from a trading journey to the Chilcotin River barrière with 3,000 salmon and the prospect of obtaining more when the Natives returned from their root grounds.

Salmon was not the only winter food available to the Dakelh of Fort Alexandria; they also foraged for many of the wild plants that grew in the grasslands around the fort. "The Tza-Chin or edible Bitter Root of N.C [New Caledonia]," Anderson wrote of one root the Dakelh harvested, "(which by the way appears to me to be nearly identical with the Tiger Lily of our gardens) might perhaps be entitled to some little notice as a bonne-bouche if cultivated in England. The mode of preparing it is either in small subterranean kilns, or by steaming until soft and mushy."[4] Carefully steamed, Anderson reported, the lily was an excellent substitute for potato, its flavour somewhat like that of a roasted chestnut, with a slight bitterness that made it very palatable.

When winter finally fell and the cycle of fishing was finished, the Company men could assess whether the Natives had enough food to allow them to enjoy a good hunting season. In 1844, it seemed they did not, especially when a storm blew in at the end of October with snow and freezing temperatures. Anderson wrote of his worry about the Natives' starving condition and what he saw as their miserable circumstances in comparison to his relative comfort in the fort:

> Would I could predict with honest Sir Hugh that 'there are pip-pins & cheese to come'—but alas! I fear cold fingers and hunger will be the more probable lot of many in the interior, and we, who are comparatively in comfort, have reason to be thankful that we are so. . . . T'is a glorious privilege to be able to write nonsense now & then, when there is no censor of the press, or rather of the pen, to check one—Enough! A good fire, a warm house, & divers acceptable concomitants, with a foot of snow around one, are circumstances that may well occasion a momen-tary glimpse of contentment in a mind not always swayed by cheerful emotions.[5]

In early December 1844, the Fraser River choked with ice below the fort, as it did every year. The Dakelh made snowshoes for the winter hunt, and the Thleuz-cuz employees rode into Fort Alexandria with a good supply of furs. However, missing and water-damaged pages in the Fort Alexandria journals suggest that autumn 1844 was a season of mishaps. A great part of the disorder was probably caused by the first of two land-slides that occurred in the area during Anderson's years there. He had an opportunity to view one of the slides soon after it fell and described it as having a "vertical depth approaching 500 feet at the time of rupture and a complete bouleversement like an ill-ploughed field gigantically magni-fied."[6] The second slide occurred in 1845, and on that occasion Anderson reported his party narrowly escaped destruction, but gave no other details. No landslide is mentioned in the surviving pages of the post journals, but Anderson's eldest son described one of them many years later:

> The land slide whereof mention is made, occurred below the fort where the bank was carried bodily into the river completely blocking its course and flooding all the lands adjacent to the river. So sudden was the occurrence that an Indian village was swept away entirely. My recollection is that it occurred at night as I remember my father coming into my room in the early morning wet and his coat, a cotton one, torn beyond recognition, he having

torn bandages from it to bind up the wounds of those natives most badly hurt. I do not remember that there was any great loss of life, one or two only I think, but I do remember the story told by my father to the effect that a child who was missing was found after the subsidence of the water, suspended by its clothes in a tree, safe and sound. These land slides called by the French Canadians Les Eboulis were not infrequent on the high banks of the Fraser, but luckily not often of such a serious nature as that I have recorded.[7]

The men of the fort carried out their usual winter chores, cutting wood, grinding and sifting wheat and hauling hay from the nearby lakes. Christmas Day dawned fine and frosty and the voyageurs celebrated their holiday by firing their guns into the air. In return for being startled out of bed by the blast of gunfire, Anderson gave his men their regale of meat and rum, with a day off work.

Sometime over the long, quiet winter of 1844–45, Anderson wrote a letter to his uncle Alexander Seton, telling him that both he and his brother James patiently awaited their expected promotions to chief trader. He also gave his uncle a short description of his life at Fort Alexandria:

My amusements here are, in the intervals of more serious avocations, gardening, shooting and reading. I have got a pretty good library, including some of the best of the Latin authors. Greek I do not pretend to [know]. I derive great satisfaction from the possession of a moderate acquaintance with the former language, which affords the solace of many a weary hour. I hear the study of the classics often decried, as implying a waste of time in the acquisition, which might be employed to better purpose. This is a view of the question which I am nowise dissuaded to admit; and which, as regards the education of my own children, I shall certainly not act upon. But my sheet warns me to conclude . . .[8]

At the same time he wrote to his uncle, Anderson reported to Governor Simpson that, in spite of being short of food as the result of the poor salmon run of the previous summer, the Dakelh traded more martens than they had in previous years. Fortunately, the vegetable and grain crops at Fort Alexandria had been "copious; a circumstance which

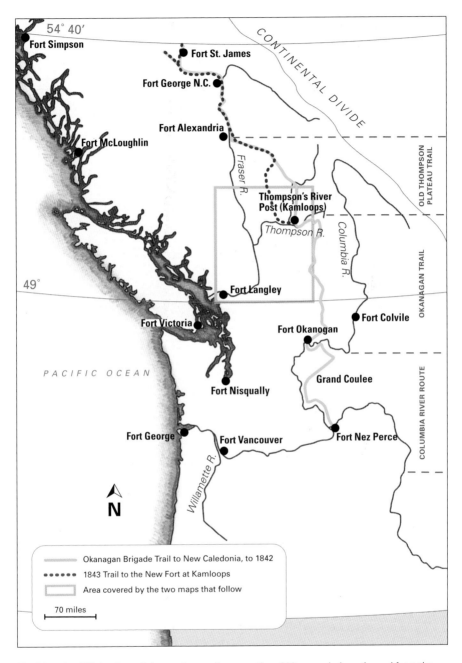

The historic old brigade trail, in regular use for more than 200 years, led northward from the Columbia River to the Thompson's River Post and continued up the east bank of the North Thompson River. In 1843 a new brigade trail bypassed the rugged Thompson plateau route, heading southward to the new fort at Kamloops. MAP BY JACQUI THOMAS

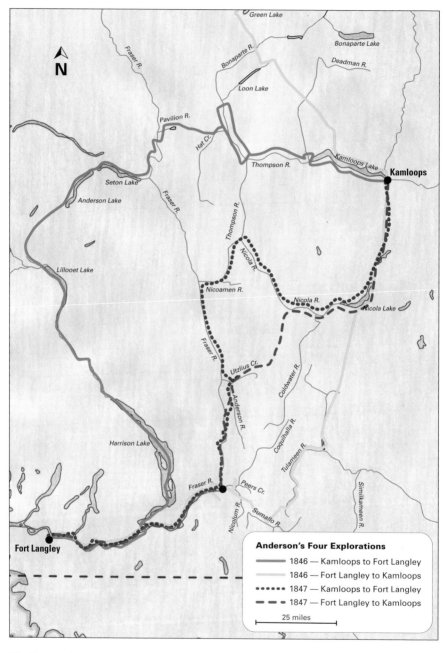

Anderson's Four Explorations

— 1846 — Kamloops to Fort Langley
— 1846 — Fort Langley to Kamloops
•••• 1847 — Kamloops to Fort Langley
– – – 1847 — Fort Langley to Kamloops

25 miles

The distance between Kamloops and Fort Langley was only 200 miles, but Anderson was expected to uncover a trail that avoided the dangers of the rapid-filled Thompson and Fraser rivers and broke through the continuous mountainous ridge that rose more than 4,500 feet above the Fraser River on its east bank. MAP BY JACQUI THOMAS

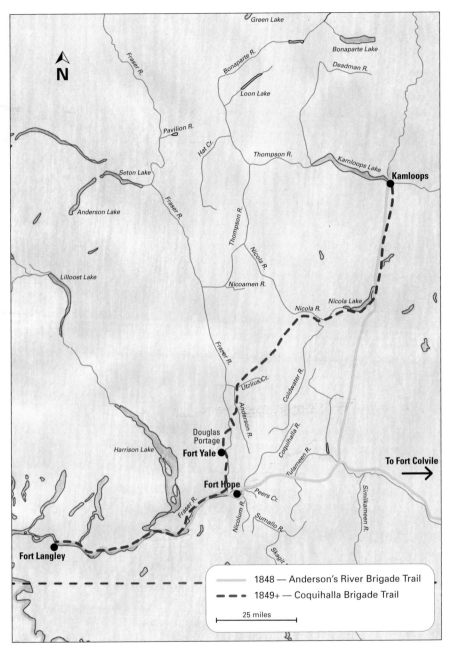

When the Cayuse War suddenly erupted along the Columbia River, the fur traders of New Caledonia and Fort Colvile were forced to use the Anderson's River trail, long before it could be prepared for horses. When that trail proved too difficult for man and horse, the fur traders fell back to using the trail that Anderson explored on his return to Kamloops in 1846, and with information garnered from Chief Blackeye and his son, opened up a new horse-friendly trail over the ridge that separated Kamloops from Fort Langley. MAP BY JACQUI THOMAS

Painted by Anderson in June 1848, this watercolour shows Mount Baker from below Smess (Sumas). Anderson's 1867 map of British Columbia identified Smess as being a large swampland or lake on the south bank of the Fraser River, a few miles west of the mouth of Chilliwack River.
BC ARCHIVES PDP1236

This unfinished sketch, made by Anderson in 1849, looks north toward the new Kamloops fort on the west bank of the North Thompson River, and the old Thompson's River post on the right, or eastern, bank. What appears to be the horse guard is in the foreground.
KAMLOOPS MUSEUM & ARCHIVES NO. 7862

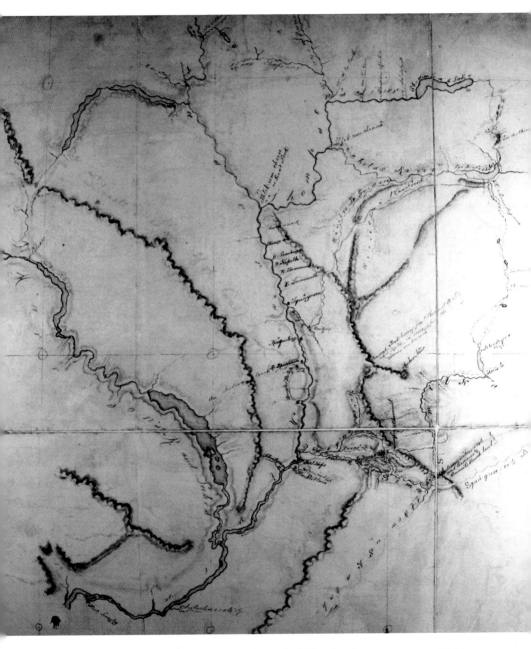

Anderson probably drew this exquisite map in the early 1860s, when he was encouraged in his map-making by the Royal Engineers he had befriended.

A.C. ANDERSON, MAP, "ORIGINAL SKETCH OF EXPLORATIONS BETWEEN 1846 AND 1849," BC ARCHIVES CM/B1094

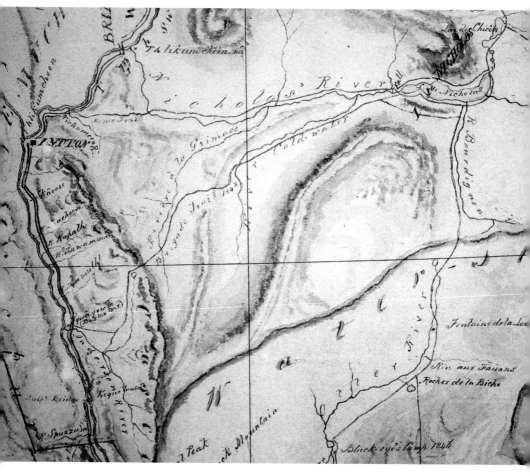

In 1847, Anderson intended to follow the red-lined trail that split from Nicola River to reach the Thompson River through a cut in the hills east of spectacular Nicoamen River waterfalls. Later that same summer he returned to Kamloops via the Coldwater River to Nicola Lake, and in 1848 that trail became the beginning of the short-lived Anderson's River brigade trail. Finally, to the south, Anderson marked in the route his exploration party took as they travelled north from Blackeye's Camp—a route that later served as the brigade trail to Kamloops from the Coquihalla mountains.

A.C. ANDERSON, "MAP OF A PORTION OF THE COLONY OF BRITISH COLUMBIA, COMPILED FROM VARIOUS SOURCES, INCLUDING ORIGINAL NOTES FROM PERSONAL EXPLORATION BETWEEN THE YEARS 1832 AND 1851," BC ARCHIVES CM/F9

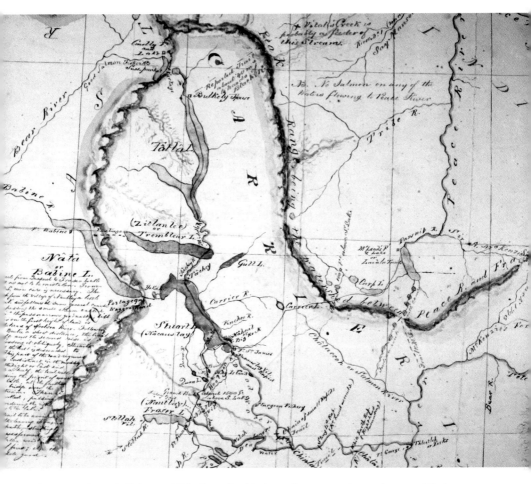

This map, drawn in February 1870, showed gold miners the route to the newly opened Omineca goldfields. It maps details of the area around Stuart and Fraser's Lakes, where Anderson spent four years in the fur trade. In the blank spaces of his many maps, Anderson wrote extensive notes that often told stories not recorded anywhere else.

A.C. ANDERSON, PORTION OF "GUIDE MAP TO THE PEACE RIVER MINES, FEB. 1870," BC ARCHIVES CM/13665A, MSS 1912

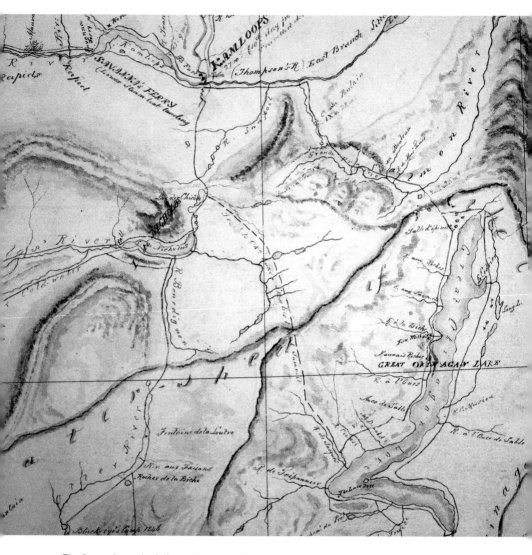

The fur traders who followed the early Okanagan brigade trails travelled along the west shore of the lake and rode over the hills that separated Okanagan Lake from today's Monte Creek and the south Thompson River, east of Kamloops. Anderson's map shows the later trails that mounted the hills on the west side of the lake to find easier paths past Okanagan Lake. Though regular use of the trails by fur traders slowed after 1848, the twice-yearly express would still have travelled the many trails to Fort Colvile.

A.C. ANDERSON, "MAP OF A PORTION OF THE COLONY OF BRITISH COLUMBIA, COMPILED FROM VARIOUS SOURCES, INCLUDING ORIGINAL NOTES FROM PERSONAL EXPLORATION BETWEEN THE YEARS 1832 AND 1851," BC ARCHIVES CM/F9

has once more placed us entirely beyond the reach of want."[9] Fur traders and Natives alike lived off the fort's harvest until the ice left the lakes in March and freshwater fish could be caught. Sturgeon and rainbow trout fed the Natives near Fraser's Lake in the early spring, while at Fort Alexandria it was a fish that Anderson called the carp.[10]

In June 1845 the Dakelh abandoned the lakes to assemble at their various salmon fisheries. A heavy rain in mid-July flooded the river, and Anderson suspected that the first flood of salmon had already passed by. There was not a whisper of any being caught. In the post journal he expressed his frustration with the weather and the many interruptions to the work of the place:

> With our multifarious operations at this place it is a difficult matter to go on regularly with any particular job. Like drunken men, we make one step forward & then a half-halt in arrears. I cannot help it.[11]

Ultimately, however, 1845 was a very good year for salmon on the Fraser River. In September, Anderson reported that Michel Ogden arrived from Atnah Rapids with 75 horses loaded with dried salmon, about 15,000 fish. Four days later Ogden set out again with 60 horses to pack in the fish he planned to trade for at the Chilcotin River barrière. At the end of the month he returned with 11,000 salmon.

There was nothing to prevent the Hudson's Bay men from fishing for their own pleasure, and Anderson sometimes walked down to the riverbank to entertain himself with the scoop net. On one memorable occasion he caught 50 or 60 fish in a single evening.

⇒ ⇐

In late August, Peter Skene Ogden and Donald Manson arrived at the fort, riding at the head of the incoming New Caledonia brigade. Manson, who had been in charge of Fort McLoughlin when Anderson served there, had come north from Fort Vancouver with the brigade to take charge of New Caledonia. Peter Skene Ogden planned to leave New Caledonia with the outgoing express in the fall, and he would not return.

For the most part, the gentlemen who worked the New Caledonia fur trade remained in the territory for a number of years, but change occasionally occurred. Peter Skene Ogden hoped to leave New Caledonia in

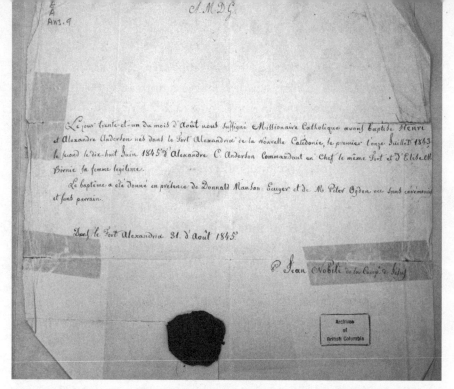

Two of Anderson's sons, Henry and Alexander, were baptized by the Jesuit Missionary Père Nobili in August 1845, as recorded on this baptismal certificate. Henry grew up to become Constable Henry Anderson of the British Columbia Provincial Police and was well known in the Kootenays at the end of the century. BC ARCHIVES MSS. 559, VOLUME 1, FOLDER 9

1844, but abandoned his plans when John Lee Lewes, who was to replace him, lost his hand in a shooting accident. John Tod remained in charge at Kamloops and never visited Fort Alexandria, and Donald McLean took charge of the distant McLeod's Lake post when the Chilcotin post closed. Thomas Charles, the new clerk assigned to the charge of Thleuz-cuz, was a young man and, though Anderson liked him, they may have shared few interests and were separated for months at a time. But one man new to the territory shared many of Anderson's interests. Jesuit missionary Père John Nobili entered New Caledonia in August 1845 with the brigade, and as he passed through Fort Alexandria on his way north, he baptized two of Anderson's children. Nobili returned that winter to live under Anderson's roof, and the fur trader took advantage of the missionary's constant presence to practise his Latin, more important than ever now that he owned a Latin Bible. Nobili also taught Anderson Italian, and Anderson's son James later reported that his father spoke the language fluently.

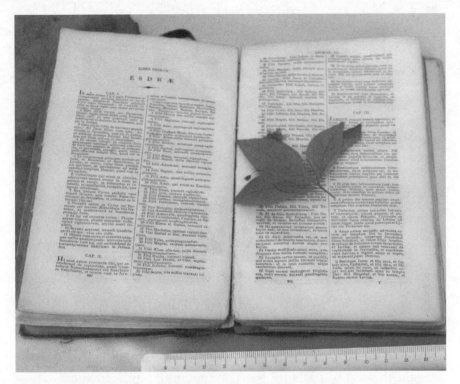

Anderson purchased this Latin Bible at Fort Vancouver in 1840. He may have carried it with him on his 1846 expedition, as the leaves found in the Bible are tentatively identified as California rhododendron, which he saw growing wild along the trail.

A.C. ANDERSON'S LATIN BIBLE AND CARRYING CASE, ROYAL BRITISH COLUMBIA MUSEUM, ITEM #973.177.1 A&B

Nobili left Alexandria with the outgoing spring express, returning to spend the late summer and winter of 1846–47 at Fort St. James with Donald Manson. But the missionary had a stubborn streak that frustrated the fur traders. In March 1847 he left Fort St. James against Manson's advice and travelled on snowshoes down the frozen Fraser River to Fort Alexandria, arriving so exhausted that Anderson removed his tattered leggings and shoes for him.[12] For Nobili's safety, Anderson arranged that a retiring employee, Jean Baptiste Vautrin, accompany the missionary for the remainder of his journey south.

[14] THE FUR TRADE, 1845-46

Although it was rarely mentioned in the Fort Alexandria post journals, the fur trade was the reason for the post's existence and always rumbled on in the background. In May and June pelts flooded into the post when the Natives brought in the results of their winter's trapping. Even during the slow months of fall and early winter, trappers who had held furs back earlier in the year brought them in to trade for guns, ammunition, tobacco and trapping supplies. Only the salmon fisheries halted the trade in furs for a few months in the summer.

Fort Alexandria's furs came from numerous Native trappers who travelled a considerable distance to trade at the fort. The hunters stretched and dressed their furs before presenting them for trade. As in other posts in the territory, the actual trade was likely a lengthy and ceremonial affair. Natives everywhere traded their furs one at a time and took payment for each pelt separately, so it could take several days for the trader to determine the price for the pelts from an individual trapper.

Once they'd agreed on the price for a pelt, the trader gave the trapper tokens, or "castors," which represented the value of the fur. No paper money or coin changed hands. A castor might be a piece of wood or a porcupine quill, but it represented value to the Natives, who exchanged it for needed trade items. Trades were rarely entered in the post journal, but Anderson kept track of the furs received in a ledger he called the "blotter." All the furs received were entered on one side of the trade blotter's page, and the products purchased with the castors were listed on the other.

Indian trade books, or trade blotters, such as this one containing information from Fort Rupert for the years 1876–1881, can contain many stories not found in post journals, but few survived to be stored in archives. BC ARCHIVES A/C.20/R2.3

The real standard of the fur trade was Made Beaver (MB)—the value of a one-pound prime beaver skin worn by a Native for at least a season so that most of the long outer hair was rubbed off. Other animal pelts, such as muskrat, otter and bear skins, were given a value based on the Made Beaver standard. For example, a collection of "55 mart[en]s, 9 sil[ver] foxes, 8 cross do. [cross foxes] & 3 red, 10 large beaver & 9 small – 5 lynxes, 5 wolverines, 4 fishers, 3 minks & 6 [musk]rats"[1] was equivalent to 98 MB. A later listing of 60 MB of furs included "13 large beavers & 4 small, 2 otters, 15 martens, 4 bears, 7 fox . . ."[2]

The prices of all trade goods were set at a certain number of MB. A Native hunter might purchase five pounds of shot, a length of tobacco or one blanket with one MB. Even the castors represented an MB value. Made Beaver was an estimated value that could vary from place to place and from time to time, and its value sometimes depended on how skilled the Company fur trader or the hunter was at negotiating a trade.

Tobacco was, of course, a valuable item and something the Natives would always work for. In the early days the Company imported it from Brazil, a leaf tobacco twisted into ropes an inch in diameter and wound into massive leather-wrapped rolls from which lengths were measured. In the early 1700s the HBC began importing "North West Twist," a new leaf tobacco from Virginia, which was delivered in rolls, pressed blocks or string-wrapped carrots weighing one-and-a-half or three pounds. In 1821 Governor Simpson considered sending tobacco from Quebec, and when Anderson was trading furs for tobacco at Fort Alexandria, his tobacco could have come from either Virginia or Quebec.[3] The tobacco came into the territory in massive amounts; in 1848 the brigade carried in at least twenty-four 90-pound rolls of tobacco to be distributed between the forts in the districts of New Caledonia, Thompson's River and Fort Colvile.[4] Tobacco still came in carrots, too. Anderson recorded that he "traded the 2 beavers left here by Petite Oeil together with 3 skins martens for a carrot Tobo. of 5 MB."[5] Later, another Native was paid "½ carrot Tobo. (3 ½ MB) for the 11 martens . . ."[6]

Leather and guns were other important trading items. In April 1844, Anderson traded "20 MB martens from Patissos for leather to be delivered on arrival of brigade,"[7] and in one case a hunter traded 25 miscellaneous furs for a gun. The trade guns sold to the Natives were smooth-bore flint-locks, not as well built as the fur traders' guns but always decorated with a brass serpent on the side and a seated fox engraved on the back of the lock. These animals had a spiritual significance for the Natives, who also believed the symbols would bring them good luck in the hunt.

Once they purchased a gun, the hunters also needed ammunition, which was not cheap. "The Chilcotins traded 20 or 23 MB furs—foxes, martens &c for blankets and ammunition,"[8] Anderson wrote on one occasion, and on another: "Traded 3 beavers (large) from Old Hunter's son of Chilcotins for ammunt."[9] Anderson also traded a "filly with Capot Bleu for 10 beavers."[10]

In 1845 the martens were numerous and the quality of their fur excellent. When Anderson took inventory, he found there were 214 large beaver and 93 small, 45 otter, 726 marten, 91 mink, 15 fishers, 8 wolverines, 61 marmots, 15 bear of various kinds, 150 muskrats and 14 fox. It was early in the winter and already this was a considerable improvement over the previous year's take. Anderson anticipated a good winter hunt. He was correct. At the end of April 1846, Fort Alexandria had 15 packs of furs, containing 1,800 martens and other pelts to be taken out in the brigade. The Natives around the fort more than doubled their usual catch of martens over the winter of 1845–46, though the New Caledonia returns show the fur traders brought in fewer beaver and muskrats.[11]

Not everything went well that winter, however. In November 1845 one of Anderson's French-Canadian employees, Marineau, returned from Fort George with some horses that had been loaned to Chief Trader Paul Fraser as he made his way north. Fraser had driven the horses hard through deep snow; one horse was dead and five other tired animals had been left behind in a place where there was good grass. Anderson was furious and scribbled in his journal, "Disorder seems to be advancing on all hands with seven league strides. However, let me cease lest I trespass upon critical ground."[12]

The fort's regular routine continued through the winter months. Anderson gave the local Dakelh chiefs their usual present of tobacco, and his men enjoyed a holiday and their regale on Christmas Day, as well as drams of liquor on New Year's Day. As spring approached, Anderson

A view from the south looking up the Fraser River at the point of land on the east bank where Fort Alexandria stood after 1846. In 1842, when Anderson first arrived at the fort, the post stood on a small flat of land on the west bank of the river. BC ARCHIVES A-08012

decided to move Fort Alexandria from its old location on the west bank of the Fraser River, where it was prone to flooding, to a new site on the river's east side, atop the hill overlooking the Fraser. Anderson's eldest son, five-year-old James, later recalled helping with its dismantling:

The fort was removed to the upper bench, and well I remember getting hold of an axe and proceeding to demolish the apology for a mantelpiece in one of the rooms, in the belief that I was assisting in the general removal.[13]

The construction of the new fort continued through the spring as weather and time allowed. The voyageurs dismantled the stable at the old post and brought it across the river in pieces. At the end of March, Anderson took possession of his new house, and the men stored the furs and trading goods in the new fort. The cook now occupied the kitchen, but the employees remained at the old post until their residence could be built.

The outgoing brigade left Fort Alexandria on May 1, 1846, and Anderson travelled south with them. He was not going all the way to Fort Vancouver, however, as Governor Simpson and Peter Skene Ogden had given him a new task: finding a good horse road over the range of hills that separated Kamloops from Fort Langley on the coast.

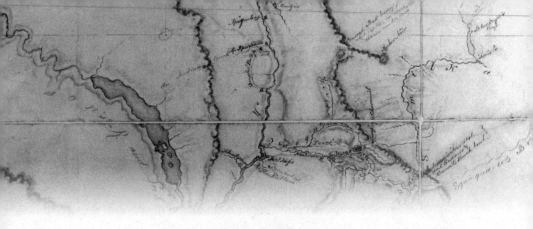

[15] THE SEARCH FOR
A NEW BRIGADE TRAIL, 1846

In 1846 the British and American governments began to negotiate
the placement of the American border through traditional Hudson's
Bay Company lands west of the Rocky Mountains. Some Company
men optimistically expected the new boundary to pass south of the
Columbia River, leaving all the territory to the north in Company hands.
Americans hoped the boundary might be placed as far north as the bottom of the Russian Territories, which meant that much of New Caledonia
would fall into American hands. Wherever the boundary ultimately ran,
it was certain to interfere with the business of the fur trade. The nervous
Company men planned to enlarge the new post at Fort Victoria, on the
south end of Vancouver's Island. Fort Langley was already serviced by the
HBC ships, but no one knew how the rich furs of New Caledonia would
reach the lower Fraser River. The impassable Fraser River canyon and a
rough, unexplored range of mountains lay between New Caledonia and
Fort Langley.

In 1845 Anderson wrote to Governor Simpson to volunteer himself
for the job of finding a new brigade route across the mountains from
Kamloops to Fort Langley on the Fraser River. The letter reached Simpson
at Norway House, and he discussed the issue with Peter Skene Ogden,
who happened to be there at the time. In October 1845 Ogden wrote from
Fort Colvile, giving Anderson instructions to confer with John Tod of
Kamloops before exploring potential routes between Kamloops and Fort
Langley. At the same time, Ogden wrote to Tod, suggesting that the most
feasible route might be "starting from Thompson's River, across land to

the Nicoutimine Country, and from thence to Harrison's River then with canoes nothing can intervene to prevent reaching Ft. Langley."[1]

Anderson's 1845 letter to Governor Simpson no longer exists, so it is not known whether he suggested the routes that should be explored. Nor do existing records give a clear idea of what motivated Anderson to volunteer for this task. In 1845, no one was discussing the need for a new brigade trail; it appears to have been entirely Anderson's idea. He may have believed he was the only fur trader in good enough condition to conduct the search, or he may have sought the adventure of a journey across unknown country without knowing the difficulties of the terrain. It appears that Anderson considered the trail necessary, and he alone made the offer to explore—an offer that was quickly accepted by Simpson and Ogden.

In early January 1846 Anderson visited Tod at Kamloops to discuss possibilities. The route Tod suggested followed the path of an earlier Thompson's River fur trader who, in 1827, explored two lakes at the end of a little river that flowed east into the Fraser and partially explored the Lillywit (Lillooet) River beyond. Tod believed that the Lillywit River might be the northern end of a river the Company already knew as Harrison's River, which flowed through Harrison's Lake into the Fraser River just above Fort Langley. If the river that flowed into the north end of Harrison's Lake was indeed the Lillywit, it might prove to be a good route around the canyons of the Fraser River.

Besides considerations regarding the route itself, the Hudson's Bay men had developed strict requirements for an overland brigade trail, based on experience, good and bad. The Company was looking for a trail that hundreds of horses could travel safely without injury. A path that might work for a man on foot would not necessarily work for the heavily loaded brigade horses. Sharp rocks on the trail bed would damage the horses' delicate hooves and cut their fetlocks. If the ground was too soft, the passage of so many horses would turn the trail into a quagmire that later brigades could not cross. Safe fords over rivers and creeks were essential, especially as so much of the travel was done in early summer, the season of high water. Gradient was important, but they could accept a steep slope if the hillside allowed room for switchbacks. The horses needed food and water, and trail builders could sow alfalfa and white clover along the edges of the horse road if the ground was good, but they could not manufacture streams. Anderson would have to keep all these concerns in mind as he explored the potential brigade trails.

On the early afternoon of May 15, 1846, Anderson rode away from the Kamloops post with five voyageurs and a few Native guides. One of the men who accompanied him was Édouard Montigny, the 34-year-old Métis who had guided him over the new brigade trail to Fort Alexandria in November 1842. Montigny had remained in Anderson's service since then and was his most experienced and trusted employee.

Anderson rode ahead of his men along the south shore of Kamloops Lake, following the first of a series of Native trails westward. At the lake's end, the party crossed to the north shore of the Thompson River in borrowed canoes, swimming their horses across. A few miles west, flood-waters filled the steep-sided stream bed of Rivière du Défunt (Deadman's River) and blocked their passage.

The men were still in the territory of the Secwepemc people who "principally do their travelling on horseback & have very little knowledge of the art of constructing canoes, the only use they ever make of them being just for the purpose of ferries where the water is too deep to ford."[2] Familiarity with the Secwepemc habits illuminated the Company men's course of action.

> *Found River du Defunt much swollen; and having searched in vain for a tree suitable for a bridge, we went at length to the mouth of the river and having procured a crazy old canoe, we succeeded in doubling the end of the impediment upon the main stream. After several successful trips with our sorry vehicle we nearly experienced an accident at last, for Montigny with [another] of the men and several Ind[ian]s narrowly escaped missing the eddy, and being swept into the boiling rapid some hundred yards below. Having crossed safely myself at the first trip, my feelings at witnessing the imminent danger of these people may be conceived.[3]*

In Anderson's journals of exploration, he describes a number of occasions when he risked his life to lead his men through dangerous situations. Probably all fur traders behaved in this manner. By crossing first, a trader encouraged his employees to follow him places they might otherwise have been unwilling to go. But more important, the trader showed his men that he was willing to take the same risks he asked them to take, and so earned their respect. In this country, filled with life-threatening dangers of every sort, a trader like Anderson must successfully lead his men where he wanted them to go. Moreover, because good men were so hard to come by, he also had to ensure that his employees arrived safely at their destination.

The explorers followed the north shore of the Thompson River under the looming Cache Creek Hills westward until they were stopped by the high waters of the flooding Bonaparte River. The next morning the men "succeeded in making a bridge, and crossed over by 9 am: but it was not till late in the afternoon that we got the horses across; having had to go up nearly as far as the Loon River Fork to find a suitable spot. Encamped upon the R. aux Chapeaux; then NW through a cut in the hills, 4m: to a small lake."[4]

The Native guides led the explorers westward through a spectacular rockbound canyon (Marble Canyon) where many small waterfalls tumbled down limestone cliffs into two jewel-green lakes. At the end of the first lake:

We arrived upon a camp of Indians; the inmates of which upon our approach rushed out tumultuously with their arms, yelling very vociferously. Judging, as it proved correctly, that their hostile demonstrations were not intentionally directed toward ourselves, I rode up and enquired their meaning. The tumult forthwith subsided; and the leader of the party, a one eyed blackguard who is known as the Batailleur, excused himself, saying: that they had taken their arms under the impression that we were enemies. It appears that a murder has recently been committed upon one of the Batailleur's relatives by an Ind. of the lakes; a close connection of N-poomsk, the Indian who accompanies our party, and who is to guide to Harrison's River. I therefore judged it prudent to wait for the arrival of N-poomsk, who being an indifferent horseman had fallen behind; and the Indians, perceiving our intentions of protecting him did not attempt to offer any molestation.[5]

From the west end of the second lake, the party followed Le Pavillon [Pavilion River], a river named by the French Canadians for a British flag once conspicuously hoisted here.[6] At its mouth, Le Pavillon flowed into the Fraser above a Native fishing village where Kamloops employees traded for salmon. Below the fishing village, the Fraser River poured into a steep-sided, rock-bound trench that curved around the base of Fountain Ridge, a rounded hump of land that nosedived into the Fraser on its east bank and forced the river to bend to the west. Tod had proposed that Anderson's horse trail should lead over the ridge, but Anderson saw it was impossible to take horses there. He and his men turned their animals over to the Native guides, who would return them to Kamloops, and set up camp near the fishing village.

On the morning of May 20, the exploring party crossed the Fraser River in canoes borrowed from the Natives. By 7 a.m. the men were walking down the west bank of the river, following its rocky shore toward Fountain Ridge. They crossed the mouth of Rivière du Pont (Bridge River) by the Native footbridge that had existed there for many years, and after a 10-mile hike down the Fraser's rough banks they arrived at the mouth of a rapid-filled watercourse. "The Indian name applied to the outlet of

The Fraser River from the east bank of the river, in the area of the Gibbs Creek Rapids, looking south toward the bulk of Fountain Ridge. Anderson and his men would have walked toward Fountain Ridge on the west bank of the Fraser River (the right-hand side of this photograph).
BC ARCHIVES I-57871

Anderson and his party would have walked down the shoreline shown on the right side of this photograph, taken at the Seton Lake salmon weir where Seton River flows out of the east end of Seton Lake. BC ARCHIVES A-03965

Seton Lake, as far as my recollection serves," Anderson later wrote of this tumbling river, "has a [name] so cacophonous that I scarcely dare write it. 'Pap-shil-qua-ka-meen'—ie., the River of the Lakes."[7]

The river tumbled from two isolated bodies of water that wound between high mountain peaks. The party broke for a meal at the head of the first lake and looked at the narrow stretch of water that lay before them, curving between precipitous mountains that reached 1,000 feet into the air. Anderson saw that the unbroken tops of the ridges were white with snow, precluding once and for all the route's possibility as a brigade trail. Now he needed to assess its potential as a river route on which the Company men could transport supplies both up and down river by boat.

The men believed they were halfway to Fort Langley at this point, and as they had no alternative route, they walked along the sloping north shore of the mountain lake, camping that night where it jogged westward. Anderson wrote in his journal:

> A ripe strawberry was picked here this evening. But the background
> is the most rugged and dreary-looking tract I ever met with; nor

had I any previous conception that so mountainous a region could exist so near the banks of a large stream like Fraser's River.

We are encamped near an Indian village, containing at least 100 men, with a proportionate number of women & children. These one and all express their delight at our presence by every possible demonstration. So much so, indeed, that what with handshaking and laudations of every conceivable description, I am heartily wearied out. They behave in the most orderly manner, and if at all troublesome it is unintentionally so, from a desire to conciliate and please: killing one with kindness in short. They are now all returned to their lodges to smoke, upon receiving intimation that it was our hour for bed.[8]

The following morning broke fine and clear, and the party hiked to the end of the lake and crossed over a wooded point of land to another large lake beyond. A second camp of Stl'atl'imx people welcomed the fur traders with expressions of joy, but the party quickly bypassed the village and stopped for breakfast on a low point of land some distance up the lakeshore. The steep, bare mountains that had ringed the first lake now gave way to rounded tree-covered hills, and at the end of the lake the salal of the coast appeared for the first time. Soon the explorers found themselves walking through dense coastal forests of enormous timber and thick undergrowth as they followed eastward-flowing streams up the ridges of land that separated the two lakes from the Lillywit River.

On the second day, the Native guides showed Anderson a "large isolated block of granite, bearing the impression closely resembling that of a human foot. The Indians call it 'the Foot-stone,' and have, of course, a marvelous tradition connected with it."[9] Anderson heard the story of the Transformers, two magical groups of people who came from opposite directions to meet at this place. After transforming the lives and cultures of all the people they had found, one Transformer stamped his footprint into the stone to indicate the boundary between the Upper St'at'imc, who lived on the Fraser River and the lakes that Anderson had already passed, and the Lower St'at'imc or Lil'wat tribes on the rivers and lakes he had yet to reach.

The Company men left the height of land and followed the stream until they reached a village at the north end of a lake Anderson called

Lillooet Lake. He noted that the Lil'wat people had no food to spare, but "they possess . . . some good cedar canoes, made after the model of those seen on the coast. After some parlaying I succeeded in hiring a couple of these, together with the necessary conductors."[10] On May 22, the combined parties paddled past the rapids that blocked the lower end of Lillooet Lake and reached the lake Anderson's guides called Little Lil'wat Lake. Two Native canoemen refused to go farther, so the HBC men loaded their goods into the single canoe that remained and walked down the riverbank. At a second Lil'wat village, Anderson hired another canoe and men to paddle them downriver, and the party made camp that night at the head of a rapid where they would have to make a portage.

The river on the other side of the portage was rough and filled with rapids. "At this stage of the water it is a perfect torrent; and at a higher stage . . . must afford a very precarious navigation. In fact, but for the expertness of our Indian boutes, who are thoroughly versed in the intricacies of the river, we should, I fear, have much difficulty in getting through."[11] A few short portages avoided fierce rapids that blocked the river, and on the second day of river travel the two canoes floated into a large lake, "its upper end bounded by steep rocky shores affording few if any harbours."[12] They made camp halfway down the length of the 40-mile lake and the next day travelled through heavy rain to Harrison's River, at the bottom of the lake. Three hours later the Lil'wat paddlers brought their passengers into the Fraser River south of its barrier of rapids and falls, and that evening they delivered Anderson's party to Fort Langley (for a map showing the routes of Anderson's explorations, see the colour-photo section in this book).

Peter Skene Ogden was now chief factor in charge at Fort Vancouver, so it was to Ogden that Anderson addressed his report the following morning. Anderson condemned the route as altogether useless as a brigade trail and told Ogden he was returning to Kamloops by a route long known to the fur traders but never explored—a Native trail that led over the range of mountains running parallel to the Fraser on its east bank. Anderson hoped that this trail would take him to the area the fur traders called the Similkameen.

[16] THE RETURN JOURNEY OVER THE MOUNTAINS, 1846

On the morning of May 28, 13 paddlers carried the exploring party upriver in the Fort Langley boats, threading their way through the wooded islands of the Fraser River on a fine, clear day. From his evening's camp at the mouth of the Chilwhae-ook (Chilliwack) River, Anderson saw that the northern slopes of the hills that surrounded the river valley were coated with snow.

The party set off early the next morning, and at eleven o'clock arrived at the Tlae-Kullum (Silverhope) River. The Company men followed their Stó:lō guide, Pahallak, up the river's narrow defile until they crossed a steep mountain ridge and entered a narrow, boulder-strewn valley. Anderson knew immediately that this route could never be used as a brigade trail and ordered the party to retrace its steps. They set up camp that night in the dark, a few miles from the banks of the Fraser River.

On their passage up the Fraser, Pahallak had pointed out another possible route up a second river he called the Que-que-alla (Coquihalla), and Anderson now decided to explore that route. Early the next morning they crossed the Fraser in borrowed canoes, and Pahallak led them up the north bank of the large stream, through a broad, thickly wooded valley where vetch and horsetail grew. Anderson took the presence of these wild plants as a good sign, for both would provide feed for the hard-working brigade horses. At noon the men crossed a gravelly stream on a logjam of driftwood that was wedged in so tightly it made a secure bridge. They lunched where the Que-que-alla turned sharply northward and another river, the N'Calaownm (Nicolum), flowed in from the southeast.

The explorers followed the N'Calaownm up its valley. The mountains closed in, looming high above them, and steep, rocky banks made passage difficult where the cliffs butted up against the river. But Anderson saw that the riverbanks offered a soft surface for the horses' hooves, and at day's end, he was optimistic that this trail might become the new route into the Interior.

Early next morning the explorers followed the south banks of the stream and climbed an easy hill into a valley, where they rested. At noon they continued upriver with the stream on their left, and crossed over another height of land, arriving on the shore of a little lake nestled in a mountain valley. The open meadows had groves of large cedars and soft, mossy ground, and Anderson knew it would be a simple job to build a horse road through this valley.

No names for the little lake appear in Anderson's journal of that time, but by the time he drew his 1867 Map of British Columbia, he had named the lake for his cousin, General Sir James Outram, who had garnered fame in London and India. Anderson's Outram Lake was part of the Sumallo River system, but sometime between 1867 and the early 1900s, settlers or surveyors transferred the name westward to a lake, once the source of the Nicolum River, that was later buried under tons of rock and rubble from the massive Hope Slide of 1965. Anderson's Outram Lake still exists as anonymous Cedar Lake, a few miles east of the Hope Slide, and remains as quiet and peaceful as it was when he and his men walked its tree-shaded shoreline. (See map at top of page 113.)

Anderson's party followed the river the Native guides called the Simallaouch (Sumallo) toward the east, and where the stream joined another that flowed in from the south they met a Native hunter from Thompson's River who had crossed the mountains to hunt. "As he appears to possess a knowledge of the country superior to our other pseudo-guides (who are miserably at a loss), I have engaged him under the promise of some Ammunition & Tob[acc]o, to accompany us for a day or two."[1] The Thompson's River man guided them eastward along a track that followed the banks of the Simallaouch through country obstructed by fallen trees. "Our progress is slow," Anderson noted, "owing to the dilatoriness of our Indians, who are miserable walkers—for my own part, having a great deal of extra walking in the worst parts, in order to determine the practicability of doubtful passages, I have enough to do, in this sultry weather. Unfortunately for my efficiency, I this evening find myself suffering considerably from stiffness of my right leg, arising from varicose veins—an evil contracted some years back, and which threatens to be attended with painful, if not altogether alarming, results."[2]

There were any number of Native trails over these mountains, and the Stó:lō guides from Fort Langley advised Anderson to follow the easternmost fork of the river to the mountaintop. Because Anderson had found the Thompson's River trapper's information more accurate, however, he chose to follow the route he had recommended, a well-marked trail that ascended the mountain from a grove of trees where wild rhododendrons bloomed. The explorers followed a stream to the top of the mountains, and Anderson noted that "the ascent is very gentle, and perfectly clear of impediment throughout the greater part; frequent fires having destroyed the timber that heretofore encumbered the ground."[3]

At the top of the hill, however, it appeared that all the work they had done that summer might be for naught: "A dreary prospect met the view. The whole surface of the valley, as well as of the confining mountains, was white with accumulated snow."[4] Anderson thought the heavily laden brigade horses could not travel through the deep snow that would lie here in the early summer.

The Thompson's River trapper had left them at the bottom of the trail, and most of the Stó:lō men turned back at the summit. Anderson and his men now had no guide familiar with the country and were forced to find their own way across the top of this plateau and down its north side. They hiked north for three hours through snow that lay three or four feet deep. For the most part the men walked on the snow's frozen surface, but as the crust softened in the sun, travel became more difficult. At last, exhausted, they set up camp in a clear spot among the pines, on the banks of a creek that flowed from a little round lake Anderson named the Council's Punch Bowl.

In a map drawn more than 10 years later, Anderson indicated the position of Anderson's Tree, which stood slightly southeast of the Council's Punch Bowl.[5] It is probable that Anderson's Tree was the French Canadians' maypole—a tree lopped of all its branches except for a puff of greenery at its top. Making a maypole to honour a man or a special occasion was a tradition among the French-Canadian voyageurs, and like all traditions it was done to inveigle a drink of rum from the gentleman the tree honoured. On this occasion the voyageurs almost certainly succeeded in their goal. It was, after all, a historic moment: they had reached a height of land that no other fur trader had seen.

On June 4, the men set out at three in the morning, following the creek that flowed out of the Council's Punch Bowl across the plateau. A cold night had frozen the snow's icy crust again, and the men slipped and slid their way across until they reached land clear of snow. The creek bore away to the northwest, and they followed its narrow canyon down the side of the mountain. Anderson reported:

> The Indians are quite at a loss as to our position, knowing nothing of the country, and puzzling themselves and the Interpreter (Montigny) with fifty silly conjectures, sometimes supposing themselves upon a fork of the branch of the T[hompson's] R[iver] that falls in near its junction with Fraser's River. In fact, all of them seem to be much dispirited, but as I feel pretty secure, from the course which the river seems to follow (apparently bending round eastward in advance of us), that we are upon the right stream, so I have no anxiety on the subject.[6]

Anderson was correct in thinking they were on a tributary of the Similkameen River; the stream they followed was the Tulameen. That night the men set up a rough camp in the river defile and the next day they felled trees across larger streams that rushed in to join the mainstream they followed. Soon the country opened up and the occasional Ponderosa pine appeared. They continued down the east bank of the river, knowing they needed to cross the mainstream eventually. At one point they dropped a few trees across the stream, but when the makeshift bridge was almost secured the river rose rapidly and the water flowed dangerously over the logs. Discouraged, the men continued downriver until they located a natural logjam at a narrow spot a few miles away.

> Fearful of its being soon swept off, we placed hurriedly an extra tree or two to connect the sides more firmly; and taking off our shoes to avoid slipping on the wet drift wood, succeeded in our object. Altogether our bridge was a tremulous and marvelously unsteady affair; and my mind was relieved of no small degree of anxiety when I saw the whole party safely across. The old proverb tells us to "bless the bridge which carries us safe over," and I

say not do less than this, our friend in need, however dubious its
pretension to security.[7]

The exhausted men had travelled only 10 miles that day, and it was abundantly clear to all that this river defile was far too rocky to be considered for a brigade trail. After breakfast the next morning they felled another tree for a bridge and at its lower end followed horse tracks along a rough road until they met two Native men well known to them—"Blackeye, the Similkameen, and his son-in-law, on their way to visit their deer snares."[8] To Anderson's delight, Blackeye told him they were only a few hours by horse from Red Earth Fork (Princeton) where the Kamloops men had left horses for their return. Blackeye sent his son-in-law to bring the animals forward and offered to guide the explorers to Kamloops by a shorter route than the one regularly used by the Company men. On June 7, Blackeye led the explorers upstream past a five-mile-long lake (Otter Lake) to his camp at a smaller lake. The chief gave Anderson's men fresh fish and loaned them additional horses to carry them to Kamloops.

Finally, Blackeye told Anderson that a good Native trail led across the height of land they had just passed over, ending at the meadow where the rhododendrons grew. "He states that it is a wide and good road, with plenty of pasturage at the proper season; and that but for the depth of the snow, we could not have missed seeing it after crossing the height of land."[9] Blackeye agreed to show the company men the trail to the top of the mountains later in the summer, when the snow had melted.

The explorers made their way toward Kamloops through open country and set up camp where Bourdignon's River (Quilchena Creek) flowed into Lac de Nicholas (Nicola Lake). On the morning of June 9 they forded the creek at its mouth. Four miles later they unloaded their horses to cross the deep stream that flowed into the east end of Lac de Nicholas. At eleven o'clock the men climbed the range of hills that separated them from Kamloops, arriving at the fort a little after six o'clock that evening.

Twenty-six days had passed since Anderson left Kamloops in May, and on his return he wrote his report. He stressed that if this route were approved, a summer establishment would be required at a place where the horses must remain, probably at the junction of the Fraser and Que-que-alla rivers.

Anderson returned to Fort Alexandria, not entirely satisfied with his second exploration but confident that his work was done and a new route between Kamloops and Fort Langley had been at least partially uncovered. Opening Blackeye's trail to the plateau would be easily accomplished when needed, and as the route down the south side of the plateau and through the river valleys to the mouth of the Que-que-alla was already passable, there was little more for Anderson to do but return to the normal work of running Fort Alexandria.

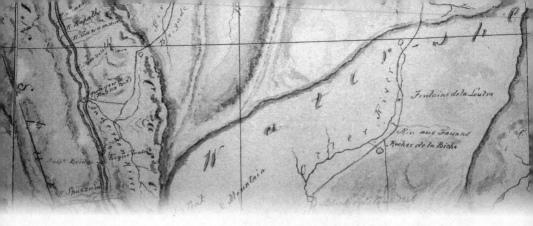

[17] THE NEW
CHIEF TRADER, 1846-47

Anderson rode into Fort Alexandria on the last day of June 1846, and the work of the fur trade continued. In late August, Chief Trader Donald Manson led the incoming brigade into the fort. A few weeks later, Manson wrote from Fort St. James to tell Anderson that two men had abandoned his brigade. Anderson discovered two saddles missing from Fort Alexandria's stores and suspected the men were well on their way to Kamloops. To prevent their escape, he hired Natives to steal their horses.

Within a few weeks the starving deserters stood outside the gates of Fort Alexandria. Anderson ordered the men back to Fort St. James but was not surprised when they showed up on his doorstep again. He chastised them, but relented when one of the frightened men fell to his knees and begged forgiveness. Anderson knew these French-Canadian deserters would never willingly return to Fort St. James because the hot-tempered Manson would thrash them. To keep their services for the Company, he put them to work at Fort Alexandria.

At Fort Nisqually, Anderson had been punished by Chief Factor McLoughlin for striking a voyageur. But in New Caledonia, the rules were different. In earlier years, both John Tod and James Murray Yale had beaten their New Caledonia employees, and club law still reigned under Donald Manson 25 years later. "You really must put a check on the 'Club-Law' which prevails in your district," Governor Simpson wrote Manson in June 1853. "It makes the service so unpopular, that it is difficult to entice men to join it. I can easily understand that the men are very

Donald Manson is remembered for the club law that ruled in New Caledonia, but punishment like his occurred at all fur-trade posts. As a student at the Fort Victoria school in the early 1850s, Anderson's son James watched as one of the Company's men was stripped, tied to a post and flogged with a cat-o'-nine-tails.

BC ARCHIVES A-00901

troublesome and difficult to control, at times richly deserving punishment which you are right to inflict but let it be in any other shape than corporal chastisement."[1]

Part of Manson's problem was that New Caledonia received the least able men and those with the worst attitudes. York Factory and Red River got the first pick of the new men every year, and most of the unskilled men were sent across the mountains to New Caledonia and the Columbia district. In 1844, Chief Factor McLoughlin complained to Simpson about the quality of the men who arrived at Fort Vancouver. Some were already too old and weak to carry out the heavy work of the fur trade, and a few were physically disabled—one man was missing three fingers on one hand, another had a withered limb. Economy now ruled Governor Simpson's fur trade. The voyageurs' wages had been reduced over the years and more work was expected of them; as a result, fewer good men joined the trade.

The hard work and the long years in isolated posts took a toll on the men, as well as on the gentlemen. Punishment was a necessary part of the fur trade: the men must be made to perform their duties as there was no one available to replace them. In December 1846, Anderson punished a man who had spoken rudely to him:

> I have to record that today I was under the disagreeable necessity of chastising one of the servants under my command—the more disagreeable to me, I may add, since it is the first occasion of my having to do so for some years past; and the only one since my sojourn in N.C. Having occasion to reprimand J. Bte. Vautrin for disrespectful language, which I did quietly in my sitting room, the man replied in so improper a manner that I was compelled to strike him a couple of blows, in order to maintain that authority without the possession of which one's efficiency in this country is more than doubtful.[2]

Over the winter of 1846–47, Anderson received his commission as chief trader in the Hudson's Bay Company's service. There were only three positions available to the gentlemen of the Company—clerk, chief trader and chief factor—and it was considered an honour to be named chief trader, for it was a public recognition of the good work done for the Company. It also meant a marked increase in wages. Even more important, chief traders shared in the profits of the Company. Since 1821, the Company's dividends had been divided into 100 shares, with 40 of those shares going to the men who worked in the field. These 40 shares were immediately divided into 85 shares, which were then distributed among the chief factors and chief traders. Each chief factor was entitled to two shares (or 2/85th of 40 percent of the total dividends of the Company) and each chief trader to one.

In 1831, when the two Anderson boys joined the fur trade, the chief traders' shares were high and a full 20 percent of the Company's profits went to dividends. However, the dividends dropped to 16 percent of profits in 1832, and a year later fell to a new low of 10 percent. By the time Chief Trader Alexander Anderson earned the right to take his share, the dividends were permanently set at 10 percent.

Governor Simpson also reduced the numbers of chief factors after 1834, and increased the numbers of chief traders. Reducing the numbers of expensive chief factors and putting more responsibility on the shoulders of less expensive chief traders saved the HBC money in dividends paid out. But retired chief traders received dividends for a full six years after they left the Company, and until a retired chief trader no longer received dividends, no senior clerk would be granted his commission as chief trader. Many a clerk did the work of a chief trader without ever earning a promotion, and some men were never considered, as was the case for Anderson's father-in-law, James Birnie.

Immediately upon receiving the letter that advised him he was now a chief trader, Anderson wrote of the joyful news to his brother James, now in charge of the Lake Nipigon post. In his response, James expressed his pleasure that at least one of them had received their long-awaited chief tradership. "Since one of us was to suffer disappointment and disgrace . . ." James wrote, "I rejoice that the blow has fallen on me, not on you."[3] Although James had never had a complaint lodged against him, he had been superseded in his department by three junior officers, men who in his opinion could never have properly run a fur-trade post and who were, in addition, relatives of either Governor Simpson or the powerful McTavish family. James was so angry at the slight that he considered leaving the Company's service. And he was so humiliated he could hardly show his face in the fort.

However, James pulled himself together enough to warmly congratulate his younger brother and to advise him that his first dividends should

James Anderson's fur-trade career took him from Moose Factory to Nipigon Lake in 1841. He made chief trader a year after his brother Alexander and by 1851 was in charge of the Mackenzie River district and lived at Fort Simpson, NWT.

GEORGINA PIONEER VILLAGE & ARCHIVES

be excellent because the returns in the east had been especially high. James's prophecy did not prove accurate, and within a year or two the fur traders suggested that a fixed amount of 400 pounds a year be permanently established for chief traders' dividends. But as James wrote, "Who will bell the cat?"[4] Governor Simpson had a free hand to do whatever he wanted to do, and no one had the power to prevent him from keeping dividends low. In the years after 1840, a chief trader's dividends averaged little more than 300 pounds sterling annually.

⇒ ⇐

On April 23, 1847, clerk Montrose McGillivray arrived at Fort Alexandria with dispatches from Fort Vancouver, including orders from Peter Skene Ogden. Anderson was to find another route to Fort Langley from Kamloops, this time through the rugged canyons and rapids of the Fraser River.

> *Recent information received by Chief Factor Douglas a short time since induces us to hope that a route can be opened from Langley to Thompson's River even more favorable than the one you returned by. The great objection to it appears solely to arise from the depth of snow that the Brigade might be liable to meet with and while there is a prospect of another route being found preferable we feel most anxious to ascertain if it be so ere we decide on commencing operations we consider it highly expedient that it should be explored and we see none more fit or suitable for the Expedition than yourself.[5]*

Anderson's party was not the first to attempt to follow the Fraser River south through its canyons to the ocean. In 1793, Alexander Mackenzie had begun the journey downriver, but the Natives had advised him to turn back and follow the Blackwater River to the sea. Fifteen years later, Simon Fraser and John Stuart set out to complete the exploration of the river that the men of the North West Company still believed to be the Columbia River. Fraser's party flew from one danger to another as they paddled through the series of rapids that impeded river travel south of Fort Alexandria. At the Iron Rapids, one canoe had its stern twisted off by the force of the rapids, and at French Bar Creek they followed each other down the rapids "in awful silence."[6] At last the men walked down the banks of the Fraser on foot. On June 26 they traversed the precipices of the Fraser Canyon on scaffolds and paths wide enough for a single man's passage, and on July 2 they paddled to the mouth of the Fraser. There, where the north arm of the Fraser reached what appeared to be the ocean, Fraser's men felt threatened by the hostile Musqueam and quickly escaped upriver. Fraser decided that the river, which was later named for him, would never have commercial value to the North West Company.

In 1828, Governor Simpson of the Hudson's Bay Company decided that the Fraser River should be explored once more and with the help of Chief Traders James Yale and Archibald McDonald, then in charge of Thompson's River post, made a two-pronged descent of the Fraser and Thompson rivers. At the Thompson's juncture with the Fraser, the parties met up and exchanged horror stories, then frightened themselves badly in the descent of the river through the canyons. Everyone survived, but Governor Simpson declared that descending the Fraser River by boat would result in certain death 9 times out of 10.

Now James Douglas and Peter Skene Ogden asked Anderson to explore a route through the Fraser Canyons to Fort Langley. While it had been years since Douglas left the comfort of a major fur-trade fort, Fort Langley's Chief Trader Yale knew how frightening the rapids were. But Yale also knew that the Stó:lõ around Fort Langley travelled through the canyons fairly regularly, and that Nlaka'pamux from above the Fraser River Canyons sometimes traded at Fort Langley. There must be a practical route past the canyons, and Anderson was expected to find it.

On the brigade's arrival at Kamloops in May 1847, Anderson was astonished to learn that the long-discussed Boundary Question had been settled a year earlier, with the new American border firmly fixed along the 49th parallel. This decision made it even more crucial to find a good horse road across the mountains to Fort Langley. But there was still no urgency, as the Hudson's Bay men expected to use their Columbia River route for a few more years.

On the morning of May 19, Anderson set out on his third journey across or around the mountains that lay between Kamloops and Fort Langley. He and McGillivray and four employees, including Michel Ogden and Edouard Montigny, rode over the hills to Lac de Nicholas, passing over the same Native road Anderson had travelled a year earlier on his return from Blackeye's camp. Almost immediately, Anderson met with one of the many hazards this type of journey risked:

I met with an untoward accident this afternoon which nigh put an end to my explorations for the nonce. My horse stumbled & rolled completely over, I narrowly escaping a broken leg. Fortunately, though painfull [sic], the injury is less severe than I first feared.[7]

The party set up their first camp at the west end of Lac de Nicholas. From there, Anderson had planned to take the Native road that ran from the west bank of the Nicola River across the valley to a gap in the surrounding hills near where the Nicoamen River flowed into the Thompson.[8] But the overflowing Nicola prevented their crossing at the usual ford and forced them along a path on the river's east bank. Anderson noted that this trail was littered with broken rocks and cactus and "quite unsuited, indeed, for the passage of many loaded horses."[9]

That night they camped a few miles from the junction of the Nicola with the Thompson, and set off again early the next morning, reaching the junction by 7:30 AM Anderson sent the horses back to Kamloops with their guides and crossed the Nicola River in canoes borrowed from the Nlaka'pamux people who lived here.

From this point, Anderson led his men on foot along the rocky shores of the Thompson River's south bank. The river foamed with white-topped rapids as it flowed swiftly past them, and the hot, sultry air was cooled a little by a breeze from the west. Though their path led up and down the hills of the uneven riverbank, Anderson considered it suitable for horses.

The tired men camped that evening close to the banks of the Nicoamen and rose before four o'clock the next morning to cross the mouth of the river on a fallen tree. The day was hot, and they walked past many rapids before stopping to enjoy the first meal of the day, close to the place where the Thompson River forced its way through a narrow channel into the Fraser. There they were joined by their Native guides.

Pahallak, the chief engaged by C.T. Yale, made his appearance shortly after our arrival accompanied by a large Concourse of Indians of every age and sex. A general handshaking took place. Before our little arrangements were completed part of the day had elapsed and at the earnest entreaty of the Indians I consented to encamp there. They are on their good behaviour and show every external desire to conciliate, but they are a scampish looking set of vagabonds; nor does their ordinary conduct, I believe, at all belie their looks; and though there is little to be apprehended from them under present circumstances, we are of course, as usual, on our guard.[10]

Pahallak, the Stó:lō chief who had guided Anderson's party the previous year, had been sent by Yale to guide them down the Fraser River. The next morning, the combined parties set off down the rocky eastern bank of the Fraser River.

4 miles further cross a stream from E. very impetuous. Owing to the height of the water, we did not cross at the usual ford, but on a tree higher up. To regain the road it is necessary to scale the edge of a precipice which is effected with the aid of a long withe of plane, fixed there permanently by the natives for the purpose.[11]

As in places farther downriver, the poles were probably supported by ropes strung down from the cliff tops. Travel in this rugged country was not easy and not for the faint of heart. Farther down the rocky banks of the Fraser River the party stopped for a meal a little beyond a palisaded Native village their guides called Skaoose.[12] The villages along this stretch of the Fraser River belonged to the Nlaka'pamux, people whom the fur traders considered treacherous because they were constantly occupied feuding with their neighbours. On this occasion, however, the village occupants greeted their visitors with "clamourous vociferations of welcome, expressed in a peculiar and amusing style of oratory."[13] Later, Anderson offered a better description of his experience with the warlike Nlaka'pamux:

Congregated for mutual protection in villages, frequently pallisaded, they had, until lately, a very limited intercourse with the whites . . . Yet while exploring with a small party toward Fort Langley in the summers of 1846 and 1847, I was received among these people with the kindest demonstrations, certainly at the time sincere, and whereof the notion is still possibly undisturbed. Man, woman and child at every village, brought a trifling present of welcome, whether of fish, wild fruits, or other local production. It was of course impossible to convey away the enormous

piles thus accumulated; so after a present of trifles in return,
the offering remained for a general scramble on our departure.
Everything was couleur de rose on these occasions; but then one
felt constantly as if seated on a powder magazine which a spark
might at any moment ignite.[14]

Because the path they followed was studded with pebbles and sharp
fragments of rock for long distances, Anderson wrote that the report of
"the country we have passed through I must, I regret, be unfavorable . . .
And though I do not condemn these passages as <u>impassable</u> with horses,
in the strict acceptation of that term, I decidedly think them quite imprac-
ticable for a loaded brigade, or loaded horses, however limited in number,
or indeed for anything beyond possibly, a light horse or two."[15]

That night they set up camp on the banks of the Fraser "near a popu-
lous village, one & all, I believe, fairly wearied out. A days march among
the arid hills of Fraser's river, with the thermometer between 80 & 90° in
the shade, is a trying matter, however willing the spirit."[16]

The men started off early the following morning, and crossed the Tse-
wamnia (Ainslie Creek) at its mouth in canoes. At noon they arrived at a
partially stockaded village of Squâ-zowm (Boston Bar). But even before
he arrived at this village, Anderson had heard of the recently opened
Native trail that led over the hills behind Squâ-zowm to Lac de Nicholas.
Before he left Kamloops, Anderson had arranged to meet Blackeye at
Lac de Nicholas. The Similkameen chief had not arrived when Anderson
made his journal entry for the day, but sometime before Anderson's party
reached Squâ-zowm, Blackeye's son and Tsilaxitsa, the nephew of the
powerful Chief N'kwala after whom Lac de Nicholas was named, joined
his party.[17] Now these two Native men showed Anderson the beginnings
of their newly opened road to Lac de Nicholas:

At 2.10 we set out to ascend the hills, by the horse road to the
Similkameen country. At 4 we reached a rivulet the banks of
which abound in fine pasture; thence in ¾ hour the spot where
the track we are to follow in the direction of the Falls, diverges
from the Similkameen road. In this vicinity I have appointed our
horses to meet us on our return. Hence to Nicholas Lake the
country is well known to Montigny who has passed through it
with horses several times. Michel Ogden too has passed through

it and their united testimony goes to represent it as favorable for
our purpose, after the bestowal of some labour on it . . . The fea-
sibility of a horse communication with Squâ-zowm is established
more successfully than I at first anticipated, having always under-
stood that no practicable passage for horses existed down the hill
to the river side. Such indeed appears to have been the case by
the road once followed. It is only recently that the Similkameens
have examined the country, and opened the new road, which the
height of the hill alone excepted, is unexceptionable in its facili-
ties of ascent or descent.[10]

But the most difficult part of their journey to Fort Langley still lay
ahead as they approached the part of the river that was squeezed between
upright rock walls. Below, the canyons and rapids were rough and dangerous. Early the next morning, the Stó:lō guides led the exploring party
up the banks of the Squâ-zowm (Anderson) River, which flowed into the
Fraser River south of the village, and followed its narrow canyon to a
place where impetuous Utzlius Creek tumbled in from the northeast.
They crossed the creek on a fallen tree and continued up the narrow river
valley, wading across a larger tributary (East Anderson). To cross the
mainstream of the river they constructed a temporary bridge, then continued along its southwestern bank for a few more miles. At last the Native
guides led them up the rough, sloping side of the high, rocky saddle that
separated the Squâ-zowm River from the Fraser. "The ascent is tedious,"
Anderson noted in his journal, "but by making the road deviously, the
inconvenience of the hill may be easily overcome."[19]

At the top of the rocky saddle (Lake Mountain), the explorers found
a level plateau, free of undergrowth, where a few patches of snow still
lay. A short diversion to the west brought them to the top of bluffs that
overlooked the heavily forested side of the mountain that tumbled all the
way to the Fraser. Anderson saw, far below him, the maelstrom of rapids
and whirlpools churning through the narrow, deep canyons that made
this part of the Fraser impassible. The fur traders had always called this
The Falls, but as Anderson noted, "There is no such abrupt descent as the
name implies."[20]

The party camped that night on the top of the rocky plateau and
next morning "descended the hill in a slanting direction to the village of

Kequeloose upon Fraser's River which spot we reach after 2 hours slow travelling. The track may be easily improved and by making an occasional circuit a good horse road may be constructed."[21]

From Kequeloose (Alexandra Lodge) the men followed their guides down the banks of the Fraser until they looked across the river at Spuzzum, the Nlaka'pamux village that stood at the mouth of a busy creek (Spuzzum Creek) that flowed in from the west. Pahallak suggested that it was safe to cross the river at this point, but in Anderson's view, the wide Fraser flowed far too swiftly here and provided no sloping banks that would allow the horses to clamber out of the water.

The party "procured a canoe and after some delay succeeded in crossing."[22] They were now on the west side of the Fraser, but three miles of rapids lay between Spuzzum and the wide, smooth river that led west to Fort Langley. Anderson took a two-pronged approach to this final leg of the journey.

> *I determined on ascertaining whither the navigation in the direction of the falls, was so bad as I was led to believe, for the information I had recently received from the Indians, induced me to hope that means of overcoming the obstacles, by portage & otherwise might possibly be devised. Accordingly I dispatched Mr. McGillivray to pass the party by the land track marked on Pahallak's sketch, while with Montigny & some Indians I proceeded in a canoe by the river. In 35 minutes we reached the head of the Falls, running a small rapid by the way. Several hours after the party arrived, Mr. McGillivray [arrived], reporting very unfavorably of the road.*[23]

Beyond this point, the Fraser rushed through a narrow gorge between high walls of rock. In a later report to Governor Simpson, Anderson expressed his horror when he first viewed the rapid-filled canyon:

> *The scene wears indeed a formidable aspect, and I was at first inclined to despair of success. For a distance of three miles the torrent rushes between rocky precipices, towering in parts to a height of 600 feet or more. From these lofty escarpments, however, enormous fragments have toppled down, which, protruding on the stream, present a perpendicular, and apparently unbroken, front of solid rock.*[24]

The party ran their canoes down the first set of rapids. The rough, tumbling rapids were interspersed with open stretches of fast-running water, and although this part of the Fraser appeared to be relatively free of hazards, Anderson knew it would be difficult to bring loaded boats upriver on the return voyage. However, he considered it might be possible to carry the boats over a long portage through narrow ravines that bypassed this first set of rapids.

Once the first rapids were run, the river widened, and rock ledges, smooth or broken, slanted under the waters. Along the shoreline of this stretch of river stood the empty wooden scaffolds where Natives dried their fish in the summer fishing season. They found a portage that bypassed the second set of rapids; a third portage led over a point of land opposite an island in the river, avoiding another set of rapids. The men finally set up camp below the last portage on the west side of the river, and Anderson made his journal entries while his voyageurs smoked around their fire.

This image of the Fraser River shows the rapid-filled river above Spuzzum, a little north of the place where Pahallak suggested the fur traders cross with their horses to reach the tiny post they called Simon's House. BC ARCHIVES C-09593

This aerial view of Yale looks northward up the Fraser, and shows the cliffs above Yale where the dangerous Native trail led fur traders to the southern part of the Fraser River. BC ARCHIVES B-01916

The explorers noticed a major change in the country's appearance on this day's travel. A day or two earlier they had been travelling through the hot and dry interior climate of the Thompson's River, where sagebrush and other shrubs, such as cactus and wormwood, grew close to the riverbanks. Beautiful prairies stretched away from the riverbanks in places, bordered by lofty hills and sparsely scattered with timber. Ponderosa pine, aspen, cottonwood and bunchgrass grew where they could find a foothold. South of the Thompson's junction with the Fraser, wild vetch covered the dry, bare hills, and the radiant dwarf sunflower bloomed everywhere. But at The Falls, where the Fraser River appeared to break through the mountain ridge, heavy coastal rains had encouraged a thick growth of cedar and large firs that Anderson found monotonous.

On May 28, the men threaded their way downriver through the broken rocks that protruded from the foaming river. After two more portages, the Native guides led the explorers via a stony path up the cliffs to a narrow causeway that Anderson described as "dangerous cedar boards connecting the several projecting points of a precipice."[25] These "boards" were probably poles, with one end resting on the broken rocks of the narrow trail, the other suspended by deer-hide ropes from the top of the overhanging precipice, joined by one or two more poles hung in the same fashion and tied together. The men crossed these flimsy bridges by clutching the face of the cliff and inching across, knowing that one false step would cause the poles to sway and drop them into the murky Fraser that rolled in angry waves 100 feet below. Thirty years earlier, Simon Fraser had ventured over these same fragile bridges, noting that his men "had to pass where no human being should venture."[26]

Shortly after this terrifying portage was completed, the explorers followed the rocky trail to solid ground and waded across a stream close to a village that belonged to the Stó:lō tribes of the lower Fraser. Here the explorers obtained fresh potatoes and salmon for their breakfast, and Anderson hired canoes to bring his men to Fort Langley. That evening Anderson and his men set up their tents outside the walls of Fort Langley.

As he always did, Anderson refused the comfortable bed offered him by Chief Trader Yale. There was no need to remain with his men to prevent their escape (a precaution required in later years, when the fur trade was a less appealing occupation), so sharing the relative discomfort of camp was probably another example of Anderson's style of leadership. But while he declined the bed, he almost certainly enjoyed a meal in the Big House with the chief trader.

[18] THE ANDERSON'S
RIVER TRAIL, 1847-48

A
nderson and his men left Fort Langley on the morning of June 1, 1847, heading back to Kamloops, and two days later stood at the foot of the first set of rapids, on the west bank of the Fraser River. They travelled in two canoes—one the Northwest canoe that had carried them upriver the previous year, the second borrowed on their way downriver. "The first will be left with its owner below the Falls," Anderson noted. "The second it is my wish to take as far as Kequeloose, the spot where I propose the horse portage to commence, thus to afford evidence that the navigation is available so far."[1]

Anderson's guides led the party by a short portage over a rocky point of land and past a rocky island in the middle of the river (Lady Franklin Rock), to the east bank of the Fraser. That night Anderson expressed his optimism in his journal:

At present, light boats, might, I conceive, be taken up with a line, or at most require to be transported for a short distance at the worst part. A series of eddies conducts to a second portage upon the same side (right ascending). It is 700 paces in length & very favorable in its nature. Carried our canoe here, or rather dragged it, for the overhanging branches prevented our carrying. It would be necessary to discharge at this portage, but the lightened boats might, I am of opinion, be taken up with the line with comparatively little trouble.[2]

On its way upriver in 1847, Anderson's party camped at the foot of the rapids where Lady Franklin Rock squeezed the river into a narrow channel. BC ARCHIVES B-01921

From the place where an isolated grove of oaks (Yale Garry Oak Ecological Reserve) stood on the river's east bank the Native guides led them across the Fraser River again, and the party breakfasted below a new set of rapids created by rocky islets exposed by the low waters of the summer. They portaged through a small channel and over rocky points of land to another quiet patch of water where they crossed the river, before lining their boats up the river's east bank to the last set of rapids. Anderson noted that neither portage offered "serious obstacle to our boats, light or at half cargo."[3] But his optimism was short-lived:

> *All went very well, when after almost every obstacle, except the last rapid, had been surmounted, an untoward accident occurred. The line . . . suddenly broke, owing to the canoe taking a sheer out while the steersman was disembarked. An Indian, the bowman, was alone in the canoe. It was swept downwards with rapidity, in spite of the lad's exertions to propel it to shore. Fortunately, after running some of the worst of the rapids, he succeeding in getting into an eddy, the canoe half full of water . . . At first some of the near relations became a good deal excited, taking their arms apparently disposed for evil . . . By prudent*

management we contrived shortly to dissipate the momentary chagrin, and after some parley & a smoke the Indians consented to assist us as before.[4]

The Natives were no longer willing to trust the rotten boat line, so they carried the canoe upriver by an overland path that bypassed the rapids, while the Company men walked ahead with their axes, cutting branches to clear the way. It took five hours to reach the village at Spuzzum Creek.

On June 5, Anderson's party paddled their Northwest canoe upriver, hugging the riverbanks to take advantage of the swiftly flowing river's many eddies. At Kequeloose they hid the canoe in the bushes for Pahallak to find and return to Fort Langley. Then Anderson distributed axes to all hands, and everyone chopped down trees to clear a wide path that zigzagged up the hill behind Kequeloose. That evening they set up camp at the top of the hill, overlooking the rapids and whirlpools of the Fraser River canyon.

The next day the party descended the cliffs to the upper reaches of the Squâ-zowm River. For three more days they climbed the series of hills on their way to Lac de Nicholas, carving a trail through the wooded landscape along the path of the Similkameen trail. On the third day they hit lightly wooded hills, and Anderson told his men to mark the trail with blazes to indicate the approximate route.

At this point, a Nlaka'pamux youth realized their path was not going to take them to the junction of the Thompson and Fraser rivers as he had believed.

The scamp in question seized one of the men's guns & attempted to pull off the gun cover. Discovering, however, his action, Montigny and myself advanced to prevent him; Mr. McGillivray with the others standing aloof, in readiness to repel any treachery on the part of the rest, would they have shown symptoms of interference.

They, however, betrayed no signs of sympathy. The chief actor in the scene upon being grappled with, evinced evident marks of trepidation, and after a momentary hesitation yielded up the gun. I afterwards spoke to the Indians in plain terms, enquiring once for all whether we were to look upon them as enemies or friends in order that we might regulate

our conduct accordingly, and whether I was to judge their dis-
position in general, from that manifested by the individual in
question. They all denied in strong terms having any desire to
side with him, condemning his conduct, and loading him with
long winded objurgations with all the energy of their cacopho-
nous dialect.[5]

When the speechmaking ended, Anderson led his men up the hillside
trail. They set up camp that evening at a horse rendezvous, where they
found none of the expected horses waiting for them in the corral. On
June 9, Anderson paid the remaining Natives with ammunition, tobacco
and other items of value to them. But as the explorers walked away, the
troublesome youth slipped behind a tree and aimed his gun at them.

This morning, after all the party had set out from the enc[ampmen]t,
as I was bringing up the rear with the interpreter, our friend of
yesterday, who had been sitting during the morning moodily aside,
ensconced himself behind a tree and cocked his gun. Montigny
and myself advanced upon him to ascertain what his intentions
might be. Seeing his gun cocked, I took off the cover of my own
gun, as a precautionary measure, and then directed Montigny to
examine that of the Indian, to see if it was primed. The fellow
got quite confused, and suffered Montigny to take the gun out of
his hand. Eventually the affair assumed rather a ludicrous aspect,
since the arm proved to be neither primed nor loaded.[6]

Anderson did not punish the boy, but rejoined his party. They soon
met the Kamloops men bringing the horses. On the next day, Anderson
left McGillivray behind with some men to finish marking the trail, while
he and Michel Ogden rode through the wind and rain toward Kamloops.
They crossed Maka Creek and Coldwater River, following the east bank
of the latter river through open country until it flowed into the Nicola
River. At five that evening the two men reached Lac de Nicholas and two
hours later they camped at Bourdignon's River. The following day heavy
thunderstorms and hail slowed their travel, but they reached Kamloops
in mid-afternoon.

Anderson wrote his report to the Board of Management at Fort
Vancouver. "It is difficult to realize a conception of the ruggedness of the

extraordinary region without actual observation," he noted. "One is surprised rather at finding any practicable passage, than disappointed in the reverse."[7] He concluded that the Fraser River route could be used to carry furs downriver and trade goods and supplies upriver, but he knew there was a big difference between clambering up and down this river with lightly loaded canoes and travelling with the heavily laden bateaux of the Company's brigades in the freshets of early summer. Much work would have to be done before this could be a good route, but no one expected that it would be needed immediately.

When James Douglas received Anderson's report, he travelled to the Fraser River to investigate and was horrified at the violence of the river rapids. He explored the river canyon for himself, discovering a rough and rocky passage through a mountain defile on the west bank of the Fraser that entirely bypassed the rapids and came out below the Spuzzum village. Douglas knew it would take a tremendous amount of work to make this rugged passage a satisfactory horse trail, but he thought the work might be completed over the next two years, in time to be used by the outgoing 1849 brigade.

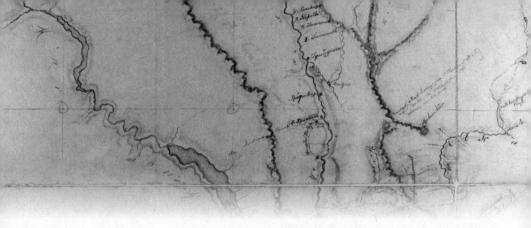

[19] A YEAR OF
GREAT CHANGES, 1847-48

At Fort Alexandria, the September weather was cold and overcast. Because of the drought of early summer, the wheat grew thin and scanty, though there was a good harvest of other grains. The mill needed repair, and a shortage of good men in the territory meant that Anderson depended on Native employees to get the work of the fort done. The early summer's rush of salmon had been encouraging, but at the end of summer the Dakelh fishermen had caught only a few salmon in their weirs. In 1847, both agriculture and the salmon run failed, and over the winter the fort's food supplies dwindled.

The normal rations for each employee were two salmon and one pint of flour a day, with four gallons of potatoes and a half-keg of turnips a week. When the flour ran out, Anderson substituted a quart of barley and increased the ration of turnips. The Fort Alexandria men worked cheerfully, for they knew they were better fed here than at other forts in the district.

Measles began to sicken a few Dakelh around the fort, and Anderson took the precaution of teaching the chiefs how to treat the illness. In January 1848, a few women and children inside the fort took to their beds, and two weeks later the houses were crowded with the sick. By the end of the month, everyone at Fort Alexandria had recovered, but all around the fort the Dakelh succumbed to the virulent epidemic that spread rapidly.

In mid-February, Anderson learned that every man at Kamloops had been laid low by the measles, and 35 Natives had died. At Fort Colvile,

100 Natives were dead, but Anderson believed those reports were exaggerated. They were not. The measles epidemic had begun months earlier in the Columbia district, and the results had severe implications for all the posts west of the Rocky Mountains.

A few Natives who visited the Waiilatpu Mission, near Fort Nez Perce, died of a particularly malignant mix of measles and dysentery. Although the missionary treated the sick with whatever medicines he had available, his patients continued to die. A Cayuse chief set a test for the missionary, demanding he treat a boy who lay sick. The boy died, and the Cayuse attacked the mission house with guns and axes, murdering 14 residents and taking many hostages.

When news of the massacre reached Fort Vancouver, Peter Skene Ogden gathered together trade goods to ransom the prisoners and set off with a well-armed party of voyageurs. The Company men forced the Cayuse into an uncertain peace, but out of this uprising came the Cayuse War of 1848, when all the tribes along the Columbia River went to war. It became clear to the Hudson's Bay men that the New Caledonia and Fort Colvile brigades could not use their Columbia River route to Fort Vancouver, and James Douglas gave orders for the men to come out by the unfinished trail Anderson had explored the year before. He also instructed the Fort Langley men to build an unstockaded post, Fort Yale, near the Stó:lō village just south of the cliffs that divided the north river from the south. Men improved Douglas's passage through the rocky defile, now called the Douglas Portage, and constructed another post, Simon's House, at its north end.

At Fort Alexandria, Anderson received orders to take over the command of Fort Colvile, on the Columbia River. This meant he not only had to prepare to bring out his brigade over the unfinished route he had explored the year before, but he must also pack up his belongings and bring his family to spend the summer at Kamloops. On May 5, 1848, the New Caledonia brigade left Fort Alexandria, with Anderson and Donald Manson riding in the lead. They arrived at Kamloops later that month, where they joined the Thompson's River and Fort Colvile brigades. Donald Manson commanded the combined brigades, with Anderson acting as Manson's guide over the rough trail that few other men had seen.

It was not usual for the Fort Colvile men to bring out their furs by horseback, and the result was a combined brigade twice its normal size. Fifty men had to bring out 400 loaded horses, many of which were unbroken. The various brigades made their way over the hills south of Kamloops and followed the well-used Native trail past Lac de Nicholas to the beginning of the new brigade trail.

This 10-foot-wide road wound its way through the sparsely wooded hills along the banks of the Coldwater River and mounted the forested slopes of the ridge of hills that blocked the way. The brigaders followed the trail along the base of these mountains to a pass, before descending the hills on the west side to the banks of the Squâ-zowm River, now called Anderson's River. They followed the mainstream south, to the place where bridges had been hurriedly constructed earlier that spring by the Fort Langley men so the horses could cross the river.

The men and horses then clambered up the rocky bluff that led to the height of land between Anderson's River and the Fraser. This was where they experienced the most difficulty. From the rocky saddle of Lake Mountain, the horses came down the zigzag trail of the Big Hill and reached the banks of the Fraser River near Kequeloose. A few miles down the riverbanks, the brigaders looked across the Fraser at Simon's House.

The boats or scows used to carry the goods across the Fraser River to Simon's House proved to be difficult to handle, and a number of horses drowned as they swam across the river. Manson remained at Simon's House to organize the men and horses while Anderson led the first traverse of the Douglas portage. At the south end of the 13-mile portage, the brigade men stumbled into the newly built Fort Yale.

No one in this outgoing brigade kept a journal, and no one wrote a detailed report of the downward journey. All Anderson wrote was:

It is needless to enumerate the difficulties which we had to encounter and surmount, suffice it to say that we continued to reach Fort Yale, which had meanwhile been established, with our packs, and thence ran down speedily to Langley.[1]

Anderson arrived at Fort Langley on June 8 with the nine Fort Vancouver men who had been sent to Fort Colvile to assist with the outgoing brigade. These men were to return to Fort Vancouver, and Anderson, after a brief visit to Fort Victoria, returned to Fort Langley.

On his arrival at Fort Langley, Manson discovered that six of his men had deserted his brigade rather than face the hard work of their journey home. The brigade was already returning across the mountains without the nine Fort Vancouver men who had assisted them on their way down, and the desertions would make the trip more difficult. No one looked forward to the return journey to Kamloops.

On July 15, Anderson travelled as a passenger in the first of eight or nine boats that carried almost identical loads upriver to Fort Yale. In addition to a large square-headed axe, a cooking kettle and a boat line, the boat carried 47 pieces of luggage, including a few bales of iron-works, 5 rolls of tobacco and 13 bags of ball and shot. Provisions included 90 pounds of fresh beef, 100 pounds of pork and 100 pounds of flour.[2] Anderson later described the difficulties of the upriver voyage:

Hitherto, bateaux of about three tons burthen have been employed by the Hudson's Bay Company, for transport below the Falls—a slow method when the water is high, as the ascent can then be effected only by warping along shore, with the aid of Indian canoes to pass the lines. By this tedious process, an ascent was made during the freshet of 1848, to the foot of the Falls, in eight days; under ordinary circumstances, it would occupy five.[3]

Two days after Anderson left with the first four boats, Manson loaded his grumbling men into five bateaux and two riverboats, all deeply laden and manned by Stó:lō paddlers, for the voyage to Fort Yale. Manson's new clerk, a young Englishman named Henry Newsham Peers, kept a journal that recorded many of the difficulties he and Manson endured in their overland journey to Kamloops.[4]

The high water of the Fraser River flowed heavily against them, and Manson's men warped their boats through the throngs of startled Natives who now swarmed the riverbanks, fishing for salmon. When the brigaders finally arrived at Fort Yale after eight days of chaotic upriver travel, they discovered that some of their horses had been wounded or killed by the fishermen, while others were starving and weak from lack of grass.

Because of the shortage of healthy pack animals, Anderson and Manson hired some Stó:lō men to carry more goods upriver by their old trail, which clung precariously to the rocks at the edge of the river. Then they picked out the healthiest horses and sent them over the portage with the first loads of trade goods. The trail began with a gentle rise and continued over a long hill that climbed upward to the height of land, where

Many different Native tribes travelled up and down the Fraser River to gather on these rocks and fish for their supply of salmon every year. BC ARCHIVES A-08917

another steep hill cut sharply down 700 feet into the ravine of a little river (Sawmill Creek). A bridge carried the horses across the river, and the land rose gradually and levelled off to run gently into Simon's House. It was not a particularly difficult portage, but when Manson and Peers finally crossed it with the last loads on August 2, two of their tired horses fell as they climbed the big hill, and the trail lost itself in the swamp where many passages had churned the area into a sea of mud. Manson joined Anderson at Simon's House that night, just in time to set up camp as darkness fell.

It took the Company men three days to ferry their packs across the Fraser River and swim the horses across. Everything arrived on the east bank of the river safely, and on August 6 the journey to Kequeloose began.

The horses were divided into groups or brigades, with each brigade in the care of a few men who were entirely responsible for all horses and the loads they carried. Typically, a Company brigade was made up of seven to nine horses only, but due to the shortage of employees, these brigades contained an average of 18 horses, in the care of only two men. The men were overworked and overwhelmed, and it did not take long for disaster to strike. On the morning of August 7, the brigaders found Jacob Ballenden dead on the outskirts of camp, shot through the heart with his gun at his side. The Fort Colvile man had apparently committed suicide, unable to face the difficult road ahead. The men carried Ballenden's body back to camp, and the priest, Père Nobili, who travelled with the brigade, said a brief prayer before he was buried.

The remaining voyageurs spent most of that day gathering together the scattered horses that had strayed off after dark to find grass, many still carrying their loads. By the end of the day, all but six packs had been found and one horse lay dead.

Next morning they started up the hill to the top of the plateau that divided Kequeloose from the Anderson's River canyons. The first brigades set up camp by late afternoon at the bridges that crossed Anderson's River; later brigades arrived well after dark or camped at the top of the hill. The brigaders spent the following morning waiting for the last brigades to catch up and recovering lost trade goods, for an inventory showed that 80 packs were missing. Many packs had fallen down the dangerous cliff faces into the river and would never be recovered, and some horses had been killed by falls. While Anderson waited for the arrival of the last few brigades, Peers fished for supper in the river that bore Anderson's name.

At last the men packed the horses and set off down the bed of Anderson's River before crossing turbulent Utzlius Creek and ascending the steep hill on the other side. At the top of the first rise lay a little prairie with fine grass, but the brigades passed this by and climbed another steep hill to a miserable horse guard close to the shores of a little lake. Again, many of the rear brigades arrived after dark, and their horses wandered off before they could be unloaded.

That night a thunderstorm rolled through, and heavy rain soaked everything. The brigaders herded the starving horses into the park for an early start the next day, and the gentlemen sent Natives out to find the missing packs. All but two pieces were found, and Manson paid the Natives for their hard work.

August 12 dawned fine and clear. The exhausted men captured and loaded the horses, setting off at midday. They followed the winding trail up the steep hills, hoping to reach the hilltop. But the starving and exhausted horses limped from their travel over rocky paths, forcing the leading brigades to stop in the woods five miles short of their destination.

Three brigades were left behind to set up camp in the dark a few miles down the hill.

The next morning, Anderson loaded the strongest horses and set off for the height of land, while Manson waited for the delinquent brigades and the return of packs that had been lost. At the crest of the hill, Anderson found fresh horses waiting for them and immediately sent some back to Manson's camp. Manson and Peers finally reached the hilltop in the early afternoon of August 14 and set off after Anderson, who had ridden ahead with most of the brigades. They spent the first part of the following day trying to catch and load the fresh young horses. That night Manson set up camp on the banks of Maka Creek.

On August 16, Manson left some of the brigades behind in Peers's charge and caught up to Anderson at Coldwater River. Here, in the narrow grassy valley where there was good food for the horses, everyone relaxed and the men became quite cheerful. At last Peers's brigades marched in to join them, and five days later the reunited brigades rode into Kamloops.

No one arrived at Kamloops in a good mood. Because of the scarcity of horses, the employees had been forced to walk almost all the way in moccasined feet, and they considered this a severe infringement of their rights. Thirty-five horses had been lost—27 died on the return journey alone—and 14 bales of goods were missing. The gentlemen held a meeting, and Donald Manson condemned the route. Anderson defended his road over the hills but agreed that it appeared more rugged from horseback than it had when he travelled it by foot the year before. In his letter to Manson, written on his arrival at Kamloops, Anderson reported on some of the problems.

> From the traverse to Kequeloose the tract (about six miles in length) characterized by me in my report last year as practicable only through much labour and many painful circuits is very bad and dangerous. It is in this part that our chief loss of horses by maiming occurred, both in outgoing and incoming. There likewise, property was lost by falling down into the river from the precipices.[5]

Anderson suggested that the brigades should use Blackeye's trail over the mountains to the Que-que-alla River and Fort Langley—the trail he had partially explored in 1846. The other gentlemen agreed and together they wrote a letter of instruction to Henry Peers, ordering him to take Montigny and ride south to Blackeye's camp, where he would have the Similkameen chief show them the trail to the top of the mountains.

The gentlemen spent three days at Kamloops, separating the loads for the various posts and exchanging property and horses. Then Donald Manson's brigades left for New Caledonia, while Anderson led his men toward Fort Colvile.

⇒ ⇐

In the late summer of 1848, Henry Peers and Edouard Montigny located Blackeye at his village on the lake south of Kamloops. Blackeye kept the promise he had made to Anderson two years earlier and arranged for his son to guide the two men over the trail to Council's Punch Bowl Lake at the top of the mountain. Together the three men rode up the side of the Que-que-alla plateau by way of a small river valley, arriving at a round lake that resembled Council's Punch Bowl but was, in fact, a different lake. Anderson's Tree did not stand on the shores of this round lake, and Montigny did not recognize the place and could not locate Anderson's trail down the south side of the mountain. Instead, the two men followed their guide across the top of the plateau to the west and down the mountainside by a steeper and more difficult path than the one travelled two years earlier. At a stream he called Soaqua (Sowaqua), Blackeye's son pointed out the path that Peers and Montigny should follow to reach the valley of the Que-que-alla and, eventually, the Fraser.

The trail led across a ridge and down the banks of a rushing mountain stream into the valley of the Que-que-alla River. They followed the Que-que-alla to the stream that Montigny finally recognized as the N'Calaownm—the river he had followed upward with Anderson. From that point it was a quick downriver walk to the banks of the Fraser River where they paid Stó:lō Natives to transport them by canoe to Fort Langley. Peers arrived at Fort Victoria in December 1848 and reported to James Douglas that the new road was quite feasible as a brigade trail.

Douglas immediately ordered work to begin on the new trail, instructing John Tod of Kamloops to send as many men as possible to open up the road from his side of the mountains. Peers was to build the trail from the west side, and Douglas dispatched 10 Fort Langley men to build a small summer establishment at the mouth of the Que-que-alla River. When the new post was finished, it was named Fort Hope.

Douglas believed the road could be cut to the mountaintop before winter set in, and the trail would be finished for the outgoing brigade of summer 1849. But an early winter brought in a deep, heavy snow that buried the Que-que-alla River valley all the way to the top of the mountains, and Peers accomplished nothing in the way of road building that season.

[20] FORT COLVILE,
1849-50

Fort Colvile stood in a beautiful horseshoe-shaped valley surrounded by steep, wooded hills, on terraced land above the east bank of the Columbia River, and three-quarters of a mile north of turbulent Kettle Falls. A dwelling house, three or four storehouses and some smaller buildings, all one-storey high and built of squared logs, formed the main part of this orderly post. Behind the houses stood the cattle yards and hay sheds covered in bark, and three warehouses that stored the farm's produce. Fifteen hundred acres of arable land supported crops of wheat and corn. The three pigs that had been brought up from Fort Vancouver 10 years earlier now numbered in the hundreds.

At Fort Colvile, 35-year-old Anderson was in charge of three important posts and supervised 6 clerks and 30 employees. Joachim Lafleur was in charge at Fort Okanogan, the small post on the Columbia River used by the New Caledonia brigade as a transfer post in normal years. On the banks of the Kootenay River to the east of Fort Colvile stood the three tiny buildings of the HBC's Kootenais House. A husky young Scotsman, Angus McDonald, was in charge at Fort Connah, which stood south and east of the old Flathead House it had replaced in 1847. No palisades circled Fort Colvile when Anderson first arrived, and he immediately ordered that new stockades be built around the main part of the fort. The US Army, now in the Columbia District, had been unsuccessful in settling the Cayuse War, and the fur traders felt less secure than they had in years past.

Normally 200 horses grazed on the grasslands around the fort, but in 1848 the winter blew in with snow and extreme cold, and all over the territory livestock suffered and died. At Fort Colvile alone, 60 cattle and 50 horses perished. The hard winter, combined with the heavy loss of horses during the recent brigades, so depleted the stocks at Fort Alexandria and Kamloops that John Tod feared there were not enough horses to supply the brigade.

However hard the winter was for the Fort Colvile horses, the cold was a boon for the business of the fur trade. Badger, bear, fox, lynx, marten, muskrat, otter and red fox were trapped around Fort Colvile, and Anderson's trade in furs easily surpassed anything he had accomplished at Fort Alexandria. The 1848 outfit came to an end in May 1849. At Fort Colvile the fur traders took in larger than usual numbers of beaver skins and grizzly bear, fisher and red fox pelts.

In April 1849 the York Factory express, coming upriver from Fort Vancouver, was slowed by sickly horses and deep snow northeast of Fort Nez Perce. The New Caledonia men were also delayed, and while Anderson awaited the express's final departure from Fort Colvile, he wrote his annual reports to Governor Simpson. This year he indicated his decision to delay taking the furlough that was generally earned with a chief tradership:

> *I have for some years past had a strong desire to visit home; and it was at one time my intention to apply for leave of absence next year. The unsettled state of affairs, however, has induced me to defer doing so until things are in a fairer train. I have now been so long a resident in the Columbia, that I almost begin to identify myself with its interests; and now that there is a prospect of its affairs on American Territory being finally wound up, I should like, having followed the chase so long, to be in at the death at last.*[1]

On Sunday, March 22, Anderson held divine services in the fort, and early the next morning the men of the express departed for Boat Encampment. Soon afterward spring blew in, the snow melted away to leave the valley floor ornamented with flowers and Anderson turned his attention to other concerns. Because the Cayuse War still raged in the territory south of Fort Colvile, the brigade men could not take the risk of travelling down the Columbia between Fort Okanogan and Fort Nez Perce. The winter that had killed so many horses at Fort Colvile and Thompson's River had prevented the Fort Langley men from finishing the new road over the mountains to Fort Hope, and there was not another route available. By March it became obvious that, once again, the brigades must travel out by Anderson's River and Douglas Portage, to Fort Yale.

With sinking hearts, the brigaders assembled at Kamloops in May 1849. For the Fort Colvile men, it had been a nine-day journey from their post, following the Kettle River west until they could cross the hills to Osoyoos Lake, then over the ridge to the Similkameen River valley and north to Kamloops. As Anderson waited for his men to assemble their brigades for the last push over the hills to the Fraser River, he sat on the hillside above the fort and sketched the scene.

⇒ ⇐

No improvements had been made on the unsatisfactory Anderson's River trail, and the brigade spent 10 days making the crossing from Kamloops. When they arrived at Fort Langley on July 10, James Douglas awaited them to ensure that all ran smoothly. The brigaders left Fort Langley on July 25, planning to return to Kamloops over the new Que-que-alla road, but when they reached Fort Hope, no horses waited to carry them home. Without wasting any time, the men set to work widening and clearing the new brigade trail to ease their return journey over the mountains.

The animals that eventually arrived at Fort Hope may have been the same horses that had carried the loads down the Anderson's River trail and over the rocky saddle to the banks of the Fraser at Kequeloose. The extreme shortage of horses in the territory meant there were not enough pack animals to carry the supplies away from Fort Hope, and both the New Caledonia and Fort Colvile brigades were forced to leave a portion of their trade goods behind. It was a worrisome and stressful time for all the men at Fort Hope, especially for the New Caledonia men who had to travel all the way north to Fort St. James before winter set in. After a heated argument with Donald Manson, Anderson packed up his brigades and travelled over the trail without waiting for the New Caledonia men. When news that Manson and Anderson had exchanged "high words" reached Fort Vancouver, Chief Factor Ogden worried about the divided brigades among the numerous Natives he envisioned on this high plateau.

However, the Fort Colvile men rode over the mountains with little difficulty and, bypassing the long diversion north to Kamloops, arrived at Fort Colvile 18 days after leaving Fort Hope. In his letter to Governor Simpson, Anderson reported, "I subsequently to our separation, received a note from Mr. Manson, stating that he had safely passed the Mountains with his Brigade."[2]

Fortunately for the Fort Colvile trade, the post at Fort Hope was close enough that Anderson could send his men and horses back over the new trail to pick up the remainder of their supplies, and they made their second trip in only 27 days. Donald Manson was not so fortunate. He was forced to leave 55 packs at Fort Hope, and the shortage of trade goods caused him considerable trouble the following winter.

The quarrel between Manson and Anderson worried the Board of Management for many months afterwards, but as neither gentleman made any reference to the disagreement in their various reports, Douglas was unable to discover the cause. However, Manson reported on the argument in a letter to Governor Simpson the following spring. When Manson left Kamloops on his outgoing brigade, he arranged for a number of Okanagan and Secwepemc men to travel over the new mountain trail to Fort Hope, opening it up on their way. Manson also planned that Anderson would remain behind at Fort Hope to work with a party of French Canadians, opening up the new trail from the west end. Anderson refused to do the work unless Manson assigned him clerk Henry Peers as his assistant, and even then he would only do it after he'd had a chance to visit Fort Langley. Manson complained that "by this arrangement much time was lost."[3] After Anderson's departure from Fort Hope, the Thompson's River Natives rode into the post and reported positively on the trail's possibilities. Immediately, Manson hired a strong party of Natives to widen the new road.

⇒ ⇐

On his return to Fort Colvile in late summer 1849, Anderson found the harvest almost secured and the fur trade promising. News of the California gold rush now flooded the fort, but all of Anderson's men chose to complete their contracts before escaping to the goldfields. The next spring, Anderson reported the California gold rush's effect on the Fort Colvile fur trade to Governor Simpson:

Truly, sir, much as the important combination of the four small letters sounds sweetly to the ear at most times, one wearies of it through satiety here:—"Gold, Gold, Gold" is the cuckoo cry on all hands. Everyman has his eye open for that. The whole land is frighted from its propriety; and the bed of every Columbian stream and rivulet, within the range of Brother Jonathan has, I dare affirm, been pertinaciously scraped in the hope of new discoveries.[4]

In early spring 1850, an important visitor arrived at the fort. Eden Colvile was a member of the family after whom Fort Colvile had been named and son of Andrew Colvile, the man with whom Anderson's uncle, Alexander Seton, had been long associated. Andrew Colvile was now deputy governor of the Company in London, and Eden Colvile had been appointed associate governor for Rupert's Land in Governor Simpson's temporary absence in Europe. In late 1849, Colvile made a quick overland journey through New Caledonia and via the brigade trail to Fort Victoria. After a short visit at Fort Vancouver, he set off with the outgoing express and spent a week with Anderson at the fort named for his father.

Anderson told Colvile of the shortage of affordable horses in the territory and suggested that some be brought across the mountains from Edmonton House. Colvile had already noticed the poor condition of the New Caledonia horses, many of which were so exhausted from their multiple journeys over the mountains that they might not survive the winter. He agreed that it might be profitable to import animals from Edmonton and, later that year, made arrangements for 100 Edmonton House horses to be sent across the mountains. Colvile later reported to Governor Simpson that: "I have written stringently to Manson & Anderson to take care of these horses, as we cannot promise them a regular supply by this route."[5]

The winter of 1849–50 passed slowly. In the spring James Douglas worried about the brigades due to come over the new route, where snow remained until early summer on the mountaintops. Ogden reported to Simpson that Douglas planned to be at Fort Langley to direct affairs, as "without a conductor, the Gentlemen are not competent to conduct their own affairs, trifling as they are, and a separation is absolutely necessary as Pugilistic affairs between the two leaders is not exactly the proper

mode of conduct in Brigades in presence of the Company's servants."
In this same letter, Ogden told Simpson he had offered Anderson a promotion to chief factor and a marked increase in pay if he would agree to "superintend the affairs of New Caledonia for the remainder of the service, provided he would consent to remain there." But Anderson was "deaf to the offer," and refused it.[6]

The reason Anderson gave Ogden for his refusal was that the education of his children was too important for him to isolate himself at Fort St. James. But the real reason may well have been that the problems Donald Manson had encountered in running this difficult and isolated territory were compounded every year by the increasing difficulty of getting good men to work the fur trade. James Douglas wrote that "the agony and suspense of this life is torturing, wealth is truly no compensation, except it leaves one at liberty to seek a change."[7]

There were many good explanations for the dearth of good men in the fur trade. First, with all the American settlers arriving in the Columbia district, some men chose not to renew their contracts with the Company and retired to set up businesses in the area. In a few cases the news from the goldfields lured the men away to California. But many of the staffing problems the Company now suffered began years earlier, in London.

In the mid-1840s, the Company made some powerful enemies. Influential men who were eloquent speakers argued against the Company's monopolistic practices in Parliament, and even the new publisher of the *Albion*, a British newspaper that all the fur traders read religiously, proved to be no friend of the Company. When a Métis ex-employee appeared in Britain's Parliament to charge the Company with oppressing the mixed-blood Red River settlers, the story appeared in British newspapers and caused a scandal in London. More cries of outrage rose from London streets when the newspapers revealed that the new colonial secretary, the 3rd Earl Grey, had granted the Hudson's Bay Company the exclusive use of the lands and minerals of Vancouver's Island, all without the consent of Parliament. As a result of these scandals and the many that had preceded them (for years the London directors of the Hudson's Bay Company had been plagued by charges of monopoly), the pool of educated and able-bodied men willing to join the fur trade dried up, and the Company was forced to hire less talented men.

In April 1850, Anderson reported lower returns in the fur business than in previous years. The bonanza of 1848–49 was over and the trade was in decline. Eighty-five Flathead men had died as the result of wars with their enemies from the prairies to the east, who had grown so bold they murdered a Company employee, David Finlay, three miles from Fort Connah. Because the man was the child of the botanist David Douglas, who had explored the Columbia district in the late 1820s, Anderson told Governor Simpson of Finlay's death:

He was met by a party of Blackfeet who had just been repulsed from an attempt on the establishment. They shot, stripped, and scalped him.[8]

The clerk at Kootenais House reported lower trades because of the influenza that swept through the area and killed 30 men of the small Kootenay (Ktunaxa) band. At Anderson's own post the Colville Natives abandoned the low pay of the fur trade and worked for the nearby American settlers for the comparatively high pay of three dollars a day.[9]

With the outgoing spring express, Anderson applied for furlough, though he knew his chances were slim. Many men had requested time off before him. John Tod was sick at Fort Nisqually, and Paul Fraser had taken his place at Kamloops; Donald Manson planned to take furlough 10 years after his last, and Peter Skene Ogden had permission to go on furlough, though he had returned from his last in 1846. By 1850, Anderson had worked in the Columbia district's fur trade for 19 years without a break, and every year the territory's problems had increased while the rewards lessened. No one now expressed optimism for the future of the fur trade, nor did anyone express appreciation for a job well done. "I am sometimes tempted to wish that the good old times were back again," Anderson wrote. "If profits were less, they were more secure; and we had the benefit of tranquility into the bargain, which is out of the question now-a-days."[10]

In addition to worrying about the fur trade, Anderson had personal worries. His widowed mother, whom he had not seen since he left London in 1831, was sick, and his wife, Betsy, had been suffering for some time from an unidentified inflammation that may have resulted from her most recent

In the early 1860s, HBC employee Angus McDonald visited Anderson at his new home in Saanich. The noise of McDonald's bagpipes brought Betsy and Anderson to tears and frightened the Natives, who thought a battle was going on. BC ARCHIVES A-01495

pregnancy. But there was no one to replace Anderson at Fort Colvile. Henry Peers had refused the position, and all the gentlemen agreed that Fort Connah's Angus McDonald did not have the necessary experience to take over the charge of such an important post.

[21] FORT COLVILE BRIGADES, 1850-51

When the brigaders rode out of Fort Colvile in June 1850, no one knew whether the new road over the mountains could be crossed with horses so early in the season. The Fort Colvile men swam their horses across the Columbia River and followed the Kettle and Similkameen river valleys west to the base of the mountains, where their trail intersected the new brigade trail from Kamloops. At Campement des Femmes (Coalmont), the brigaders rested for the night.

The men and horses began their journey up the narrow river valley to the top of the mountains early the next morning. Snow lay everywhere, but the men crossed the plateau without difficulty on its frozen crust. The first stop was on the shores of Lodestone Lake, 12 miles from Campement des Femmes. Another 12 miles brought them to their camp on a bend on the east bank of the Tulameen River at Podunk Creek, and the next day they travelled to Encampement du Chevreuill (Deer Camp), just below the summit on the Soa-qua Creek side of Manson Mountain. Nineteen miles farther on, Manson Camp lay at the head of Peers Creek, and on the next day a 15-mile journey brought them down Peers Creek and the Que-que-alla River valley into Fort Hope. After a night's rest at Fort Hope, Anderson and his men boarded the boats and journeyed downriver to set up camp at the mouth of Harrison's River. The air was thick with mosquitoes, which so annoyed the men that they abandoned the land and, lashing their boats together, drifted downstream with the current. The sentry woke the brigaders in time for them to paddle around the last bend in the river, their voices raised in song.

In 1850, two of Anderson's children, 12-year-old Eliza and 9-year-old James, rode away from Fort Colvile with their father for Fort Langley. James Douglas had convinced Anderson to enroll his children in the school established inside the walls of Fort Victoria. Chief Trader Yale welcomed the Anderson family and quickly installed them in the gentlemen's quarters.

The next morning was a day of great excitement for the Anderson children, as the ship that carried James Douglas to Fort Langley sailed majestically up the Fraser River and dropped anchor in front of the fort. The sailors offloaded the trade goods, and Douglas came ashore to be ceremoniously greeted by the gentlemen and voyageurs at the fort. Two days later, the New Caledonia brigades arrived, with Donald Manson in charge, and Paul Fraser leading the Kamloops men. Fort Langley sizzled with excitement as the men unloaded the boats and the voyageurs celebrated their arrival with the regale.

Fort Langley buzzed with the news of the gold rush in California. To deter desertions, the gentlemen allowed a shorter break than was usual, and the work of the return journey soon began. There was no disagreement between Anderson and Manson this year, but Douglas reported to Governor Simpson that Anderson and Paul Fraser had argued:

> Fraser as usual promises great things, more I fear than can be reasonably expected from him. He has an unfortunate tongue, which is a never failing source of trouble to himself and all around him. Anderson was very bitter with him at Langley about some reports to his prejudice and was disposed to go to great lengths with him but I advised him to drop the matter and patched up a reconciliation on Fraser's solemn promise of amendment for the future—which I fear was forgotten as soon as the parties separated.[1]

At length the day of parting from his children arrived, and Anderson consigned them to James Douglas's care. While Anderson led the Fort Colvile men eastward to Fort Hope, James and Eliza began a rough two-day journey to Fort Victoria, in James Douglas's canoes. In October, Douglas reported to Anderson that Eliza and James were doing well in school and were favourites of Mrs. Staines, wife of the schoolmaster.

What he did not write was that when Eliza arrived at Fort Victoria, Mrs. Douglas took away the sack-like garment she wore and gave her a new dress and hat. James's leather pants proved more suitable, but his leather shirt was exchanged for a belted moleskin blouse with enormous buttons down the front.

In the same letter, Douglas complained of that quarter's paltry dividend—"some one hundred pounds, just about enough to keep us in tobacco money."[2] As Douglas was a chief factor, he would have received twice the money that Anderson, a chief trader, received in quarterly dividends. Earlier that year, Peter Skene Ogden had commented to Governor Simpson:

> *What inducement does the fur trade hold out? None. They look around them on all sides and behold nothing but old men covered with grey hairs, having given forty years servitude and still steeped in poverty.*[3]

In the late fall, Simpson wrote to Ogden, reporting that Anderson had put in an urgent application for leave of absence so that he could cross the mountains to visit his mother in Canada. Simpson said that there was no suitable officer in the east to replace Anderson. Could Ogden find a man? But Ogden could not; there was a shortage of qualified gentlemen in the Columbia District.

There was little news from Fort Colvile over the winter, but in early 1851 Anderson renewed his urgent request for leave. He wanted to spend the next winter in the Columbia district so his sick wife would have access to the doctor at Fort Vancouver. Again the Board of Management expressed its willingness to grant him his application but found no one in the territory to replace him. All the other gentlemen in the district had requested furlough, and almost all had received it. Donald Manson was leaving New Caledonia for a year, and Chief Factor John Ballenden was crossing the mountains with the incoming express to relieve Ogden at Fort Vancouver.[4]

Anderson was stuck at Fort Colvile. His fur-trade returns were in decline, and he worried about keeping his men until their contracts were finished. His wife had been ill for more than a year. His eagerly anticipated chief trader dividends had proven to be less than his brother had optimistically forecast a few years before. Anderson may have been able to set some time aside for private interests such as hunting or map making, but those pleasures were less stimulating when there was no one to share them with. The lack of support from the Company, his isolation from the other gentlemen of the trade with whom he could discuss the problems and share the pleasures of the business, his distance from any people other than his French-Canadian and Iroquois employees, and the lack of time for hobbies or interests outside the fur trade all contributed to Anderson's exhaustion.

Anderson was so isolated at Fort Colvile that he did not hear of the changes happening in other parts of the territory. At Fort Vancouver, so many men had abandoned the fur trade that Ogden depended upon the Natives to carry out necessary work at the fort. The few employees who remained could not prevent the American settlers from stealing the fort's fences to use as building material for their houses, nor could they protect the livestock, which were lost to theft or butchery. In a letter to Governor Simpson, Peter Skene Ogden complained:

> *I have just received letter from Colvile—the returns fair—Mr. A. C. Anderson is in great trouble for want of a linguist, a whole page on the subject—it is truly ridiculous and still more calling on me to supply him with one. I have not six white men in this establishment, and we are reduced to Indians to cook our victuals, while these men, Anderson & Manson, are enjoying their ease and comfort, and calling on me for Interpreters & Horsekeepers just as if I had nothing else to occupy me than dance attendance on these gentlemen, while they have abundance of resources within themselves if they could only use a little exertion.[5]*

In the summer of 1851, when Anderson and his Fort Colvile brigades arrived at Campement des Femmes, they discovered the brigade trail was much improved. The men of Kamloops and Fort Hope had constructed bridges through boggy ground, felled trees to widen the trail and built long switchbacks up steep slopes. On sharp corners, where the horses liked to rub their loads against the trees, protruding triangles of wood placed a foot or two above the ground forced the animals to swing wide

The Interior Salish who camped near Fort Colvile called Angus McDonald Oops-chin, probably because of his whiskers. Anderson also earned a Salishan name that is difficult to translate— S'gath poose. BC ARCHIVES B-01483

and prevented damage to the goods they carried. Alfalfa and white clover now flourished alongside the trail, and eight acres of alfalfa grew outside Fort Hope. The rough trail of previous years had been made into a good horse road.

On July 15, Anderson arrived at Fort Langley and enjoyed a brief visit with his children, who had travelled from Fort Victoria in James Douglas's canoe. The return journey over the mountains was quick and easy, and the Fort Colvile brigade arrived home on August 15. In September, the clerk-in-charge of Kootenais House rode away from Fort Colvile, and Angus McDonald set off for Fort Connah. On November 15, 1851, when the incoming express boats drifted into Fort Colvile, Chief Factor John Ballenden found Anderson seriously indisposed. His entire family and all the employees of the fort were sick or slowly recovering from the fierce influenza that raged through the district, sickening Natives and fur traders alike. Ballenden, who had crossed the mountains to take over Fort Vancouver while Peter Skene Ogden was on furlough, ensured that everything was in good order at Fort Colvile before continuing down the Columbia River in the express boats, taking the Anderson family with him.

[22] NO FUTURE
IN HIS PAST, 1851-52

On November 20, 1851, Ogden met the incoming express on the beach in front of Fort Vancouver. The influenza-stricken Andersons had mostly recovered by the time they reached the headquarters, but Betsy remained sick. Anderson had arranged with Ballenden that if Ogden disapproved of his leaving Fort Colvile, he would take his wife to her father's residence and return to his post. But Ogden was pleased to see Anderson as it meant he was free to depart on his furlough. Chief Factor John Work was coming to Fort Vancouver to train Ballenden, but Ogden left Ballenden's immediate training in Anderson's hands and boarded a ship for the east coast.

Anderson was shocked to see that Fort Vancouver was no longer the sprawling, bustling headquarters he had left 10 years earlier. Only a few dozen employees now worked at the fort, and its fields had been taken over by well-established American settlers. On the hill that overlooked the fort, the soldiers of the US Army had constructed their rough barracks, best described as corrals with roofs.

Before he left Fort Vancouver, Ogden instructed Anderson to take the express packet and furs to Nisqually, where they would be forwarded to Fort Victoria. On his arrival at Nisqually, however, Anderson found a crisis in the works. At the new Oregon Territory capital of Olympia, American customs agents had seized two Company vessels and impounded their cargos. John Work, one of three members of the Board of Management and the man who had been travelling south to train Ballenden, had been a passenger on one of the seized vessels and was now delayed at Fort Nisqually.

British spies Henry Warre and Mervin Vavasour travelled with the HBC express to Fort Vancouver with Peter Skene Ogden in 1845. When Anderson first saw Fort Vancouver in 1832 it was probably only 318 feet square. By 1836 it was 318 feet x 638 feet, and additions during the early 1840s extended its stockaded length to 733 feet. BC ARCHIVES PDP05241 (ARTIST: HENRY JAMES WARRE)

Anderson's old friend of Fort McLoughlin days, Dr. Tolmie, had long been in charge at Nisqually. The two friends took a quick trip north to Olympia to deal with the immediate problem of the seized vessels. On their return to Nisqually, Anderson stayed with Work while Tolmie delivered the news to Fort Vancouver. Work thought it more important he remain to deal with the crisis of the seized ships and he now gave Anderson the Board of Management's instructions for Ballenden.

On Anderson's return to Fort Vancouver, he and Ballenden addressed the many problems caused by the influx of American settlers and the decline of the traditional fur trade. At first Ballenden thought Anderson to be "proud and restrained."[1] But his first impressions changed as the two men worked together, and Ballenden reported that Anderson was open, helpful, intelligent and very familiar with the problems of the department. Together the two men ordered new items to sell to the American settlers who now lived in the environs of the fort, and cut back on farming operations. They also worked with agencies that either purchased HBC products at wholesale prices or sold them on commission. Anderson looked into exporting salmon and timber directly to Chinese ports (an idea that Simpson had already tested and rejected), while Ballenden's letters suggested replacing Fort Colvile with a line of posts north of the boundary line to capture the rich furs traded in the Kootenais district while avoiding the duties the Americans now charged on their trade goods.

From Fort Victoria, Douglas told Anderson that he must return to Fort Colvile in the spring. "I regret our inability to relieve him at once," Douglas told Ballenden, "but able men like Anderson are not easily replaced."[2] In his letters to Governor Simpson, Anderson had expressed his thoughts of retiring from the Company many times over the past few years. He now decided the time had come, but because Ogden was away from Fort Vancouver, he delayed writing his final letter of resignation.

For 38-year-old Anderson, there were many reasons to leave the fur trade. One of the most obvious was that he saw how well his father-in-law was doing in the new business he had set up on the north shore of the Columbia River, halfway between Fort Vancouver and the new settlement of Astoria that had sprung up outside the gates of Fort George. After his retirement from the Company in 1846, James Birnie opened a store that

In 1846, James Birnie opened a successful business in Cathlamet, Washington Territory, which he ran until his death in 1864. This photograph of his store was taken many years after it closed, but before the building was torn down in 1926. PRIVATE COLLECTION DAVID K. HANSEN, VANCOUVER, WA

served the many American settlers in the new Oregon Territory. Moreover, Anderson's friend Archibald McKinlay had retired from the Company in 1851 and was now actively engaged in Allan, McKinlay and Lowe, a general store that was doing so well its principals planned to expand into San Francisco. The settlers needed supplies, and storekeeping appeared to offer a brighter future than the traditional fur trade these men knew.

Anderson recognized the effect the interference by American settlers and government officials was having on the profits of the Columbia district's fur trade and he saw no benefit in working for the Company for 20 more years. The dividends the Company paid to the fur traders who had worked for so long in the field showed no signs of increasing. Finally, for Anderson, the desire to set up a home for his family was another reason to leave the service. When he expressed this sentiment in a letter to James Douglas, the latter agreed, although with reservations:

> *I rather fancy your plan of preparing a future home for your family, but I trust you will not decide on abandoning the fur trade till you have some equally certain source of income in prospect. Small as our incomes are, they are too valuable to be lightly thrown aside.*[3]

For a while Anderson enjoyed a break with his family at his father-in-law's residence at Cathlamet. But in January 1852, Ballenden suffered a stroke, and Anderson returned to Fort Vancouver to take charge of the district until his recovery. Ballenden and Anderson agreed that the Fort Colvile brigade should come down the Columbia River by boat rather than making the cross-country journey to Fort Langley. There were many good reasons for this decision: there was a continued shortage of horses in New Caledonia and at Fort Colvile; the Cayuse War had finally wound down, and the Columbia River was deemed safe for travel; and finally, Fort Vancouver's warehouses bulged with trade goods on which American duties had already been paid.

The heavy customs duties the Americans charged on the HBC trade goods imported from England severely affected the profits of the Company forts south of the American boundary line, and had done so for years. From Fort Colvile Anderson had commented on the losses to the district when American customs duties halved the profits of £14,000. He rounded off his report with the words:

Gentlemen will not fail to perceive that the above statement of profit and loss by no means exhibits a true view of the profits on Lower Oregon—it was all very well last year to carry the amount of duties paid, to Gen'l Charges; for the reason, simply, that they (the duties) were then virtually a suspense account, and it was supposed they might be refunded—Not so with Outfit 1850, when that hope no longer exists, and we are evidently bound to pay the piper, however little disposed to dance withal. Permit me to subjoin a brief statement of your affairs below, which will considerably reduce the apparent amounts and relieve poor General Charges (who, poor fellow, has certainly a very broad back and a marvelous stock of patience) from the heavy burthen with which he has rather unmercifully been saddled.[4]

Anderson left Fort Vancouver with the outgoing spring express and arrived at Fort Colvile to find the agricultural work underway and the returns in furs excellent. In a private letter to Governor Simpson, written from Fort Colvile, Anderson suggested that a small post be located on the Arrow Lakes north of Fort Colvile. Such a post would secure the valuable furs of the Fort Colvile district while avoiding payment of duties on trade goods imported through Fort Vancouver. "It is obvious that the system of business in the Columbia District demands a radical alteration," he told Simpson, and continued with a criticism of Fort Victoria's place in the fur trade as he knew it.

The utility of Victoria, as a fur trade depot, seems more than questionable. Fort Langley is the ritual depot for the British interior; and might with ease be made to suffice for the North West Coast likewise. It seems clear that a vessel, touching at Victoria from England; and receiving an ordinary pilot there, could, if of a size not exceeding the usual burthern of our ships, reach Langley with little additional risk or difficulty—thus obviating the present costly necessity of intermediate craft; and reducing the demand for an establishment at Victoria to the simple requisites for the sale and trading shops—the sole possible source of profit there.[5]

The fur trade of the isolated New Caledonia and Fort Colvile districts had remained as traditional as it had always been, but Anderson was unaware that the trade on the Pacific coast was anything but. Fort Victoria was surrounded by grasslands that were quickly converted into large farms; it was close to the provisioning forts on Fraser's River and the northwest coast, and it had an excellent harbour that allowed sailing vessels to set sail at any time, and under any weather conditions. But it was the Company's agency in the Sandwich Islands that made a real difference, as the islands offered a huge market for many products that were not a part of the traditional fur trade. Hundreds of barrels of pickled salmon were shipped there from Fort Victoria, as was whale and fish oil, coal, cranberries, shingles, timber, cut and planed lumber, masts and spars for sailing ships, and agricultural products such as wheat and flour, potatoes and butter. The Company's products were sold into the local markets or to the many whaling vessels that gathered in the Sandwich Islands, but they also reached markets in Sitka, San Francisco, Chile, Manila and China. The salmon and timber sales on the Pacific coast soon became a very profitable branch of the Hudson's Bay Company's business. This Pacific trade through Fort Victoria and the Sandwich Islands agency was the culmination of the dreams of the early explorers of the North West Company, but it took Governor George Simpson's drive to make a successful business from that dream. Not only was Anderson not a part of this new business; he didn't even realize there was room in his traditional fur trade for this new economy.

⇒ ⇐

Before Anderson left Fort Colvile with the brigade boats that were to carry the furs downriver to Fort Vancouver, he had work to do. The Edmonton House men were delivering 150 horses through the mountains to Fort Colvile over the summer, and Anderson made final arrangements for the distribution of these animals throughout the district. Finally, as a result of the American agreement to purchase all the Company's properties south of the border, he had to survey and value all the lands and improvements in the various fur-trade posts.

On May 30, Anderson brought the Fort Colvile brigade onto the beach in front of Fort Vancouver. Sometime over the past few months the members of the Board of Management had overcome their objections to Angus McDonald's inexperience and had given him the charge of the

Fort Colvile district. McDonald would lead the brigade boats home and Anderson was free to take his furlough.

In July 1852, the Anderson family moved into a house immediately east of James Birnie's home at Cathlamet. In August Anderson took charge of Fort Nisqually for a month while Tolmie visited Fort Victoria. Tolmie returned with Anderson's two children, Eliza and James, and the Anderson family was united once more. Anderson had already written to Governor Simpson, advising him that "recent news did not reconcile me to a continuance in the fur trade."[6] In November, Anderson travelled to Fort Vancouver to visit Ballenden, who was disappointed to find that Anderson's intentions had not changed. "I think he will leave," Ballenden told Simpson. "The appointments of junior clerks over his head, first as a Chief Trader, and now as Chief Factor, galls him much, and I must say I can sympathize with him."[7]

In December Ballenden suffered another stroke, and the doctors warned him to refrain from work and stress. Anderson took over Ballenden's duties until Ogden's expected return in 1853, while Ballenden made plans to leave with the outgoing express in March. But Ogden did not return to Fort Vancouver in January as expected, and for two months the gentlemen anxiously awaited his arrival. By March, Ballenden had received a letter from Simpson that warned him not to leave Fort Vancouver in Anderson's hands. It is unlikely Anderson knew of this letter, and fortunately for Ballenden's plans to leave, Ogden reached Fort Vancouver in time for him to take the outgoing express across the mountains.

On the day Ogden arrived, Anderson gave him his notice of resignation in person. Anderson had made plans to enter Birnie's business at Cathlamet as a partner, selling Company goods on consignment as Simpson had suggested some months earlier. In June 1853 Simpson remarked to Ogden that "Anderson I think might have done better by holding on to the service a little longer, it is useless to say anything further on the subject." Simpson's letter to Ogden finished with the question:

> Pray, what do you think of Anderson as an agent, as far as I can judge he would do us justice, as although a little flighty, he is perfectly upright and honourable.[8]

10 - Walter Birnie, their 7th son, born
at Cathlamet W. T. 26th July 1856 - Bapt
by the Revd Dr McCarthy   November 1856.

11 - Rose, their 4th daughter born   at Cathlamet
28th August 1858 - Baptised by the Revd
McCarthy, 4th Jany. 1859.

12 - Allan Ottram - their 8th son, bo
at Victoria

[23] LIFE AND DEATH
IN NEW OREGON TERRITORY, 1853-57

As Peter Skene Ogden re-established himself at Fort Vancouver, Anderson returned to Cathlamet to enjoy the remainder of his furlough. He and Birnie took over the fort's salmon fishery, preserving fish for export to the Sandwich Islands. The work that the men of Fort Vancouver were no longer able to do often fell into the hands of private individuals such as Birnie and Anderson.

The first steamships chugged their way up and down the Columbia River between Fort Vancouver and the new town of Astoria, and every boat or canoe that travelled the river stopped at the Birnie store. Across the river from Fort Vancouver, the town of Portland slowly grew, and steamers pushed their way down the smaller rivers to Oregon City and up the Columbia to the new town of Cascades. By this time, everything north of the Columbia River was part of the newly created Washington Territory, but Cathlamet remained isolated from that territory's northern communities by hundreds of miles of trees, rocks and brush.

By late 1853, Ogden had convinced Anderson that he should remain in the Company's service. But Anderson placed conditions on his return, telling Simpson that he would stay with the Company only if he were promoted to chief factor. In 1854, Ogden told Simpson that Anderson had consented to go into the Snake River district for the summer, and in his appointments for the department he listed Anderson as responsible for the Snake Country for Outfit 1854.

In April, Anderson began his upriver journey to Fort Walla Walla (Fort Nez Perce). But in May he returned to Fort Vancouver with the news that almost all the Walla Walla horses had died over the previous winter. Ogden arranged to send goods that could be traded for horses from the Nez Perce, and he reported to Simpson that Anderson would return in a week's time. But ships now made mail delivery much faster than it had been in the past, and a few days before Anderson began his second journey into the Snake District, a letter arrived from Governor Simpson that reminded Ogden that the Company had no claim on Anderson's time after May 31, 1854. Governor Simpson was a man who needed to control all aspects of his fur trade, and granting Anderson a chief factorship on demand not only set an expensive precedent but was a sign of weakness he would not allow. So Ogden dispatched another man into the Snake district, and Anderson returned to his farm at Cathlamet.

In July, Ogden complained of feeling ill, and a month later Anderson wrote to Tolmie that "Ogden is very low. If he does not recover his spirits and appetite I entertain serious fears for him."[1] On August 18 Ogden moved to the house of his son-in-law, Archibald McKinlay, and six weeks later, Peter Skene Ogden died. On September 30, Anderson attended the final ceremony to say goodbye to the man he had worked with for much of his life.

⇒ ⇐

As early as January 1852, Anderson had declared his intention of becoming an American citizen, and he was naturalized in October 1854. This was a legal step he had to take to obtain the 320 acres the United States government gave every adult American citizen in the Oregon and Washington Territories under the Donation Land Claim Act of 1850. In January 1855 he became a commissioner of the court, able to take bail and affidavits, and a month later he was appointed a justice of the peace in Wahkiakum County. He also applied, through Governor Simpson, for the position of Oregon Territory agent for Lloyd's of London, the insurance market. Simpson described the job as "almost a sinecure without pay, it might at any moment become one of great importance."[2]

In May 1855, the man in charge of Fort Vancouver, Dugald McTavish, reported to Governor Simpson that most of the agencies in the area had closed. However, the Cathlamet agency thrived, and Allan, McKinlay and Lowe of Oregon City was also doing well. Anderson was involved in both businesses. Because one of Allan, McKinlay and Lowe's focuses was

supplying gold miners with goods and provisions, Anderson and his partner, Archibald McKinlay, decided to take a run into the Interior to assess
the opportunities that might exist for expanded trade in the territory once
owned by the Hudson's Bay Company.

They began their upriver journey in August 1855 and spent some time
at The Dalles, preparing four wagons to carry their trade goods. In a letter to his father-in-law, Anderson asked that Birnie brush up the large
gold scales to ship with the next load of supplies. Anderson's last words
told Birnie there were rumours of unrest among the Yakima people, and
the letter ended with the phrase, "One will require to look sharp."[3] A
large Native party had set out from Yakima River, and the American settlers above the Cascades were nervous.

Anderson and McKinlay travelled up the Columbia River as far as the
Arrow Lakes, north of the boundary line. In the past, Anderson had suggested to both Governor Simpson and John Ballenden that a post on the
Arrow Lakes would allow the Company to trade for the Kootenais' furs
without paying the Americans' crippling duties on trade goods, as Fort
Colvile was forced to do. Though he and McKinlay were probably selling
goods to the American gold miners who were working their way north
from the California mines, their future plans likely included setting up a
post that competed directly with their old employer's Fort Colvile.

On their way downriver, Anderson and McKinlay stopped near the
Spokane River, close to a camp of 100 or more gold miners. In the quiet of
the evening, a Spokane chief Anderson had known in the past approached
him to warn of an ambush that had been set by some Natives on the
Yakima River shortcut. "I do not wish to hear of bloodshed," the chief
said. "Tell these men not to cross the Columbia and take the Yackland
(Yakima) route—if they follow it not one will reach Olympia."[4]

Anderson and McKinlay spoke to an American official camping
nearby who called a meeting to tell the miners to take the longer route
home. McKinlay and Anderson followed the Spokane chief's advice and,
bypassing the Yakima shortcut, reached Fort Vancouver just before the
Yakima War commenced.

The conflict that erupted in the eastern part of Washington was not a
local war, for the Salish people of Puget Sound and Cowlitz were closely
related to the Yakimas. In September 1855, the first attack against a settler
occurred near Seattle. Four months later two settlers died in a skirmish

called the Battle of Seattle. There were small clashes all around the Puget Sound area, and the nervous residents of Cathlamet stayed close to home, keeping a careful watch. Their nervousness intensified when a red-painted box appeared in the top branches of a spruce tree near their houses. This was supposedly a signal for war, but no attacks occurred.

The US Army had little success in settling down the rampant Native tribes, and two years later the territory of the Upper Columbia was as turbulent as it had ever been. Although the Hudson's Bay men had no trouble and were always treated politely by any Native man who had known them in the past, the wars forced Anderson and McKinlay to abandon their plans for expansion into the Arrow Lakes district.

The Métis wives of the retired fur traders played an important role in protecting their communities, and none more so than Anderson's mother-in-law, Charlot Birnie. No Native man could plot an attack without Charlot being aware of it, and while the settlers who surrounded Fort Vancouver remained in a constant state of alarm, those who lived near Cathlamet were calmed by Charlot's steady hand. In spite of the

Charlot Birnie, Betsy Birnie's mother, was born in Red River about 1805. She might have been the daughter of Joseph Beaulieu, who crossed the Rocky Mountains with North West Company explorer David Thompson in 1807. OREGON HISTORICAL SOCIETY ORHI 101076

constant state of war, Charlot hosted many grand parties in the Birnie house. Guests included fur traders such as retired Chief Factor McLoughlin, and American soldiers from the camp outside Fort Vancouver. (One such guest was Captain Ulysses C. Grant, who, to Anderson's surprise, soon after became the President of United States.) On these happy occasions, Charlot decorated her house with candles and evergreen boughs and took her place at the head of the table with the self-confidence of an Englishwoman of long pedigree.

Anderson occasionally wrote letters to Governor Simpson to let him know how matters were proceeding in the Oregon Territory. In March 1857 Anderson reported that his sister Margaret, who had arrived at Cathlamet in May 1853 with Simpson's help, now planned to marry. He went on to add:

> I am happy to say that my family are well; and I know it will interest you to learn from me—though in such case possibly a partial witness—that my children conduct themselves in such-wise as in no way to dishonor the grizzled crown with which Time is liberally endowing me. My sister [Margaret] teaches the younger branches; I myself the elders; in a loose scrabbling way, but not ineffectually.[5]

In the same letter, Anderson broached the subject of returning to work for the Company. By this time the California gold rush had died down. A few miners were quietly finding gold as far north as the Thompson River, and so many miners were asking Anderson for information on the various routes into the Thompson's River district that he published a booklet containing the information they needed to access the new gold-fields. The *Hand-book and Map to the Gold Region of Frazer's and Thompson's River* was published in San Francisco in 1858, and it guided the Washington and Oregon miners northward via the Okanagan brigade trail or over the coastal mountains to Thompson's River—routes that Anderson had travelled many times as a Hudson's Bay fur trader.

Around the same time his book was published, Anderson approached the British government with a view to becoming its consul in the region. There was no British representative in this part of the United States, although there were many settlers of British ancestry. However, Anderson was diverted from this task. In April 1858, John Work wrote from

Fort Victoria to thank him for the package of seeds he had sent north, ending his letter with a hint of opportunity:

> *We have some difficulty getting proper efficient conductors for the operations now being commenced in the interior—had you not left from your knowledge of the country and experience and qualification generally, you would have been just the man to have done every justice to it and have insured...and likely benefited yourself, but it is too late now, this I have often regretted.*[6]

The letter spurred Anderson into action. He had grown dissatisfied with his quiet life at Cathlamet, where few opportunities existed and where Hudson's Bay men were never fully accepted by the American settlers. Fort Vancouver was almost abandoned, and his fur-trade friends had either died or moved to Fort Victoria. Anderson decided to visit James Douglas at the new headquarters of the Company on Vancouver's Island.

[24] THE CURSE
OF THE FUR TRADE, 1858-60

In 1849, the British Government established the new Colony of Vancouver's Island, and two years later Chief Factor James Douglas became its governor. Less than a decade later, gold was discovered on the Fraser and Thompson rivers, and the miners who had been in California began to make their way north in a new rush. As governor of Vancouver's Island, Douglas had no authority on the Fraser River or in New Caledonia, but he was the nearest British

Anderson, who delivered the New Caledonia and Fort Colvile furs to Fort Victoria every summer between 1848 and 1851, failed to realize what an important role the post played in the HBC's Pacific trade of non-traditional fur-trade items. BC ARCHIVES PDP00019 (ARTIST: MATTHEW MORESBY)

James Douglas was made governor of the Colony of Vancouver's Island in 1851, when the first governor, Richard Blanshard, abandoned the governorship and returned to England.

official, so in December 1857 he issued a proclamation declaring that all gold found in the area belonged to Britain. American miners had to purchase a licence from the colony's government before entering British territory.

In April 1858, 450 San Francisco miners streamed off the paddle-steamer *Commodore* after it arrived in Victoria's harbour. The population of the colony doubled overnight and continued to multiply as thousands of miners flooded the town's muddy streets and clamoured for transportation to the goldfields. Men hammered together rough boats in French Ravine north of Johnson Street, and hundreds found their way to the Fraser River on their own. A building boom ensued on Yates, Government and Wharf streets, and soon Victoria consisted of 70 wooden buildings, 1 brick house and 500 tents.

Two ships and hundreds of homemade boats carried miners east to Fort Hope. There they found the Fraser River so high they could not hike up its rugged banks to the goldfields, north of the same canyons that had troubled the Company's brigades 10 years earlier. Stories of miners who had discovered gold on the Bridge and Chilcotin rivers further excited the trapped miners, and Victoria sizzled with excitement.

In May 1858 Anderson arrived in this bustling shantytown to pass a few weeks with his old friends of the fur trade. Douglas offered him a position in the new government, but Anderson hesitated, for this would require him to leave Cathlamet and bring his family north. Finally, at the end of June, he accepted the position of customs collector for the free port of Victoria and committed himself fully to a future in the vibrant new colony.

When Anderson heard of the miners' difficulties in reaching the gold-fields of the Interior, he reminded Douglas of his explorations of 1846, when he had followed the chain of lakes and rivers from the Fraser River north of the canyons all the way to Fort Langley. The Hudson's Bay men would never have been able to bring their loaded horses across any trail they could have constructed between or around those lakes, but the miners had no need of horses. Once developed as a pack trail, this rough road might prove to be an efficient route around the canyons of the lower Fraser to the goldfields.

Douglas agreed. In mid-July the sternwheeler *Umatilla* arrived at Victoria under the command of Captain Ainsworth who, within a few days, set off on an expedition up Harrison's River to the north end of Harrison's Lake. News of the *Umatilla*'s successful explorations ratcheted the miners' excitement even higher, and Douglas announced his plans to build a proper trail into the goldfields by the Lillywit River route.

The government had no money, however, and hoped some private citizen would step forward to take charge of the new road's construction. The miners knew that something must be done quickly if they were to reach the goldfields before winter set in, and they presented Douglas with a proposition. They would cut a good road through from the head of Harrison's Lake to the Fraser River, on the condition that the government would furnish them with provisions while they were working. Each miner would deposit twenty-five dollars with the government to be used for purchasing the necessary supplies, and when the road was finished the miners would receive their money back in provisions. Douglas immediately accepted the miners' offer. In August, crowds of anxious men besieged the customs office to purchase their twenty-five-dollar certificates of deposit and their right to work on the road. Soon, 500 miners had signed up, and Douglas gave Anderson the job of supervising the trail construction.

Douglas also told Anderson to assign names to the lakes that were still unnamed. Most of the smaller lakes had been named by the fur traders or the Natives who lived on their shores, so ultimately Anderson named only the two large lakes at the far end of the trail. The first he called Anderson, for his own family; the second Seton, for his recently deceased cousin and childhood playmate Lieutenant-Colonel Alexander Seton of the 74th Highlanders.[1]

On August 5, "Mr. Collector" Anderson and the first detachment of 250 men sailed out of Victoria; the fort fired a salute on their departure. The next morning the miners cooked their breakfast outside the walls of Fort Langley, and by the evening of the next day the boat had paddled the length of Harrison's Lake and reached the cove at its north end. The first men off the boat dropped some trees into the lake as a wharf, and the remainder offloaded their supplies. After firing a salute to Anderson, Captain Ainsworth sailed away to pick up the second batch of miners. The road-builders pitched their tents on the narrow skirt of land a little above the water's edge, and the commissary served out rations of beans, flour, pork and coffee. After dinner, some men constructed a log storehouse for provisions, while others prospected in the creek and found a few particles of gold in every pan.

Work on the trail began early the next morning, and soon two or three miles of road stretched into the bush. On the second day they worked so quickly the surveyors could not stay ahead of the road-builders. By suppertime there were five more miles of good road. That evening the men walked back to the lakeshore and asked Anderson's permission to name the place after him. Anderson suggested it be named for Governor Douglas, and the miners gave three cheers for Port Douglas, and three more cheers for Anderson himself.

In a few days the second batch of miners arrived, and Anderson returned to Fort Victoria, leaving his assistant, R.W.D. Bryant, in charge at Port Douglas. He juggled the demands of supervising the work done on the Harrison-Lillooet trail with his continuing employment as customs collector, extending business hours for the Customs House. Douglas had hired clerk Charles Angelo as deputy collector, so the money for licences was now collected at the Customs House rather than through the Hudson's Bay Company office.

The children of Betsy and A.C. Anderson (left to right): Eliza Charlotte, 21 years old (assuming this photograph was taken in 1860); Agnes, 11; Rose, 2; and Walter Birnie, 4. The boys who did not pose for the photograph were James Robert, 19; Henry, 17; and Alexander, 15.

BC ARCHIVES A-07789

In early October, Anderson left Victoria on the *Constitution* and returned a month later with his wife and children. With the Harrison-Lillooet trail finished and the Customs House mostly run by his assistant, Anderson developed his own business interests. Thomas and James Lowe, of Allan, McKinlay and Lowe, had already moved north and expanded into shipping and shipbuilding. They built the *Governor Douglas*, the first sternwheeler constructed in Victoria, and immediately began work on its sister ship. Shares in the company sold for $200, and the shareholders' meetings were held in Anderson's office at the Customs House. As a partner in the Company, Anderson wrote to Colonel Richard Clement Moody of the Royal Engineers, now Lieutenant-Governor of the colony, and asked permission to name the new vessel after him. He signed his letter as "President of the Victoria Steamship Company."

[25] "AND I SAY
YOU LIE, SIR!" 1859

On April 13, 1859, Anderson took his official oath of office as customs collector for Vancouver's Island in front of his friend James Douglas. Beside Anderson stood Wymond Hamley, the collector for the mainland colony of British Columbia, officially established in November 1858. Before Hamley's arrival in Victoria, Anderson had acted as collector for Vancouver's Island and temporary collector for British Columbia. Anderson's first duty was to submit to Hamley the records his office had kept while he acted for the Colony of British Columbia. As no separate set of books had been established for British Columbia, all the Customs House accounts were forwarded to the new collector.

With limited means and no experience as an accountant, Anderson had set up the Customs House books himself, and they had worked efficiently through the first busy months. However, Anderson had learned his bookkeeping in the fur trade, where no money existed to tempt men to steal. His system did not allow for dishonesty, but Hamley's examination of the books revealed that eight permits issued by Deputy Collector Charles Angelo had not been entered in the Customs House books, and the money had disappeared.

The experienced accountants who represented the Colony of British Columbia began to ask questions. By the end of May, reports of "something rotten" in the Customs House made headlines in the *Colonist* newspapers, and the editor, Amor de Cosmos, suggested the Hudson's Bay Company was mixed up in the mess. The colonial government launched an investigation headed by Collector Anderson, Judge Matthew Baillie Begbie and Colonial Secretary W.A.G. Young. Collector Hamley attended the meetings, as did Captain W. Driscoll Gossett, the new treasurer of the Colony of British Columbia.

Gossett had 20 years' experience as an accountant in England, but James Douglas recorded that the new treasurer also had a capricious and volatile temper, a loose tongue and a very good opinion of himself.[1] Gossett found "undoubted proofs of Mr. Angelo's guilt" in the books, but he also recommended that Anderson be fired, for he was "most culpably negligent in attending to the pecuniary affairs of his department."[2] In June, the sheriff arrested Angelo on suspicion of being concerned in what the newspapers now dubbed the "Custom House irregularities." Two days later, the government suspended Anderson from office, and Hamley took over his duties as customs collector for Vancouver's Island.

Though suspended from office, Anderson arranged that $150 of Customs House funds be forwarded to Angelo's wife, who was penniless and unable to feed her children. "I do this on my own responsibility," Anderson wrote, "and to satisfy my own scruples on the score of humanity, for it has been intimated to me that for any payment made under present circumstances I shall be held responsible."[3] Mrs. Angelo had been his landlady during the time he first lived in Victoria, but the money he paid her was twice as much as he had been charged for his room and board.

As Hamley continued to pore over the books, he uncovered further defalcations. Gossett, in his reports, described the books as very loosely kept, full of erasures and unbalanced or torn-out pages. At last Anderson objected to Gossett's accusations of fraud and incompetence and returned the treasurer's report in disgust. His accompanying letter read:

> Penned, I am forced to conclude, in a malicious spirit, and grossly false in its conclusions, I decline to receive any such communication, directly or indirectly, from Captain Gossett or any other member of the Government. I have uncomplainingly so far submitted to petty indignities and covert insults to which a gentleman of my position and known reputation should never have been subjected. To a repetition of such indignities I now refuse, unhestitatingly, to submit.[4]

"A large quantity of sealing-wax is being used at present," the *British Colonist* blared. "Everybody is 'sealing up' everything, money, papers and all. Is it the intention to hush up or seal up all inquiry?"[5]

Many colourful people lived in Victoria, but the *Colonist* editor, Amor de Cosmos, was perhaps the most eccentric of all. He arrived in Victoria in 1858 to establish the *British Colonist* newspaper. This hard-drinking and theatrical man was not afraid of offending anyone. He loathed the Hudson's Bay Company and questioned Douglas's connection with the Company, accusing him of toadyism, cronyism and incompetence. His constant harassment of government officials caused one Company man to break an umbrella over de Cosmos's head. Douglas lived in constant fear of the man.

Through the *Colonist*, de Cosmos whipped up public interest in the scandal, and when Angelo's trial began on August 11, 1859, spectators crowded into the Court House. The charges included falsifying accounts and embezzlement of £200. Attorney-General George Hunter Carey explained the nature of the charges and in doing so remarked that "the grossest negligence had been permitted; that other parties besides the prisoner were morally implicated."[6] Immediately, Anderson stood up in the courtroom and declared, "And I say you lie, sir!"[7]

The sheriff ordered Anderson's arrest for contempt and conveyed him to jail. After a short but undignified incarceration, Anderson was released, but the trial continued. Later in August the courts declared Angelo guilty and confined him to jail. Anderson, too, returned to jail. Even after he apologized to the court for his outburst, the judge refused to release him until he could pay the £10 fine for contempt of court.

Now out of work and shamed in the eyes of his peers, Anderson withdrew from public life and cut off all correspondence with his family in Canada. In December 1859, John Palliser, leader of the British North American Exploring Expedition, which had travelled the country between the Saskatchewan River and British Columbia, arrived in Victoria. Palliser and Anderson exchanged information about the country that one had travelled through and the other had lived in for many years. The Columbia detachment of the Royal Engineers, which had arrived in the colony in 1858, also approached Anderson for information about the territory they were planning to enter. These red-jacketed men were both soldiers and engineers, responsible for keeping order in the new colony's goldfields and for building its roads. In 1860 the Royal Engineers substantially widened the Harrison-Lillooet trail that Anderson had first explored in 1846, turning it into a good wagon road. They also worked on the abandoned brigade trail that followed the Anderson River, though they found its high pass subject to landslides and deep snow late in the season.

For years the Anderson River trail was the miners' only access to the central part of the Colony of British Columbia from the Fraser River, but the Royal Engineers now carved a good road out of the cliff faces between Yale and Boston Bar, above the rapids and falls that had so troubled the brigaders of the Hudson's Bay Company in 1848 and 1849. By autumn 1862 their road reached Lytton, and in 1863 the first Alexandra Bridge crossed the Fraser River north of Spuzzum, its eastern end resting near the place where Anderson's men had buried Jacob Ballenden in 1848.

The Fraser River canyons were not the only places where the Royal Engineers blasted their roads. Anderson and his voyageurs had walked

The Alexandra Bridge was built across the Fraser River in 1863. The village of Kequeloose was at the east (right-hand) end of the bridge, and the brigade trails went over the top of Lake Mountain, on the right-hand side of the image. Anderson's River flowed into the Fraser on the other side of Lake Mountain, north of modern-day Black Canyon and Hell's Gate. BC ARCHIVES PDP01834

past the Thompson River's foaming rapids in May 1847; the engineers now carved a road here. Near the village where Anderson's men had borrowed a Native canoe to paddle across the mouth of the Nicola River, other engineers constructed a bridge that carried men and horses across the Thompson to its northern bank. From there, the new road followed the Bonaparte River north until it joined the brigade trail running between Fort Alexandria and Kamloops. In 1843, Anderson had led the outgoing New Caledonia brigade over the Interior's wooded ridges and through its open valleys. Twenty-five years later the new Cariboo wagon road replaced the Company's brigade trail and ploughed past roadhouses, cattle ranches and settlements all the way to Fort Alexandria.

The Royal Engineers encouraged Anderson to turn the rough travelling sketches he had drawn during his fur-trade years into finished maps. If Anderson drew any maps at all for them, his "Sketch of explorations, 1846–1849, Kamloops to Fort Langley"[8] was almost certainly one of them. Even after the Royal Engineers left British Columbia in 1863, Anderson continued his map-making projects. In May 1867, he completed and signed his "Map of a Portion of the Colony of British Columbia," a work in progress that showed the Collins Telegraph Trail, which was begun in 1865 at New Westminster and abandoned when the Atlantic telegraph cable was laid in July 1866.[9] In 1870 he drew his "Guide Map to the Peace River Mines," using various sources to sketch in the part of the territory he had never visited.[10] Four years later he drew a map of the Upper Fraser River based on his rough sketch of the difficult passage upriver to Tête Jaune Pass in 1835.[11] This map showed his suggested route for the Canadian Pacific Railway, through Yellowhead Pass and cross-country to Prince George, and he submitted it to engineer Andrew Onkerdonk, who supervised the construction of the railway in British Columbia. At a banquet in Victoria, Onkerdonk offered Anderson a lifetime pass to the CPR, but Anderson did not live long enough to enjoy its use.

Sometime after the death of his older brother James, Anderson drew his map of "Northwestern North America," which covered both the Columbia and New Caledonia districts, in which he had spent his fur-trade career, and the MacKenzie River district in which his brother had worked and travelled.[12] This map was certainly not drawn for any purpose other than to discover where his brother had been and was, more than any other map he drew, a personal map. But in summer 1875,

Anderson met George Mercer Dawson, a scientist and surveyor who was a member of the International Boundary Survey between 1872 and 1876. Dawson ensured that a good copy of Anderson's map was displayed in the Canadian Pavilion at the massive 1876 Philadelphia Centennial Exhibition. When that world's fair closed, the map hung on the walls of the Geological Survey of Canada for many years before it disappeared. No one now knows where the finished map is.

Fourteen of Anderson's hand-drawn maps are preserved in the British Columbia Archives, but the map that historians consider most significant is his 1867 map of British Columbia. This massive map measures 4.5 feet by 6 feet (126 centimetres x 177 centimetres), and is drawn at a scale of approximately 10 miles per inch. It shows all of modern-day British Columbia south of Fort St. James; it extends eastward as far as the HBC's Edmonton House and shows the route Anderson's party took through Leather Pass in the winter of 1835. When he drew the area around Fort Colvile, Anderson indicated his interest in NWC explorer David Thompson's earlier presence in the area when he drew in "David Thompson's River" and the location of Saleesh House.

In all his finished maps, Anderson used good-quality rag paper that aged to a warm cream colour. The black ink contained iron that rusted to a rich reddish-brown. He used watercolours to paint the larger bodies of water blue, and in red ink indicated the many trails the fur traders of his time travelled. His signature appears everywhere. Handwritten notes on the map indicate events in his personal life such as his journey from Fort Covile to Kamloops in the winter of 1842. At times he recorded information he obtained from post journals that no longer exist, as when he drew the route of a trading party led by Fraser's Lake clerk John McDonnell to Salmon (Dean) River in 1828. Probably the most interesting section of this map is the area south of the Coquihalla, which shows a portion of his 1846 exploration from Fort Langley to Kamloops (see the map in the colour-photo section in this book). Anderson's Outram Lake is clearly indicated as part of the Sumallo River system, and—though it can no longer exist—Anderson's Tree stands guard on the plateau above.

⇒ ⇐

The Customs House scandal was a crushing blow to Anderson's dreams of success among his fur-trade friends in Victoria, and he had difficulty escaping a sense of shame. In May 1860, his eldest daughter was married at Christ Church Cathedral. The wedding party celebrated the ceremony in the garden of the beautiful Anderson home on the hill above Rockland Avenue.[13] Later that year, however, Anderson's sister visited Victoria to discover why her brother had not written to her for so long. She found him sick in bed, deliriously calling for his mother. "It made me cry to hear him talk," she wrote to their family in Ontario:

> *He has his own troubles and very serious trouble in business matters. When matters were investigated not a shadow of blame was cast on him...Still, it was a great trouble to him and preyed on his mind for some time, for he is morbidly sensitive. When I went over and asked him why he had not written to me for so long, he said he did not know how it was but he had taken a distaste to writing.*[14]

In March 1861 the widow of Arctic explorer Sir John Franklin arrived in Victoria. In 1845 her husband's ship had disappeared during an attempt to navigate the North West Passage, and over the years since then, Lady Franklin had financed four unsuccessful attempts to recover her husband's body. One of those ventures had been led, in 1855, by Anderson's older brother James, who at the time was in charge of the Mackenzie River district. At Governor Simpson's request, James, with his clerk and 14 voyageurs, left Fort Simpson (NWT) in two badly built canoes, crossed Great Slave Lake on the ice, portaged over a spur of the mountains and followed the open water of the Back, or Great Fish, River north to its mouth on the Arctic Ocean. There the men investigated some nearby islands but found nothing more than scattered tools and wood fragments, one bearing the name of Franklin's lost ship. They safely negotiated the 84 rapids and falls of the Back River and arrived at Fort Simpson just as the ice closed navigation.

Lady Franklin had not come to Victoria to visit Anderson, but they were introduced, and Anderson organized a special canoe excursion to show Lady Franklin and her companion around Victoria's harbour. A large Company canoe, manned by 12 voyageurs dressed in their bright red shirts and gay ribbons, picked the women up at the shoreline in front of the fort. With quick strokes and voices raised in song, the voyageurs transported the Englishwomen up the waters of the inlet and past the

Company farm at Craigflower. They picnicked on a grassy point, and on their return the voyageurs asked Lady Franklin to disembark at the narrowest part of the inlet and watch as they shot the rapids with the outgoing tide.

To Lady Franklin and her companion, the excursion was nothing more than an interesting afternoon's entertainment. But for Anderson and his voyageurs, this canoe trip up and down the narrow waters of the inlet brought back memories of their shared life in the fur trade of the past. That life was gone, and the choices that Anderson had made could not be changed. All of his money was tied up in a farm property he had purchased in Saanich and in the shipping business he shared with his Oregon partners. Anderson's future depended on the success of these businesses.

[26] THE UNSETTLED
SETTLER, 1861-76

Although Anderson was kept busy with his steamship business, he continued to pursue his interests in other fields. One of these was firearms, which had always fascinated him. When he joined the fur trade, he purchased the best flintlock he could find in London. At York Factory he bought a pair of flintlock pistols. At Fort McLoughlin he had tested his friend William Fraser Tolmie's percussion gun, and 12 years later purchased his own. Now he followed this passion down a different path. In 1861 James Douglas wrote a letter of introduction to Sir Thomas Maitland, rear admiral and commander-in-chief of the Royal Navy, now based in Esquimalt:

> *Allow me to introduce to you Mr. A.C. Anderson, a gentleman formerly in the service of the Hudson's Bay Company, and well known to me for many years. He has recently been turning his attention to the theory of projectiles, and has invented a plan intended to give the same efforts to a ball fired from a smooth bore gun as that obtained from a rifled barrel, and as he is desirous of laying the same before you, I do not hesitate in giving him this letter of introduction.*[1]

The result of his meeting with Maitland is unknown, but Anderson continued to play an active role in Victoria affairs. In February 1861, he chaired a landholder's meeting that petitioned the Hudson's Bay Company for a reduction in the price of land sold to colonists, because the company failed to build promised roads. A few weeks later he acted as Chairman of the Agricultural Society of Vancouver Island. In September he signed a petition to form a chamber of commerce; in October he subscribed $50 to the Royal Hospital in Esquimalt, while others gave $5.

Anderson's steamship company lost money when aggressive competitors drove down prices for freight and transport to the new towns of Yale and Hope. Then the winter of 1861–62 blew in with frigid temperatures that froze the Fraser River to its mouth, and Anderson lost his business to his wealthier competitors.

Anderson had previously purchased 300 acres of land on the Saanich Peninsula, as had other fur traders who came north from Fort Vancouver when the Company abandoned its headquarters there. Five Hudson's Bay

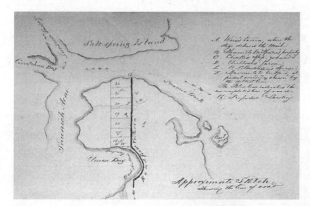

"E" marks the location of the Anderson residence on the Saanich Peninsula, Vancouver Island. Victoria merchant Richard Carr, better known for being the father of famous B.C. artist Emily Carr, held the mortgage on this property. BC ARCHIVES COLONIAL CORRESPONDENCE, F15 23A.

Anderson lived in this house on the Saanich Peninsula from 1862 until March 1882. The house was destroyed by fire sometime after Anderson sold it, and the house that replaced it is quite different in appearance. OPEN SOURCE, BRAD MORRISON COLLECTION OF NORTH AND SOUTH SAANICH MATERIAL

men owned more than 1,600 acres of farmland, and their combined properties stretched across the Saanich Peninsula from Union Bay (Patricia Bay) to Tsehum Harbour. This was the land that Anderson now farmed.

In 1862, he sold his Victoria house and moved onto the Saanich farm, which he named Rosebank. His closest neighbours were Henry Wain, a hospitable Englishman who ran the roadhouse near Deep Cove, and Thomas B. Shaw, the farmer Anderson had hired to build his new house. The Cole brothers farmed at Cole Bay, and the tiny Tseycum Indian Reserve was at the head of Union Bay. It took one full day to travel from Victoria to Rosebank along a wagon road that was a mass of tree roots and mud holes. Travel was so uncomfortable that it became Anderson's practice to stop at every roadhouse along the way.

In addition to losing his steamship business, Anderson suffered a severe business loss on the farm over the cold winter of 1861–62. In the fall of 1861 he had imported a herd of 60 cattle from Oregon and put them out to graze in the pastures that surrounded his Saanich house. The early winter brought deep snow that buried the grass until spring, and no farmer in the area was well enough established to have grown hay. Cattle do not forage for grass under snow, so only a few of Anderson's cows survived the winter.

Now almost 60 years old, Anderson was forced to depend upon the crops of his farm for his main income, although writing provided another potential source of income. The colonial government offered cash prizes for the best essays encouraging immigration to and settlement of the unpopulated lands of Vancouver's Island and British Columbia. Anderson began his manuscript, but because of the demands rising from the failure of his steamship business, he was unable to complete the essay before the competition closed. He pleaded for more time to complete the graphs and tables, but was refused, so he set the work aside. In this unpublished manuscript, Anderson philosophized on the cause of the many changes he had seen in the territory over his lifetime:

> Be this, however, as it may, one thing is evident, that Gold, under Providence, has been the great instrument in the nineteenth Century for ameliorating the condition of the human race. Powerful communities have arisen where previously a lingering state of things prevailed. Commerce has been extended

with marvelous strides. The power of England, maintained by commerce proportionately, has advanced. Colonies have become nations; but nations bound up in affectionate sympathy with and reliance on the Mother Land. And to what is all this due? The casual observer may perhaps answer, to the mere chance discovery of gold; but the philosophic mind will recognize in the chance discovery a deeper cause; and acknowledge that, retarded mysteriously until the world was fully prepared, an unseen Hand has finally revealed to human knowledge those latent treasures over which Man for ages had walked in ignorance.[2]

Anderson had always been a writer. His 1836 manuscript was rejected by the publisher and returned by Governor Simpson. Anderson edited his work and sent a copy away with Lieutenant Charles Wilkes in 1841; it disappeared. Another copy was forwarded through Governor Simpson to Horatio Hale, the American ethnologist who had accompanied Wilkes's Exploring Expedition to Fort Nisqually; it too disappeared. In 1844, Anderson wrote a history he entitled "Narrative of 13 years residence in various parts between Montreal & the Pacific"—only a paragraph or two of this manuscript was saved.[3] In 1845 an essay in letter form was published in the *Journal of the Royal Geographical Society of London* under the heading, "Some Remarks upon the Freezing of Streams in North America, in connexion with the supposed Congelation of their Sources in High Latitudes." In 1869 he had a second letter published in the *Proceedings of the Geographical Society (London)*—"The Rationale of an Open Sea in the North Polar Region." In 1855 his "Notes on the Indian Tribes of British North America, and the Northwest Coast" was published in the *Historical Magazine* and read before the New York Historical Society. This last submission embarrassed Anderson; the notes, which had never been intended for publication, contained errors, but the recipient had submitted them without Anderson's permission.

Anderson's 1858 *Handbook and Map to the Gold Region of Frazer's and Thompson's River* was intended for publication, and he wrote "Notes on North-Western America" to accompany his "Skeleton Map of North-West America" to the 1876 Philadelphia Centennial Exhibition. This essay, too, was published in Montreal, and distributed in the eastern United States. In 1872 Anderson wrote "Dominion at the West; a

Brief Description of the Province of British Columbia, its Climate and Resources," which won the Government Prize for that year and was widely distributed. In this essay, Anderson defended his position as a man of authority in this region:

> To forestall all probable conjecture on this point he may at once state, that since his youth, for the last forty years—more than two-thirds of his life-time—he has been a sojourner in various parts within the vast angle included by the Columbia River, and the Rocky Mountains: first as a clerk, then as a Chief-Trader and Wintering partner, of the Hudson's Bay Company under the old regime; and afterwards as a rather unsettled settler—till for some years past near Victoria, where he is now, probably, permanently at home. Thus there are few nooks, within the area in question, which he has not either visited in person, or of which he has not indirectly acquired a knowledge.[4]

Even while he worked as a gentleman farmer in North Saanich, Anderson continued to contribute to Victoria organizations. In 1862 the members of the immigration board, which encouraged settlement in British Columbia, named Anderson to its committee. In October 1862 Anderson exhibited his "Red June" apples at the local fair; a month later he competed in the agricultural exhibition and won first prize for a pair of work oxen. In 1864 he was appointed justice of the peace and acted as coroner for the district, investigating murders and accidental deaths for the colonial government. In 1865, Anderson was called as a witness for the British government in the British and American Joint Boundary Commission hearings held in Victoria, where he gave his occupation as "gentleman." In 1866, the new editor of the *Colonist* newspaper approached Anderson for information on the route to the Big Bend Gold Mines which were then making the news—Anderson was one of the few people in Victoria known to have been to that out-of-the-way place.

In 1867, Anderson had only just finished drawing his "Map of a Portion of the Colony of British Columbia" when it came time to pay the taxes on his property. For several years these taxes had been in arrears and now stood at about $1,000. The colonial government asked that Anderson pay them in full, and Anderson offered his map as payment. Though his offer was accepted, the officials argued about the map's value and in the end paid nothing for it. Nor did they give him credit for it, arguing that the matter of his debt and the purchase of his map must be kept separate. The debt they argued about did not appear to be Anderson's outstanding taxes; some government officials felt that Anderson still owed money as a result of the Customs House debacle of 1859. Anderson was able to pay part of his bill, probably by selling a portion of his farm. When the government renewed its demands for payment the following year, Anderson begged for additional time and was granted forgiveness by government officials who knew nothing more than that he was a respectable man. By this time, James Douglas had left the governorship, and the officials Anderson dealt with were English immigrants who had no knowledge of his history in the region.

Anderson's wife, Betsy, worked on the farm and rarely ventured into Victoria. She gave birth to their last child in 1864, and in the spring of 1872 she died quietly at home. Anderson pasted a lock of her hair in his Bible, and beside it he wrote, "On the 17th of March 1872, Sunday, about 10 o'clock a.m., it pleased God to summon to himself my dear wife. She was buried at the cemetery in South Saanich on the 19th March, the very Rev. Dean Cridge officiating." The newspaper report said the service at St. Stephen's church was attended "by the family and many friends. No recent event has so saddened the people of Saanich as the demise of this estimable wife and mother, and Mr. Anderson and his children have the entire sympathy of the community."[5]

In November 1866, the Colonies of Vancouver's Island and British Columbia merged under the name British Columbia. A year later the British North America Act established the Dominion of Canada—a country that included Upper and Lower Canada (Ontario and Quebec), New Brunswick and Nova Scotia. It was not until 1871 that the struggling territory of British Columbia joined the new dominion. Two years later, Canada called for representatives for the House of Commons, and Anderson announced his intention to run for election in the Vancouver Island district. One of his competitors was the local brewer, an affable Irishman named Arthur Bunster.

The election took place in the sitting room of Henry Wain's roadhouse, with Anderson's 10-year-old son, Walter, acting as returning officer. On

On the 17th of March 1872, Sunday, about 10 o'clock A.m., it pleased God to summon to himself my dear wife. She was buried at the Cemetery in South Saanich on the 19th March, the Very Revd Dean Cridge officiating.

Fairbank
20th March 1872

FUNERAL.—The funeral of the Mrs. A. C. Anderson, took place yesterday at the South Saanich Cemetery and was attended by the family and many friends. No recent event has so saddened the people of Saanich as the demise of this estimable wife and mother, and Mr. Anderson and his children have the entire sympathy of the community.

On the 9th of May 1884 Friday Our dear old Father breathed his last at Victoria B.C. about 3.30 P M & we buried him beside our dear Mother at South Saanich on Monday the 12th May The Rt Rev The Bishop of Columbia officiating.

On this page of his family Bible, Anderson recorded the details of his wife Betsy's death on March 17, 1872. He enclosed a lock of Betsy's hair on the same page. Anderson's own death was later recorded below the newspaper clipping announcing his wife's death.

FROM NANCY ANDERSON'S ANDERSON-SETON COLLECTION

election day, Arthur Bunster distributed free beer to the voters outside the hall, while Anderson watched as the tide of votes ran heavily against him. When one of his strongest supporters entered the hall to cast his vote for Bunster, Anderson rose to his feet and, looking the man sternly in the eye, said, "And you, too, Mr. Blank?"

"I had never properly grasped the significance of Caesar's dying reproachful question until that moment," Walter Anderson later wrote. "Well, the election was over, and Bunster's beer won the day."[6]

192

For 20 years after his disastrous dismissal from the company of men he had worked with for most of his life, Anderson led a simple life as a poverty-stricken gentleman farmer in Saanich, struggling to earn a living. While most of his English and Irish neighbours grew hops or barley for the brewery business, Anderson stuck with the traditional vegetable and grain crops he had known in the fur trade.

In his private life, he worked to improve the lot of the Natives on the nearby Tseycum Reserve, encouraging them to cultivate their clayey soil. Some of the Tseycum now raised pigs and cattle or farmed small sections of richer soil, and a few had even learned the art of grafting and owned small, thriving orchards. Anderson was also their self-appointed doctor, and this led to some major changes in his life. The Natives were now under the care of the Dominion government, and when Anderson submitted to the new Dominion Indian agent a list of medicines he needed to doctor the Tseycum, as he had always done with the colonial government before confederation, he came to the attention of Dr. Israel Wood Powell, British Columbia's superintendent of Indian Affairs. The fledgling Dominion government was looking for representatives to take on various official duties in the province it was now responsible for, and Powell offered Anderson the position of Dominion Indian Reserve Commissioner. He accepted.

Anderson was one of three commissioners appointed to establish new reserves for the Native population of the province. One commissioner was to be appointed by the Dominion government, one by the provincial government and the third by both governments. Because of a shortage of funds, however, the provincial government dragged its feet in selecting its representatives to the shared commission. In June 1876 the newspapers reported Mr. Bunster might act as Indian commissioner in conjunction with Anderson; a month later the papers stated that the province still delayed, and "poor Mr. Anderson is in a great stew."[7]

At last Archibald McKinlay, Anderson's old friend from his fur-trade days, took the position of provincial commissioner, but summer was almost over before the province finally approved the appointment of the third commissioner. An Englishman, Gilbert Malcolm Sproat, represented both the provincial and Dominion governments.

[27] THE INDIAN RESERVE COMMISSION
ON THE COAST, 1876-77

Natives everywhere knew that the government was going to set aside lands for them for their own use. In many cases, reserves had already been established, but new settlers often moved onto these reserved lands, pushing the Natives off. Certain government officials had removed prime reserve lands from Native control and sold it to settlers. And sometimes land the Natives had always considered theirs was not included in the reserves.

Over the preceding few years, Natives in the Interior had been especially vocal about their desire to have their reserves enlarged and the boundaries settled. However, by the time the Indian Reserve commissioners were ready to begin their work in October 1876, winter had set in, making travel to the Interior difficult. As a result, they decided to settle the reserves on the coast first. The retired fur traders were fully aware that the Interior Natives would learn from the coastal tribes that the commissioners had begun their work.

Anderson and McKinlay set out from New Westminster on the steamer *Leonora* on November 6, 1876, accompanied by a surveyor and a census-taker, two Native camp aides and an interpreter. Sproat was completing some business in Victoria and planned to join them later. On this expedition up the coast, Anderson took up an old habit he had followed for many years as a fur trader: he kept a journal. Anderson and McKinlay both agreed that this journal would form the basis of the official reports to the provincial and Dominion governments.

On the evening of November 6, the *Leonora* arrived at the Coast Salish Reserve of Musqueam, located on the northern banks of the Fraser River at the river's mouth. As there were no extra beds aboard the steamer, the commissioners set up their camp on shore.

Like other reserves along the coast, the Musqueam Reserve had been created years earlier, though part of its lands had been reclaimed by the government. The Dominion government wanted to grant each Native family 80 acres, but the final decision fell to the provincial government, who allowed 20 acres per family. The commissioners commenced work on November 7, confirming the boundaries of the old reserve, adding agricultural land on the island opposite the village and granting the Musqueam a right-of-way through unoccupied land to a cranberry swamp in which they gathered fruit. Finally, Anderson vaccinated the children for smallpox, with lymph provided by the Dominion government, and advised the elders on how to continue the process of vaccination as the pustules matured.

With their business finished, Anderson made a speech to explain the Dominion government's views about the Natives it now looked after, and McKinlay explained the views of the provincial government he represented. The chiefs then spoke in turn, each one assuring the commissioners of his satisfaction. When the speech making was finished, the commissioners reboarded the *Leonora* and continued on to Burrard Inlet. That night the commissioners camped on the north side of Burrard Inlet near the Roman Catholic Mission Reserve at Capilano Creek, and in the morning the smartly dressed Native residents arrived in their camps with flags flying. As it was Sunday, the commissioners refused to do business, but attended services in the mission church. When they returned to camp, they discovered that Sproat had caught up with them.

The next day the commissioners quickly finished their work at the Roman Catholic Mission Reserve, and at the False Creek Reserve they increased the area of the old reserve some distance along the shoreline. At Capilano Creek the reserve was already hemmed in by white settlers. However, the Squamish people who occupied the reserve had come from elsewhere to work in the lumber mills, and the commissioners arranged that some Squamish men travel with them to their Howe Sound villages so they could give them more land there.

On the morning of November 21, the commissioners ascended the Squamish River in Native canoes and travelled up the rapid-filled

Cheakamus River, passing by a beautiful waterfall that Anderson named Staircase Falls. At the abandoned village of Skow-a-shin they marked off a tract of land that protected several small graveyards and a grove of red cedar trees the Squamish Natives used for canoe building, and on the Squamish River north of the Cheakamus they gave them a tract of excellent land they thought would be valuable for agriculture or settlement in the future. In their camp that night, Anderson made a special note of an incident that occurred as the commissioners travelled down the Squamish River with their Native canoemen:

> *Preliminary to arrival our Indn. Canoe-men, who are in the highest spirits, brought our two remaining canoes in line, and keeping a slow stroke in unison, sang an agreeable but rather plaintive chorus in admirable time—reminding some of us of bygone days when the more lively paddle-song of the French Canadian voyageurs was a similar sound.*[1]

By November 28, the commissioners were at Trail Bay, on the west side of the Sechelt Peninsula. Here a Native path led across the narrow neck of the peninsula, and the commissioners instructed the captain of the *Leonora* to steam around the peninsula to meet them at the east end of the portage. The commissioners set up camp that night on the beach close to a large Sechelt village that surrounded a neatly built Catholic Church.

The next day they confirmed and enlarged the Sechelt Reserve and, crossing over the portage, once again loaded their baggage onto the steamer. But at the commissioners' camp at Trail Bay, Archibald McKinlay noted angrily in his journal:

> *At Muskweam I spoke a few words as is shown in Journal. At Burrards Inlet Dominion Commissioner spoke first but attempted to interfere with me when speaking afterwards. At See-shill Dominion Commissioner spoke first. I afterwards made a few remarks but while I was speaking Dominion Commissioner retired to tent . . .*
>
> *I have not had the chances of education that my learned brethren of the Commission have had. At least, I cannot quote from Virgil, Homer, Sheakspear [sic] & Byron as glibly—but I*

have had another education. I have met with numbers of men
of all classes . . . I know I understand matters as well if not
better than one of them—the one I allude to really disgusts me
by his conceited [vanity].[2]

Anderson had objected to the speeches that McKinlay made to the Natives, in which he said they were wild and barbarous and accused them of doing little to improve the land they occupied other than attacking, killing and enslaving each other. Whether Sproat objected to McKinlay's speech is not known, but Anderson's objections made little difference to the tone of McKinlay's comments at future meetings.

The commissioners' work continued. The *Leonora* carried the three men into the depths of Narrows Inlet, where they set up a new reserve on eight acres of cultivable land. On December 4 the *Leonora* steamed up the narrow channel of Princess Royal Reach, between towering cliffs of rock scarred with the Natives' petroglyphs, and in the depths of that inlet the commissioners created two new reserves containing considerable acreage of the only good land they could find. On December 7 they camped at Thunder Bay, in Malaspina Channel, and early the next morning the *Leonora* rounded the north end of Texada Island, setting a westward course for Vancouver's Island through dense fog. A little after noon, the steamer dropped its anchor in Comox Harbour, where the commissioners reluctantly left the comfort of the vessel to set up camp on the cold, hard beach.

Here they were among the Kwakwaka'wakw people who occupied the north part of Vancouver's Island and the mainland opposite, and the K'ómoks Natives who had given their name to the agricultural settlement. The commissioners remained in the Comox area until December 13, establishing reserves near the mouth of the Courtenay River, and travelling upstream to its junction with the Tsolum. The smallpox epidemic of 1862 had devastated the K'ómoks people; thousands had died, and the survivors had abandoned many of their old villages. For the most part, new settlers respected the Natives' rights to their old settlements, but at the Tsolum River the commissioners discovered that one settler had claimed ownership of what was obviously an old K'ómoks village. The commissioners listened to the settler's arguments, then consulted the local government agent and surveyor before deciding the settler's claims were invalid. They returned the land to the K'ómoks, along with what additional lands they could provide.

At Nanaimo the commissioners returned to Coast Salish territory. At the first of the Snuneymuxw Reserves, the commissioners found houses in both the old Native and new European styles. The soil was good and easy to farm, but they noticed it was little cultivated. At the upper reserve, a settler had cut some timber on Snuneymuxw lands; he quickly apologized for his trespass and offered to pay damages. The commissioners also discovered that one settler's residence intruded onto Snuneymuxw land. The cabin had been built some years earlier, with the permission of the Natives, and the cabin's present owner was a hard-working widow who had raised her children on the profits of the dairy she ran. The commissioners arranged for the widow's lawyers to transfer replacement acreage to the Natives, in exchange for the land on which her cabin sat.

At the Chemainus River fishing reserve, the commissioners discovered that the Penelakut of Kuper Island, whose fishing reserve this was, had illegally intruded upon the lands of a neighbouring settler. They informed the chiefs that the trespassing fences and buildings must be removed. Then they continued their work in the neighbourhood without settling lands on the Penelakuts. When the commissioners' deadline passed, the Natives still had not removed the fences and buildings.

Anderson, McKinlay and Sproat were aware that the government had had trouble with the Penelakut 15 years earlier, and they had previously arranged that the Royal Navy gunboat HMS *Rocket* be in the area in case of conflict. On January 11, 1877, the *Rocket* arrived at Chemainus Bay with Superintendent Powell aboard. While the three commissioners remained tactfully in camp, the gunboat steamed off to visit the Kuper Island village, and Powell had a short discussion with the chiefs. Quickly the Natives set to work removing the offending fences.

However, as soon as the *Rocket* steamed away, the Penelakut abandoned their work and prepared for a feast. Immediately, the commissioners delivered a message to the chiefs: remove the fences completely or the commissioners would depart without settling any new land on the tribe. This argument finally convinced the Penelakut to act, and within a few days the commissioners held their final conference with them.

At Cowichan, the commissioners found that lands originally assigned to the Quw'utsun' people by Governor Douglas had been regularly taken

Anderson (centre) poses with other members of the Indian Reserve Commission at Chemainus Bay. Although the party had been camping on the beach for weeks, Anderson was dressed to meet the Natives in a new suit, white shirt, tie and top hat. BC ARCHIVES C-05426

back by successive provincial governments and sold to settlers who now occupied the land. The unhappy Natives demanded that their lands be restored to them, but Anderson told them that according to the instructions from both the Dominion and provincial governments, the commissioners were unable to interfere with the rights of white settlers who had purchased their lands legally, and who had built their homes upon them. The commissioners were able to be of some help, however. When they notified a settler that his fence intruded onto the grasslands of the Quw'utsun' Reserve, he immediately removed his fences, with the Natives cheerfully assisting. In another case, the commissioners discovered that a settler whose land intruded deeply into Quw'utsun' lands was anxious to trade for different land. However, when they investigated further, they found that the Natives occupied lands the settler had purchased and had many times over disregarded the warnings of Superintendent Powell. The commissioners gave the Quw'utsun' more lands without including the settler's lands.

On February 17, the commissioners boarded the *Leonora* and sailed to Saanich, anchoring in Green's Bay at the end of the peninsula. They settled the Saanich Reserves without difficulty and confirmed some reserves on nearby islands. After confirming the Peddar Bay reserve they released the *Leonora* from service in March 1877.

Anderson wrote his report for the Dominion government, noting that, on more than one occasion, young Native men told the commissioners they did not wish to be treated as children, and they wanted to work without undue checks on their industry. He submitted his report to Superintendent Powell and discovered that Sproat had already submitted reports written without the knowledge of his co-commissioners, which Powell had assumed were the official reports of the commission. Anderson told the superintendent that, although he found nothing obviously incorrect in Sproat's reports, he disclaimed all responsibility for them.

Sproat argued that his reports were not official reports, but that it was his duty as chief commissioner to report from time to time to both governments. He then demanded that Anderson apologize for his "untruthful, irrelevant and offensive" behaviour, and in the same letter to the Dominion government reported that "Everyone is now in his place, and the Commission is in good working order."[3]

Sproat's reaction to Anderson's letter, and his outraged demand for an apology, was the first indication that he aspired to control the commission. From this point on the relationship between the three men deteriorated rapidly. Sproat turned on his co-commissioners, insulting them at every opportunity in his reports and downplaying their contribution to the work of the commission. In March and April 1877, Sproat was identified as "Joint Commissioner" in official correspondence, and Anderson referred to him by that term as late as June 4. By August, however, Sproat was referring to himself as "Chief Commissioner," and certainly he had been acting as if he were chief commissioner long before.

[28] HAWKING ABOUT
THE COUNTRY, 1877-83

As uncomfortable as the relationship between Anderson, McKinlay and Sproat had become, they still had to work together. In April 1877 the men planned their trip to the Interior, beginning at Kamloops, then covering Shuswap and Okanagan lakes and the Nicola Valley before travelling by way of Lytton to Soda Creek and the troublesome Chilcotin district. The provincial government's delays stalled them in Victoria, however, until an alarmed Okanagan resident warned of Native unrest at Kamloops. Afraid of war, the provincial government hurried the commissioners away in early June.

The three men travelled by steamboat to Yale and by horseback and stagecoach to Kamloops. On their arrival, they pitched their tents close to the reserve, which was located a little above the town. Not many Secwepemc men remained here; all the principal chiefs and most of their followers were attending a large gathering of Natives at Okanagan Lake.

A few settlers had been threatened by Native men, and many others had good reason to believe the Okanagan and Secwepemc Natives were preparing for war. Others, however, considered there was no cause for alarm. Among the first group of men was the level-headed and experienced Roman Catholic missionary Father Charles Grandidier, who told the commissioners the Natives were extremely dissatisfied with the many delays of the commission and talked of war.

The commissioners also knew that, on the other side of the American border, the Nez Perce were at war with the US Army. From their many informants in the Kamloops area they learned that American chiefs were attending the Okanagan meeting in an attempt to convince their close relatives to join their insurgency south of the border. They also heard that the Secwepemc and Okanagan tribes had formed a confederation, a union of chiefs, to force a settlement of their land claims. The commissioners recognized that affairs were as volatile as had been reported to them, but they remained confident that quick and decisive action would allay the Natives' fears.

A small number of Secwepemc chiefs returned to their villages a few days after the commissioners' arrival, but the powerful chief Petit Louis remained behind at the Okanagan meeting. On Saturday the commissioners held their first informal meeting, but the chiefs refused to talk until after the Dominion Day celebrations at Kamloops the next day. Anderson contributed a small prize for the best Native rider in the horse races.

On Monday, July 2, the commissioners held their first formal meeting with the local chiefs, outlining their plans. They then boarded a steamship and travelled up the North Thompson River to settle Chief André's reserve. The two fur traders must have taken pleasure in the view from the deck of the steamship; they knew this river by heart, and the old brigade trail by which they had entered and exited New Caledonia in the years before 1843 led up its rocky eastern bank.

The commissioners reached Chief André's village on Tuesday, and on Wednesday they rode beside the chief over his lands, travelling as far north as Little Fort where, before 1843, the brigaders had carried their loads across the river in a Native canoe. On Thursday the commissioners enlarged André's reserve, adding a large pastureland that included a coal seam the Natives especially desired to own. On Friday the commissioners returned to Kamloops, and watched as the local tribal chiefs shunned André because he had settled his lands.

On July 14, Chief Tsilaxitsa, one of the most important Okanagan chiefs, rode into the commissioners' camp and requested a private interview with Anderson, refusing to speak with the commissioners as a group until his lands were settled. As a youth, Tsilaxitsa had ridden many miles with Anderson and, in 1847, was one of the Native men who guided Anderson's party through the Fraser River canyons and up the Squâ-zoum portage to the Nicola Valley. In the privacy of Anderson's tent, Tsilaxitsa told Anderson a little of what had occurred at the Secwepemc–Okanagan gathering. He admitted that American Natives had attempted to incite the

As a youth in 1847, Tsilaxitsa (Chillaheetza) guided Anderson's party through the Fraser River canyons; in later years he became a legendary head chief of the Okanagan Tribe, providing valuable information to Anderson when he served on the Indian Reserve Commission.

BC ARCHIVES PDP02225

Secwepemc and Okanagan people to join their insurgency south of the border. Although Tsilaxitsa had prevented some of his young men from leaving for the south, he told Anderson that some Okanagan men had crossed the border to join the insurrection in the United States.

As was usual for the commissioners, Sunday was a day of rest. On Monday morning, Petit Louis and five other Secwepemc and Okanagan chiefs rode into the commissioners' camp with flags flying. The commissioners told the chiefs they would now settle their reserves, and over the next week they rode over the Natives' lands with Petit Louis, under a hot sun that fatigued both men and horses.

Petit Louis was a young and active man the other chiefs considered a leader. He was also a strong negotiator, who told the commissioners that his people knew what they wanted, but would remain silent until they heard what the commissioners had to offer. On July 21 the commissioners completed their survey and were prepared to indicate the lands they proposed to assign to the Kamloops tribes. Petit Louis, however, refused to hear the offer until the commissioners settled with the tribes at Shuswap Lake. The chiefs were all of one mind, Petit Louis stated, and he expressed his desire to ride with the commissioners to Shuswap Lake.

The commissioners delayed their formal assignment of Kamloops lands and ignored the unrest, acting as if everything was normal, though they were constantly aware of the Native messengers riding between the villages. The commissioners' plan was to detach the tribal chiefs from the Secwepemc-Okanagan confederation, one by one, and settle with each tribe before moving on to the next. There were already signs that the confederation was breaking up; three Secwepemc chiefs had returned to their lands to await the arrival of the commissioners.

An informant told Anderson, McKinlay and Sproat that the chief at Deadman's River was less firmly tied to the confederation and was likely to settle his lands should they call on him. To take advantage of this news, the three men boarded the steamer to Savona's Ferry, at the west end of Kamloops Lake, and took rooms in a tavern there. The next day they visited the chief at Deadman's River for an informal meeting; the following day they arrived at the village to be warmly greeted with a refreshing feast of freshly picked raspberries. The chief, Ceciasket, told them he had relinquished the idea of uniting with the people of Kamloops and trusted the commissioners to make adequate provision for his tribe. However, Ceciasket said, they must enlarge his reserve, for it was far too small for the needs of his people. The commissioners rode with Ceciasket over the reserve that day and the next. They saw that the Natives already owned 700 head of cattle and horses and were in desperate need of more land, so they granted the tribe a considerable extension to their reserve, including a fine stretch of pastureland for their stock.

The commissioners stayed at the Savona's Ferry tavern between visits to the reserve, and McKinlay and Anderson enjoyed a few drinks together. Sproat complained that the two men appeared drunk in front of the Natives they represented. He was so annoyed that he threatened to suspend proceedings and report both commissioners to their respective governments. Sproat then determined not to allow the commissioners to stay at any more inns, "even to save expense, but always to have our camp where we can have some discipline."[1]

It is hard to know how the two fur traders felt, as neither of them complained. The commissioners returned to Kamloops and on August 1 they visited Little Shuswap Lake, took a census of the two tribes that lived there and examined both reserves. Their work here was delayed by the death of a principal woman whose burial and subsequent feast occupied the Natives for a few days, but the chiefs made every attempt to expedite proceedings. Another delay occurred when news came that Petit

Louis, who was riding from Kamloops to join the commissioners, had been thrown from his horse and injured.

The commissioners' work continued as they visited the reserves on Adams Lake and Little Shuswap Lake, assigning new land at both places. By August 13 they were at Shuswap Lake, and on August 14 they reached the Spillumacheen Reserve, 20 miles up the Spillumacheen River from Shuswap Lake.

The commissioners spent a week there, but when they were ready to make their assignment, the chief demanded lands that were now occupied by white settlers. The commissioners told him they could not give away those lands, but offered to stay an extra day to find suitable acreage to replace them. While this offer satisfied the younger chiefs, who worried the commissioners would leave without assigning them any land at all, on the following day the older chief repeated his demands. By this time the commissioners knew this man's authority was waning. They waited in silence until a younger chief stood up to say his people were generally satisfied with their settlement.

On August 24, the commissioners arrived at Okanagan Lake. Here they now dealt with the Okanagan tribes, closely related to the Secwepemc but also to the Spokane and the Nez Perce south of the American border. There was a delay when Chief Selixt-asposem could not be found and no one knew who should represent the Okanagan. At last Selixt-asposem rode into the village, saying he had been visiting relatives south of the border so that he could check any tendencies of his people to join the American insurgents.[2]

By September 15 the commissioners were ready to make their settlement. But a few days later, Tsilaxitsa and Selixt-asposem visited the commissioners' camp and asked for a private interview. Selixt-asposem spoke of his father, Chief N'kwala, who on his deathbed had asked both his son and his nephew, Tsilaxitsa, to continue the friendly relations with the white men that he had always practised. Selixt-asposem produced two medals: one a Hudson's Bay Company medal bearing the head of King George II; the other, Queen Victoria's Coronation medal. Chief N'kwala had given these to him, telling the two young chiefs that "when they looked at these medals at any time of difficulty, they must recall his dying words."[3]

Selixt-asposem told the commissioners that previous governments had constantly taken land from the Okanagan reserve, and his people needed more land. The commissioners were aware that if they did not resolve the problem of settlers taking over lands that obviously belonged to the Natives, they would not be successful in settling any of the reserves among the Secwepemc and the Okanagan tribes. This was their test.

The two chiefs also warned the commissioners that the younger Natives were very close to rebellion, but the commissioners' words and actions over the past few days had convinced the Okanagan people to wait. As they left the camp, Tsilaxitsa asked for a gift of tobacco. Anderson's journal indicates the importance of this apparently casual request:

> We should here mention that up to this time (among the Okanagans) we have made it a point to offer nothing in the shape of a present, even so much as a pipe of tobacco, lest we might be slighted by a refusal . . . Today, however, Tila-heetza, of his own accord, before leaving us, asked for tobacco. This was of course at once given to him, as well as to his companion, and they left us in great good humour.[4]

After some consultation with other officials in the area, the commissioners removed one settler from the land he had purchased from an earlier settler and found him a piece of land elsewhere, as it was clear the original claim was illegal. Another settler's claim to his land was denied outright, and he was asked to remove his fences. In the end the Okanagan received a large piece of grazing land, part of which they were asked to share with the local ranchers for winter grazing.

In early October the two fur traders travelled south down the old brigade trail on the west side of the lake, while Sproat settled some fishing reserves on the east shore. Anderson might have referred to Sproat's absence when he wrote in his journal that night: "Till Monday we shall enjoy a degree of tranquility to which we have been strangers for some time past."[5]

Selixt-asposem accompanied Anderson and McKinlay southward, assuring the two commissioners of his people's pleasure and telling them that he and Tsilaxitsa had sent messengers ahead to let the Natives know they would get fair treatment. Selixt-asposem also told the commissioners that he had sent an American chief back to his tribe with the message that the Okanagan would not join their insurgency.

On October 8, Sproat rejoined the commission and the men rode south toward Penticton, reaching that settlement on October 22. On November 6 they arrived at Osoyoos Lake and held their first informal interview the following day. The Osoyoos Reserve was restricted in size, with one settler attempting to claim a part of the Natives' lands for himself. There was little pastureland free from settlement, and a large landowner was in the process of claiming most of the free land lying along the river. The commissioners thought this land should be given to the Natives; Sproat convinced the landowner to abandon his claim.

The weather had been inclement with violent windstorms and heavy rain throughout their travels in the Okanagan district. Now the rain turned to sleet, and the commissioners' camp became uncomfortable in the extreme. The party left Osoyoos Lake on November 17, abandoning their plans to settle the reserves in the Similkameen. Still, they considered it wise to send a man to the chief at Ashnola, and Anderson rode west through Keremeos to shake hands with him and explain why the commissioners were not coming to settle his lands that year. A quick ride over a range of hills brought Anderson back to Penticton, where he rejoined McKinlay and Sproat.

The commissioners completed their work at Penticton and Okanagan Mission on November 27, travelling through heavy snow and cold to reach Kamloops. They paid off their attendants and departed for Victoria, their work finished for the year.

Sproat complained publicly about the two men he worked with. As early as August 1877, Sproat had described McKinlay as a well-intentioned gentleman, but not bright, and said he could not remember any time McKinlay had contributed to the work of the commission. He said Powell had erred when he placed McKinlay, a cattle rancher, on a commission that granted lands to the Natives. Sproat also claimed he had forced McKinlay to apologize for his behaviour at the head of Okanagan Lake, and reported that "he has broken out again and I have had to lay my hand upon him, hard and heavy."[6]

Anderson, Sproat wrote, was intellectually superior to McKinlay but deficient in will and unable to decide what should be done. Anderson was vain and jealous and had offended everyone in the camp with his clumsy jokes and pragmatic manner. He had been drunk several times in public and had too much familiarity with the Natives, meeting privately with them. Sproat's fellow commissioners were not the only recipients of his criticism. Superintendent Powell, Sproat declared, was shrewd and capable but unimaginative and flabby and showed "too much uniform and not enough ship of war—too little rough shirt and ragged trousers."[7]

In December, Sproat offered to become the sole commissioner, while McKinlay argued that the commission did not need a joint commissioner. Anderson, who could not afford to lose his wages, remained silent. By March 1878, Sproat had succeeded in his goal of ousting the two fur traders. At about this time, a newspaper printed an article containing remarks that Anderson considered slanderous. Father Grandidier wrote to Anderson in April to advise him to "not take too much to heart the words of a newspaper Correspondent, who does not even give his name." Grandidier continued, "As far as my intercourse with you here has allowed me to judge, your private character and conduct as a commissioner is above blame and censure, and truly deserves great credit at the hands of all the settlers of the Province, for your untiring energy, firmness, patience with the natives; the qualities which you have displayed have won you the trust and respect of the Indians, who speak of you very highly."[8]

Anderson, angry and hurt by the manner in which he had been treated, forwarded Grandidier's letter to the superintendent-general of Indian Affairs in Ottawa with a note:

> I do not conceive it necessary or proper, indeed, that I, holding His Majesty's Commission for an important public office, should hawk about the Country for testimonials of character. The high character of Father Grandidier, however, and the important influence which he deservedly exercises, among the native races of the Interior, justify me, I think, in submitting his spontaneously expressed opinion for your perusal.[9]

[29] INSPECTOR
OF FISHERIES, 1876-83

In May 1876, Anderson had also been made the Dominion fisheries inspector for British Columbia, and he did his fisheries work while he travelled the province as Indian Reserve commissioner. As he made his way up and down the coast in 1876–77, Anderson investigated the use of explosives to kill fish, finding the practice generally abandoned. At Shawnigan Lake, a new dam prevented salmon from reaching their spawning beds, and Anderson arranged with its builder that a fish ladder be constructed to allow the salmon to swim upriver.

Anderson reported extensively on the important salmon fishery. Already, three canneries operated near the mouth of the Fraser River and produced one-pound cans of salmon and barrels of salted salmon for export to England and San Francisco. Anderson recommended the establishment of fish hatcheries on the Canadian section of the Columbia River to enhance production there, and he struggled to identify salmon caught in the open ocean—species that were unfamiliar to him. He also reported on the other valuable fish of the coast: halibut, large cod caught off the Queen Charlotte Islands, herring, smelt and eulachon. Dogfish, too, received their share of attention, for these fish were harvested for their oil, used both for lubrication in the sawmills and for lighting lamps at the Nanaimo coal mines and on the steamships that now frequented British Columbia waters. Lastly he dealt with the sealing business (fur seals were hunted for their skins) and whaling (porpoises and whales were harvested for their oil).

In his 1877 report, Anderson wrote of the heavy run of salmon that flooded up the Fraser River, and he used his experience as a fur trader to inform the Dominion government officials that the HBC men had long known of the fluctuation of the salmon runs. He investigated the waste of salmon by the canneries, which received so many fish the workers were unable to process them before the fish spoiled. A businessman made the first serious attempt to harvest and cure herring, exporting five or six hundred barrels of the fish to South America. The dogfish fishery at Queen Charlotte Islands failed because the owner hired white fishermen, who demanded higher wages than were paid to Natives. But elsewhere along the coast, Natives caught and sold dogfish with great success.

In 1878, Anderson reported that British Columbia canneries had put up more than 100,000 cases of salmon and upwards of 5,000 barrels of salted fish. No waste occurred that year, for if the canneries had extra salmon they could not use, they gave them to the Natives who cured them for their own use. On the Fraser River alone, there were 2,500 men working during the busy fishing season, many of them Natives. Anderson advocated protecting Native fishing rights, with the proviso that if Natives fished in competition with non-Natives, in modern boats and with modern equipment, they should be governed by the same laws that governed non-Natives.

More men now fished for herring, and one businessman pressed herring for oil on a scow that could be towed from fishery to fishery. Others leased oyster beds and improved them for future production, and there was talk of building a salmon hatchery on the Fraser River.

⇒ ⇐

In 1878, the San Francisco historian Hubert Howe Bancroft arrived in Victoria to research the history of the territory, interviewing many retired HBC men. In his published history, Bancroft noted his first impressions of Anderson:

> *In personal appearance, at the time I saw him, he being then sixty three years of age, Mr. Anderson was of slight build, wiry make, active in mind and body, with a keen, penetrating eye, covered by lids which persisted in a perpetual and spasmodic winking, brought on years ago by snow-field exposure, and now become*

habitual, and doubtless as disagreeable to him as to his friends. In speech he was elegant and precise, and by no means so verbose as in his writings, and in carriage, if not so dignified as [Roderick] Finlayson, his manner would do him credit at St. James.[1]

The end result of Bancroft's many interviews with Anderson was a jumbled and repetitive manuscript entitled "History of the Northwest Coast," made up partly of Anderson's scraps of writing, old and new, and partly of notes taken by Mrs. Bancroft. But the historian was delighted and said of Anderson's manuscript, "Almost every sentence is a jewel which finds its proper fitting."[2] The two men got along, and in his later autobiography Bancroft wrote:

But more than to any other in Victoria, I feel myself indebted to Mr. A.C. Anderson, a man not only of fine education, but of marked literary ability, of poetic temperament, chivalrous in thought as well as in carriage, of acute observation and retentive memory he proved to be the chief and standard authority on all matters relating to the country. He had published several works of value and interest, and was universally regarded as the most valuable living witness of the past. Tall, symmetrical, and very erect, with a long narrow face, ample forehead, well brushed white hair, side whiskers, and keen, light-blue eyes, he looked the scholar he was. Scarcely allowing himself an interruption, he devoted nearly two weeks to my work with such warm cheerfulness and gentlemanly courtesy as to win our hearts. Besides this, he brought me much valuable material in the form of records-books and letters. He took luncheon with us every day, smoked incessantly, and drank brandy and soda temperately.[3]

⇒ ⇐

Anderson's work was only slightly interrupted by Bancroft's visit. With Dr. Powell, Anderson set off in HMS *Rocket* to visit fishing stations at certain points along the coast. At Nahwitti, on the extreme northern end of Vancouver Island, Anderson heard that an American vessel was surreptitiously fishing for Canadian halibut. At Skeena the men visited two canneries and watched a ferocious run of salmon. Many Natives worked

Fisheries Inspector A.C. Anderson poses with officers and crew of HMS *Rocket* while on fisheries inspection patrol in 1881. Anderson stands on the left side of the group of men and is wearing his top hat. BC ARCHIVES A-00255 (PHOTOGRAPHER: EDWARD DOSSETTER)

in these northern fisheries, and Native women worked in the net lofts making salmon nets, an art in which they were expert.

In the summer of 1881, Anderson again sailed north with Dr. Powell to visit the northern fisheries. The *Rocket* steamed through the narrow channels of Milbanke Sound and dropped its anchor at the end of North Bentinck Arm, in front of the now almost abandoned town of Bella Coola. Beyond the town's borders stood the Nuxálk village of Ko-omkootz, the same village that the North West Company explorer Alexander Mackenzie had called Rascal's Village. At Ko-omkootz, Anderson and Powell listened while a Nuxálk man told them his story of Mackenzie's visit 90 years earlier. Anderson did not write the story down, but Dr. Powell did.

Mckenzie [sic] *is still talked about by old Indians, one of whom related to me an anecdote which had been handed down through successive generations, viz., that the canoe load of Indians who accompanied and followed McKenzie a short distance down the channel, seeing him take an observation with an instrument (the sextant), said that immediately after "fire came down from the heavens."*

This so frightened them that they at once declined to go farther, turning back and leaving the distinguished voyageur to himself.[4]

⇒ ⇐

The official who ran the Dominion Department of Fisheries was a parsimonious man who promised regularly to increase Anderson's wages but never did so. Anderson earned $600 a year, though the inspectors in other provinces were paid much higher wages. The Nova Scotia fisheries inspector, for example, earned $1,400 a year, and more than $100,000 was spent on wages in that province. In New Brunswick, Quebec and Ontario, the Dominion government paid its inspectors $1,200 to $1,400 annually, and total wages for the provinces hovered between $7,000 and $9,000. Only in British Columbia were the wages kept low—a little over $1,000.[5] Anderson's brother William, now employed by the Dominion Department of Indian Affairs as Indian agent in Regina and Edmonton, earned $1,035. "The duties of my office have now become very important," Anderson wrote to William, "and it is a disgrace to the Gov't that my services are not adequately remunerated."[6] Money was an important issue for Anderson, for he had never been able to pay the back taxes owed on his Saanich farm. At last Anderson sold his remaining farmland and moved into a rented house in Victoria.

[30] CROSS THE
DARK RIVER, 1884

In his 1882 fisheries report, Anderson described the increase in salmon fishing and canning in British Columbia, and reported that the industry employed more than 5,000 fishermen. Twenty canneries now operated on the coast, 13 of them on the Fraser River. Fishermen processed herring for export to Australia, and the dogfish-oil industry constantly increased. Though oyster culture had stagnated, the fur-seal fishery flourished, employing 400 Native hunters.

A year later, Anderson reported that the 1883 salmon run up the Fraser River had been small, but the salmon canneries on the northwest coast had canned enough salmon to make up for the deficiency. More than 5,000 people worked in the fur-seal fishery, but boisterous weather during sealing season reduced their catch. Also in 1883, news of the rapid construction of the Canadian Pacific Railway excited Anderson; this cross-country railway line might allow westcoast fishermen to open up new markets in the east. To test his theory that chilled fish could reach eastern Canada in good condition, Anderson packed three salmon in ice and sent them to Ottawa by Wells Fargo Express. The experiment was successful; the fish arrived in good condition and were consumed.

By this time, Anderson had identified the Queen Charlotte Island cod and knew it by its proper name—black cod. Newfoundland fishermen inquired about the deep-sea fishing on the west coast, and a Norwegian businessman approached Anderson about setting up a colony in British Columbia with 300 of his countrymen. In October 1883, Anderson travelled by boat to Pitt River to view the proposed site for a new salmon hatchery on the

Fraser River. The steam launch ran aground on a shoal in the middle of the lake, and the stranded party passed a cold night before they were rescued. Anderson returned to Victoria with a severe bronchial infection.

He recovered slowly, but by December he could eat nothing but soft food, no matter how much he might desire meat. His condition gradually worsened, and in April 1884 the doctor told Anderson's son James that a lump in his father's throat was growing larger and would eventually strangle him.

In early May, Anderson's daughters, Agnes and Rose, made arrangements for their father to enter St. Joseph's hospital. On the morning of May 9, James brought his father a bottle of champagne and, settling him in a chair, lit his pipe. That afternoon, Agnes and Rose summoned their brother back to the hospital. Anderson's last words were, "Put away my spectacles," and he asked for a drink of champagne. At the end, his suffering was intense but not prolonged. The next day's newspaper recorded Anderson's death:

> *Another pioneer has crossed the dark river and joined the Great Majority on the other side. Alexander Caulfield Anderson, who died yesterday afternoon at 3½ o'clock, after a brief illness, was one of the most intellectual and valued pioneer citizens of the province. Born in Calcutta on the 10th of March, 1814, he was consequently in his 71st year at the time of his death.*[1]

Born at Fort Nisqually in 1841, Anderson's son James R. Anderson grew up in Fort Alexandria and Fort Colvile and was an accountant in Victoria for many years. He was also British Columbia's first deputy minister of agriculture.

BC ARCHIVES G-07221

Anderson's weathered gravestone stands close to the front door of St. Stephen's Church in Saanich, BC, and bears both his name and his wife's. The woman standing next to the grave is Anderson's last grandchild, Marguerite Flora Pyner (1914–2009).

(PHOTOGRAPHER: NANCY M. ANDERSON)

The Anderson children buried their father beside his wife, in the grounds of Saanich's St. Stephen's Church. In August, James arranged that a stone be cut for his parents' grave. Almost a year after his father's death, James watched as the tall stone marker was placed on the grave.

EPILOGUE

Despite his active career in several fields," historian Derek Pethick wrote in the 1970s, "Anderson is not a well-known figure to the general public. This is surely unjust, for his discovery of a practical, all-British artery for the fur trade was to have a profound effect on the history of not only British Columbia but also of Canada itself."[1] Without Anderson's explorations, Pethick argued, British Columbia could hardly have come into being and would never have become a part of the Dominion of Canada.

The discovery of a route to the Pacific Ocean had always been important to the fur traders of the North West Company. Alexander Mackenzie succeeded in reaching the shores of the Pacific in 1793, but his route proved so difficult he considered his venture a failure. Fifteen years later, Simon Fraser paddled down the Fraser River's rapids and canyons to its mouth, but he returned to New Caledonia disappointed. Finally, David Thompson's steadfast explorations discovered the Columbia River route to the Pacific, the only route the fur traders travelled for the next 36 years.

In 1846, politics threatened to force the Hudson's Bay men to abandon the Columbia River route and replace it with another down the river that had foiled both Mackenzie and Fraser. While other fur traders wondered how the new boundary line would affect their business, Anderson offered to explore for a route across the mountains that separated Kamloops from Fort Langley. Forty or more years after Mackenzie and Fraser made their separate attempts to find a Fraser River route to the Pacific Ocean, Anderson's explorations made the new brigade trail possible.

In spite of his success in accomplishing what both Mackenzie and Fraser had been unable to do, Anderson always felt he worked in the wrong fur trade. As a young man, Anderson had joined the fur trade because he heard the stories of explorers such as Mackenzie and Fraser—men who had paddled wide prairie rivers and crossed mountain ranges to explore new territories in the west. At Lachine House he met a few of those explorers and heard their stories first-hand. In spring 1832, he followed their river trail into the country's interior and enjoyed many of their long-standing traditions—long days of travel in birchbark canoes with the songs of voyageurs ringing in his ears; meals of pemmican or corn cooked into stew over the evening campfire; and baptisms celebrated at every height of land with the firing of guns and tots of rum. Despite the many traditions that clung to the fur trade, the tightly controlled business that Anderson discovered west of the mountains proved to be very different from the adventurous trade that had inspired him. Anderson's first assignment led him north into territories that the early fur traders had never tamed, in spite of the fact that, 50 years earlier, Mackenzie had explored the depths of the sound that Anderson found himself on. A few months later, Anderson listened in awe as Peter Skene Ogden recounted his many stories of adventure in the years of conflict between the two fur-trade companies.

Anderson followed Ogden into New Caledonia, the territory that Simon Fraser had opened 30 years earlier. Under Ogden, Anderson enjoyed many of the freedoms he thought were part of the Hudson's Bay Company's fur trade. They were not. At Fort Vancouver, Anderson butted heads with John McLoughlin and lost the battle; at Fort Nisqually he angered his co-workers, argued with his French-Canadian employee and was punished for his failures. From Fort Vancouver, Anderson was banished into the territory that the fur traders had long called the Siberia of the fur trade. He suffered his punishment in silence and learned that the Hudson's Bay Company's fur trade differed from that of the old North West Company. He put aside his dreams of adventure and exploration and developed the traditional fur trade of the Hudson's Bay Company. Though he knew that Mackenzie had passed through the territory he now inhabited, he did not explore Mackenzie's path until the governor of the Company gave him permission to do so.

But his spirit of adventure did not die, and when news came that the Hudson's Bay Company might have to find a new trail to the coast, Anderson wrote to Governor Simpson, expressing his interest in exploring for that trail. Simpson granted him permission to explore, and Anderson found what appeared to be a safe route up and down the river that had troubled both Mackenzie and Fraser. However, during the difficult 1848 transport to the coast, Anderson learned that his new trail could never work for the fur trade. Another trail must be found, and Anderson's partially explored route across the Coquihalla proved good enough to be the company's brigade trail for the next 15 years.

By this time Anderson had been rewarded with his chief tradership and charge of the important post of Fort Colvile. But the isolation of the new posting distressed him, and the business's stresses and low pay wore him down, engulfing any pleasure he might have taken in exploring the territory that David Thompson had opened to the fur trade. Moreover, Fort Colvile's fur trade remained mired in the past, and Anderson was unaware of the changes that Governor Simpson was introducing on the coast. Anderson adapted to the traditional fur trade of the Hudson's Bay Company, but that trade changed around him and left him behind.

Even at Fort Vancouver, Anderson remained mostly unaware of the trade's new direction and missed his opportunity to take a part in it. Instead he retired, making his home among American immigrants who wanted his services but who refused to fully accept him in their society. Even in retirement Anderson found it difficult to leave the fur trade behind; he set up a business that closely resembled the traditional trading posts of the Hudson's Bay Company.

His old fur-trade friends eventually drew Anderson north to Fort Victoria, where his bookkeeping, learned in the trade, allowed a dishonest clerk to embezzle money and ended Anderson's career in a humiliating court case. He retreated to his Saanich farm to sow the same crops and raise the same animals he had known during his fur-trade years, though his immigrant neighbours made money growing hops and barley. Even in Saanich, Anderson saw life through a fur trader's eyes, and in his writing he constantly referred back to his fur-trade experiences.

Anderson's later careers with the Dominion government came as the result of his early work in the fur trade. As one of three Indian Reserve commissioners, Anderson earned the respect of the Natives he represented but was criticized by his co-commissioner, a British immigrant who controlled the commission's work and eventually forced Anderson out of his position. In his continuing work as Dominion fisheries inspector, Anderson dealt with issues that had always been important to fur traders west of the Rocky Mountains—the health of the various fisheries. But the department's officials in Ottawa had no understanding of the Pacific coast fisheries and refused to spend the money in British Columbia that they spent in the eastern provinces.

Anderson always knew the work he did was important. In spite of the fact that he often did not fit into the culture of the place he found himself in, Anderson's work—first for the fur trade, then for the communities he lived in and finally for the Dominion government—was aimed at improving the future of the people he lived among. No matter how out of place Anderson may have felt, he knew he was the right man, in the right place.

Sometimes the people he worked with recognized that, too. When Anderson and Powell stood in front of the Natives at Ko-omkootz and listened as they told the story of Mackenzie's visit 90 years earlier, Anderson's presence tied the two versions of the story together. To Powell, Anderson represented the new explorer who had accomplished what Mackenzie and Fraser had been unable to do; to the Natives, Anderson was the modern version of the pale-skinned, ghost-like figure whom their ancestors had followed through their waters. At that moment, Anderson was the perfect man, in the perfect place.

NOTES

INTRODUCTION: A FISH OUT OF WATER

1. Alexander C. Anderson, Report as Dominion Fisheries Inspector, January 11, 1882, in *Sessional Papers of the Dominion of Canada*, 4, no. 4, 1882, vol. XV, Marine and Fisheries Section, 206–7.

CHAPTER I: THE PROMISE OF THE ANDERSON-SETON FAMILY

1. "Sketch of the Life of Dr. James Anderson," *Gentleman's Magazine* 78, part 2 (December 1808): 1051–54.

2. Alexander Wedderburn, "The Wedderburn Firm and Suit," in *The Wedderburn* Book 1, chapter III (privately published): 441–48, in Papers of the Seton Family of Mounie Collection, University of Aberdeen Archives, Scotland (hereafter Papers of the Seton Family of Mounie).

3. Virginia van der Lande, "Bewick's Troubled Apprentice: the Work and Career of John Anderson, Scotland's First Wood-Engraver (1775–1807)," draft unpublished MS (2009).

4. Mary Frances Outram, *Margaret Outram, 1778–1863, Mother of the Bayard of India* (London: John Murray, 1932).

5. A.C. Anderson to George Simpson, February 24, 1846, D.5/6, fol. 216, Hudson's Bay Company Archives (hereafter HBCA). *The British Sovereign* was a 350-ton barque, built at Quebec in 1828 and registered in London.

CHAPTER 2: FROM LACHINE HOUSE TO FORT VANCOUVER, 1831–32

1. Alexander Caulfield Anderson, "Life at Lachine," *Beaver Magazine* (June 1952): 30.

2. Ibid., 30–31.

3. Lining was the practice by voyageurs of wading in a stream or river, towing a boat upriver with lines, while one man in a canoe held the boat away from the riverbanks with a pole. "Tracking" is another word for this practice.

4. Journal of Fort William Establishment, Outfit 1832, B.231/a/11, fol. 28, HBCA; Journal of Transactions and Occurrences at Fort William from 1st June 1832 to 1st June 1833, B.231/a/12, fol. 2, HBCA.

5. Journal of Transactions at Norway House from November 1831 to August 1832, B.154/a/21, fol. 26b, HBCA.

6. Alexander Caulfield Anderson, *Notes on North-Western America* (Montreal: Mitchell & Wilson, 1876), 11.

7. York Factory Officers Shop Book, 1832, B.239/d/422, fols. 109–10, HBCA.

8. Journal of Transactions at Norway House from 1st June 1832 to 31st May 1833, B.154/a/22, fol. 11, HBCA.

9. Fort Edmonton Post Journal 1832, entry for September 20, 1832. B.60/a/27, fol. 15, HBCA.

10. Anderson, *Notes on North-Western America*, 11.

11. Cumberland House Post Journals, 1832–3, B.49/a/47, fol. 1, HBCA.

12. Journal of Carlton House 1832/33, entry for September 3, 1832. B.27/a/19, fols. 7–8, HBCA.

13. Journal of Carlton House 1832/3, B.27/a/19, fols. 7–8, HBCA.

14. Fort Edmonton Journal 1832, entry for September 23, 1832. B.60/a/27, fol. 15, HBCA.

15. Alexander Caulfield Anderson, "History of the Northwest Coast," MSS 559, box 2, folder 3, 144 (TS, B.A. McKelvie), BC Archives (hereafter BCA).

16. Letter, A.C. Anderson to Alexander Seton, February 14, 1833, MS2787/5/2/19/5, Papers of the Seton Family of Mounie.

17. Fort George (Astoria), at the mouth of the Columbia River, was the NWC's original headquarters on the Pacific coast, established in 1812. In 1824, the HBC moved its Pacific headquarters to Fort Vancouver, built on farmland 100 miles from the river mouth.

CHAPTER 3: HOSTILITIES ON THE NORTHWEST COAST, 1833–34

1. Richard may have abandoned the fort because Manson had thrashed him. Donald Manson had a reputation for beating his men, but as this form of punishment is never mentioned in the post journals, it is impossible to know if this was the cause of Richard's disappearance. The HBC punished deserters by sending them to the northwest coast posts because there was little opportunity for escape.

2. Anderson, "History of the Northwest Coast," 9–10. Everyone but Anderson called the Native chief Kyeet.

3. William Fraser Tolmie, *Physician and Fur Trader: The Journals of William Fraser Tolmie*, ed. Janet R. Mitchell, (Vancouver: Mitchell Press, 1963), 260.

4. Ibid.

5. Alexander Caulfield Anderson, "Memorandum Respecting Millbank Sound—3rd January 1834," MSS 559, box l, folder 6, BCA.

6. Alexander Caulfield Anderson, "Notes on the Indian Tribes of British North America, and the Northwest Coast," *Historical Magazine* 7, no. 3 (March 1863), 80–81. The words collected by the fur traders were part of a local jargon used by the Natives of different tribes to communicate with each other.

CHAPTER 4: THE WRECK OF THE HOJUNMARU, 1833–34

1. George Dickey, ed., "The Journal of Occurrences at Fort Nisqually, Commencing May 30, 1833, ending September 17, 1859" (Tacoma, WA: Fort Nisqually Association, 1989), section 1, 27.

2. Tolmie, *Physician and Fur Trader*, 285.

CHAPTER 5: RELOCATING OLD FORT SIMPSON, 1834

1. Ibid., 289.

2. John Kirk Townsend, *Narrative of a Journey Across the Rocky Mountains to the Columbia River* (Corvallis, OR: Oregon State University Press, 1999), 134–35.

CHAPTER 6: THE PROMISE OF THE FUR TRADE, 1835–36

1. Alexander Caulfield Anderson, *Handbook and Map to the Gold Region of Frazer's and Thompson's Rivers* (San Francisco: J.J. Le Count, 1858), 13. The Grand Coulee was formed during the last Ice Age when the waters of a huge lake covering modern-day Montana burst their glacier dam and carved deep valleys into the basalt rock of what is now central Washington. The Coulee now lies underwater behind the Grand Coulee Dam.

2. Anderson, *Handbook and Map to the Gold Region of Frazer's and Thompson's Rivers*, 14.

3. Yellowhead Pass. Because of the scarcity of large animals west of the mountains, leather had become an important trading product for the HBC in New Caledonia. The Natives used the material for war dresses and clothing, and the Company men used leather for the moccasins they wore instead of boots. Leather sinews made snowshoes, strips of leather made heavy pack cords, and thongs of leather could be used to fashion snares and nets for catching small animals.

4. Alexander Caulfield Anderson, *The Dominion at the West: a Brief Description of the Province of British Columbia, its Climate and Resources* (Victoria: Richard Wolfenden, 1872), 28.

5. W.S. Wallace, ed., *John McLean's Notes of a 25 years service in the Hudson's Bay Territory* (Toronto: Champlain Society, 1932), 168.

6. Letter, A.C. Anderson to George Simpson, February 1, 1837, MSS 559, vol. 1, folder 5, BCA.

7. Anderson, "History of the Northwest Coast," 13.

8. Alexander Caulfield Anderson, "British Columbia," draft unpublished MS, 96, MSS 559, vol. 2, folder 8, BCA.

9. Letter, George Simpson to John McIntosh, June 24, 1836, D.4/23, fol. 41, HBCA.

10. Wallace, *John McLean's Notes*, 324.

CHAPTER 7: THE TRADITIONAL FUR TRADE, 1836

1. Anderson, *The Dominion at the West*, 23.
2. Ibid., 29.
3. Anderson, "Notes on the Indian Tribes of British North America, and the Northwest Coast," 76.
4. "Miscellaneous material relating to Fort Chilcotin," MM/C43, BCA.
5. "Fort Vancouver, Fur Trade Returns for Columbia and New Caledonia, 1825–1857," A/B/20/V3, BCA.
6. J.D.J. Forbes, "Show Week in the HBC London Fur Warehouse," *The Beaver* (April 1921): 6–8.
7. Letter, Alexander Seton to A.C. Anderson, July 9, 1838, MSS 559, vol.1, folder 1, BCA.
8. In England about this time, a Mr. Wombwell was proprietor of a famous travelling menagerie.
9. Anderson, "British Columbia," 74.

CHAPTER 8: THE FRASER'S LAKE POST, 1837–41

1. Chaplain's Report, Fort Vancouver, October 10, 1837, B.223/b/19, fol. 1–17, HBCA.
2. Letter, Reverend Beaver to P.S. Ogden, June 17, 1837, B.223/b/19, fol. 4, HBCA.
3. Letter, Reverend Beaver to A.C. Anderson, June 17, 1837, B.223/b/19, fol. 4–5, HBCA.
4. Letter, A.C. Anderson to Reverend Beaver, April 20, 1838, B.223/b/20, fol. 62–67, HBCA.
5. A.G. Morice, *History of the Northern Interior of British Columbia formerly known as New Caledonia* (Toronto: William Briggs, 1904), 182.

CHAPTER 9: COWLITZ FARM AND FORT NISQUALLY, 1840–42

1. Alexander Caulfield Anderson, "Memo relating to the Cowlitz Farm &c, 1841," MSS 559, vol. 1, folder 6, BCA. The town of Toledo, WA, is in the area that was occupied by Cowlitz Farm.
2. Alexander Caulfield Anderson, "The Origin of the Puget Sound Agricultural Company," MSS 559, vol. 1, folder 6, BCA.
3. Anderson's brother James disagreed. In a letter dated January 17, 1849, James wrote, "I do not entertain the same opinion as you do regarding the importance of the Sandwich Island[s]—allowing that the Panama Canal was cut—I think few English vessels would pass by that route." Letter, James Anderson to A.C. Anderson, January 17, 1849, A/B/40/An32, BCA.
4. Letter, A.C. Anderson to George Simpson, June 16, 1841, MSS 559, vol. 1, folder 5, BCA (also D.5/6, fol. 155, HBCA).
5. "Journal kept by Assistant Surgeon Silas Holmes during a cruise in the U.S. Ship Peacock and Brigs Porpoise and Oregon, 1838-1839-1840-1841 Exploring Expedition," 3 vols., MSS in Western Americana Collection, Beinecke Rare Book and Manuscript Library, Yale University, vol. 2, 228.
6. Letter, George Simpson to A.C. Anderson, September 5, 1841, D.5/59, fol. 21, HBCA.
7. Anderson, James Robert, "Notes and Comments on early days and events in British Columbia, Washington and Oregon: the Memoirs of James R Anderson," 200, TS, MSS 1912, box 9, folder 1, BCA. Born in 1841, Anderson's son James was too young to know Dr. McLoughlin, and only heard his father's opinion.
8. Extract of Letter to Mr. A, Fort Vancouver, Correspondence Outward, July 13, 1840–May 24, 1841, A/B/20/V, fol. 27, BCA.
9. Letter, James Douglas to A.C. Anderson, April 20, 1841, A/B/20/V, fols. 29–30, BCA.
10. Letter, William H. McNeill to John McLoughlin, June 5, 1841, Wm. McNeill's Fort Nisqually Correspondence Outwards, 1841-2, A/B/20/Ni2A, BCA.
11. Letter, George Simpson to John McLoughlin, September 5, 1841, D.4/59, fol. 22, HBCA.

CHAPTER 10: THE YORK FACTORY EXPRESS, 1842

1. Alexander Caulfield Anderson, "Big Bend," *Victoria Colonist*, January 24, 1866.
2. Edmonton House Account Book, 1842–43, B.60/d/71, fol. 102, HBCA.
3. Norway House Journal, 1st June 1842 to 31st May 1843, B.154/a/39, fols. 5-7, HBCA.
4. York Factory Post Journal, 1841–1842, B.239/a/155, fol. 51, HBCA.
5. Norway House Journal, 1st June 1842 to 31st May 1843, B.154/a/39, fol. 11, HBCA.
6. Margaret Arnett Macleod, ed., *The Letters of Letitia Hargrave* (Toronto: Champlain Soc, 1947), 145–46.
7. Anderson, "Notes and Comments on early days and events in British Columbia, Washington and Oregon," 135.
8. Letter, John Ballenden to George Simpson, April 24, 1852, D.5/33, fol. 459a, HBCA. The handwriting is hard to read; the word "restrained" might be "restraining."
9. This was an esker, the gravelly river bed of a stream that once ran under an ancient glacier. Eskers provided level and easy travelling and were often used by Natives and fur traders.
10. The Thompson's River Journal by John Tod, 1841–1843, A/B/20/K12A, BCA.

CHAPTER 11: THE SIBERIA OF THE FUR TRADE, 1842–43

1. Fort Alexandria Journal 1842–1843, entry for November 21, 1842. B.5/a/5, fol. 33a, HBCA.
2. Letter, A.C. Anderson to George Simpson, January 21, 1843, D.5/8, fol. 38, HBCA.
3. A.G. Morice, *History of the Northern Interior of British Columbia formerly New Caledonia* (Toronto: William Briggs, 1904), 213.
4. Fort St. James Post Journal 1840–46, entry for March 14, 1843. B.188/a/19, fol. 83b, HBCA.
5. Fort St. James Post Journal 1840–46, entry for April 19, 1843. B.188/1/19, fol. 88b, HBCA.
6. Anderson, "British Columbia," 11–12.
7. Prairie du Nicholas was located where the town of Summerland is today.

CHAPTER 12: AGRICULTURE AT FORT ALEXANDRIA, 1843–44

1. Fort Alexandria Journal 1842–1843, entry for July 22, 1843. B.5/a/5, fol. 49a, HBCA.
2. Fort Alexandria Journal 1843–1845, entry for April 25, 1843. B.5/a/6, fol. 3a, HBCA.
3. Anderson, "British Columbia," 27–28.
4. To the fur traders, chutes were rapids, but the barrière was a narrow canyon where the natives established a fishery. The Chilcotin River barrière was at Farwell Canyon.
5. Letter, A.C. Anderson to George Simpson, February 13, 1844, D.5/10, fol. 221, HBCA.
6. Fort Alexandria Journal 1843–1845, entry for May 10, 1844. B.5/a/6, fol. 4a, HBCA. *Verveau* was the French-Canadian name for the woven funnel-shaped basket that was a part of the Natives' weirs.
7. *En dérouine* is the practice of carrying trading goods to the Natives' villages or lodges to trade directly with them for their furs or fish.
8. Letter, A.C. Anderson to George Simpson, February 13, 1845, D.5/13, fol. 129, HBCA.

CHAPTER 13: LANDSLIDES AND SALMON RUNS, 1844–45

1. Anderson, "British Columbia," 56.
2. Fort Alexandria Journal 1842–1843, entry for July 17, 1843. B.5/a/5, fol. 49a, HBCA.
3. Fort Alexandria Journal 1842–1843, entry for July 29, 1843. B.5/a/5, fol. 49b, HBCA.
4. Letter, A.C. Anderson to Sir William J. Hooker, September 30, 1845, Royal Botanic Gardens Archives, Kew, England.
5. Fort Alexandria Journal 1843–1845, entry for October 25, 1844. B.5/a/6, fol. 13a, HBCA. The quote, "Pippins and cheese to come" is from William Shakespeare's *The Merry Wives of Windsor*, and Sir Hugh refers to the character Sir Hugh Evans, a Welsh parson.
6. Letter, A.C. Anderson to Rupert Jones (professor of Geology, Royal Military College, Sandhurst, England), December 10, 1870, MSS 559, vol. 1, folder 5, BCA.

7. Anderson, "Notes and Comments on early days and events in British Columbia, Washington and Oregon," 53–54. Though James thought the child had survived, Père Nobili, who passed the fort after the landslide occurred, reported that the child died.

8. Letter, A.C. Anderson to Alexander Seton, Spring 1845, MS 2787/5/2/19/8, Papers of the Seton Family of Mounie.

9. Letter, A.C. Anderson to George Simpson, February 13, 1845, D.5/13, fol. 129, HBCA

10. There were no carp in the lakes that surrounded Fort Alexandria at this time. The common carp (*Cyprinus carpio*) was introduced into the Columbia River system in the 1880s, and by 1928 this member of the minnow family had expanded into the Fraser River system. However, the northern pikeminnow (*Ptychocheilus orogonensis*), a bone-filled and edible member of the minnow family, had always lived in these northern rivers and lakes, as did another carp-like fish called the large-scaled sucker (*Catostomus macrocheilus*). In his youth, Anderson had become familiar with the cultivated carp in the ponds of his uncle's estate at Mounie, and he probably identified that fish's close relative, the northern pikeminnow, as carp.

11. Fort Alexandria Journal 1843–1845, entry for June 13, 1845. B.5/a/6, fol. 25b, HBCA.

12. Marie Elliott, *Fort St. James and New Caledonia; Where British Columbia Began* (Madeira Park, BC: Harbour Press, 2009), 135.

CHAPTER 14: THE FUR TRADE, 1845–46

1. Fort Alexandria Journal 1845–1848, entry for February 26, 1846. B.5/a/7, fol. 10b, HBCA. The cross fox is a variety of red fox and has black markings on its face, back and tail.

2. Fort Alexandria Journal 1845–1848, entry for August 7, 1846. B.5/a/7, fol. 16a, HBCA.

3. Marius Barbeau and Clifford Wilson, "Tobacco for the Fur Trade," *The Beaver* (March 1944): 36–39.

4. Fort Yale, Bill of Lading for Summer Brigade, 1848, A/B/20/Y1, BCA.

5. Fort Alexandria Journal 1842–1843, entry for January 17, 1843. B.5/a/5, fol. 37b, HBCA.

6. Fort Alexandria Journal 1843–1845, an entry for May, 1845. B.5/a/6, fol. 24b, HBCA. Many pages in these journals are missing; the date is probably May 3 as journal entries were rarely made on Sunday.

7. Fort Alexandria Journal 1845–1845, entry for April 20, 1844. B.5/a/6, fol. 2b, HBCA.

8. Fort Alexandria Journal 1843–1845, entry for May 25, 1843. B.5/a/6, fol. 5a, HBCA.

9. Fort Alexandria Journal 1843–1845, entry for November 4, 1844. B.5/a/6, fol. 14a, HBCA.

10. Fort Alexandria Journal 1843–1845, entry for July 30, 1844. B.5/a/6, fol. 7b, HBCA.

11. Fort Vancouver Fur Trade Returns for Columbia & New Caledonia, 1825–1857.

12. Fort Alexandria Journal 1845–1848, entry for November 14, 1845. B.5/a/7, fol. 6b, HBCA.

13. Anderson, "Notes and Comments on early days and events in British Columbia, Washington and Oregon," 50. Anderson's son James had a clear recollection of the fort yard inundated with water.

CHAPTER 15: THE SEARCH FOR A NEW BRIGADE TRAIL, 1846

1. Extract from P.S. Ogden's letter to Chief Traders Tod and Manson sent from Colvile and dated October 22, 1845, A/B/40/Og2, BCA. The Nicoutimine country referred to Nicola Valley south of Kamloops.

2. Alexander Caulfield Anderson, "Scraps of unpublished manuscript," MSS 1912, vol. 16, folder 2, BCA.

3. Alexander Caulfield Anderson, "Journal of an Expedition under Command of Alex. C. Anderson of the Hudson's Bay Company, undertaken with the View to ascertaining the practicability of a communication with the interior, for the import of the annual supplies," A/B/40/An3.1, fol. 1, BCA.

4. Ibid., fol. 2. The R. aux Chapeaux was Hat Creek, and the Loon River Fork probably Scottie Creek.

5. Ibid., fol. 3. The name Batailleur translated as "The Battler."

6. Pavilion River.

7. Anderson, "British Columbia," back of p. 14. This was Seton River that drained Seton and Anderson Lakes.

8. Anderson, "Journal of an Expedition," fols. 5–6.

9. Ibid., fol. 7. Sasquatch researchers have transformed this story into the Natives telling Anderson about the Sasquatch.

10. Ibid., fol. 9.

11. Ibid., fol. 9–10. *Boutes* was a fur-trade word that referred to the paddlers in a canoe or boat.

12. Ibid., fol. 10. This was known to the Fort Langley men as Harrison's Lake.

CHAPTER 16: THE RETURN JOURNEY OVER THE MOUNTAINS, 1846

1. Ibid., fol. 16.

2. Ibid., fol. 16–17. In a later version of his journal Anderson attributes the earlier bout of varicose veins to "overexertion on the snowshoes," obviously considering that the ailment was caused by the long hike over Leather Pass in the winter of 1835–36.

3. Ibid., fol. 18–19.

4. Ibid., fol. 19.

5. Alexander Caulfield Anderson, Map Showing the different Routes of Communication with the Gold Region of Frasers River, CM/A78, BCA.

6. Anderson, "Journal of an Expedition," fol. 20–21.

7. Ibid., fol. 22.

8. Ibid., fol. 22. Blackeye's Native name might have been Yo:a'la.

9. Ibid., fol. 23.

CHAPTER 17: THE NEW CHIEF TRADER, 1846–47

1. Letter, George Simpson to Donald Manson, June 19, 1853, D.4/46, fol. 130, HBCA.

2. [December 8, 1846] Fort Alexandria Journal 1845–1848, entry for December 8, 1846. B.5/a/7, fol. 23b, HBCA.

3. Letter, James Anderson to A.C. Anderson, Dec. 24, 1846, A/B/40/An32, BCA. None of Alexander's letters to James survived the fire that destroyed the James Anderson family home about 1875, according to letter, James McKenzie Anderson to James Robert Anderson, March 14, 1914, MSS 1912, Box 7, folder 4, BCA.

4. Ibid.

5. Letter, P.S. Ogden and J. Douglas to A.C. Anderson, January 12, 1847, A/B/20/V2Od, BCA. Twenty-five-year-old McGillivray was the grandson of William McGillivray, partner and chief director of the NWC before 1821. A Métis, Montrose McGillivray died of fever at Fort St. James in 1850.

6. Simon Fraser, *The Letters and Journals of Simon Fraser, 1806–1808*, ed. W. Kaye Lamb (Dundurn Press, 2007), 97.

7. Anderson, "Journal of an Expedition to Fort Langley via Thompson' [*sic*] Rivers, Summer of 1847," in Anderson, "History of the Northwest Coast," 77. Anderson's original journal has been lost.

8. The trail is shown on two maps by A.C. Anderson: "Kamloops Region, Nicola Valley and the upper Similkameen Valley," CM/13664A, BCA; and "Map showing the different Routes of Communication with the Gold Region of Fraser's River," CM/A78, BCA.

9. Anderson, "Journal of an Expedition to Fort Langley, summer of 1847," 78.

10. Ibid., 78a–78b. The transcript has two pages numbered 78.

11. Ibid., 78b. This was almost certainly Siska Creek.

12. Ibid., 78b. Anderson's Skaoose was just south of Falls Creek.

13. Ibid., 79.

14. Anderson, "Notes on the Indian Tribes of British North America," 77–78.

15. Anderson, "Journal of an Expedition to Fort Langley, summer of 1847," 79.

16. Ibid., 79. Anderson later reported having once owned a thermometer which he broke, possibly on this journey down the Fraser River.

17. Blackeye's son is probably the son-in-law Anderson met in summer 1846. Tsilaxitsa (Chillaheetza) would become one of the most important Secwepemc/Okanagan tribal chiefs of his time; his biography is in *42nd Report of the Okanagan Historical Society*, 1978, 59.

18. Anderson, "Journal of an Expedition to Fort Langley, summer of 1847," 79–80.

19. Ibid., 81.

20. Anderson, *Handbook and Map to the Gold Region of Frazer's and Thompson's River*, 6. The "Falls" were Hell's Gate and Black Canyon, south of Boston Bar.

21. Anderson, "Journal of an Expedition to Fort Langley, summer of 1847," 81–82.

22. Ibid., 82.

23. Ibid., 82.

24. Letter, A.C. Anderson to George Simpson, February 24, 1848, D.5/21, fol. 292, HBCA.

25. Anderson, "Journal of an Expedition to Fort Langley, summer of 1847," 83.

26. Fraser, *The Letters and Journals of Simon Fraser*, 117.

CHAPTER 18: THE ANDERSON'S RIVER TRAIL, 1847–48

1. Anderson, "Journal of an Expedition to Fort Langley via Thompson' [*sic*] River, Summer of 1847: Return Journey," in "History of the Northwest Coast," 84.

2. Ibid., 85.

3. Ibid., 85.

4. Ibid., 86.

5. Ibid., 87–88.

6. Ibid., 88.

7. Letter, A.C. Anderson to Board of Management, June 21, 1847, in "Journal of an Expedition to Fort Langley via Thompson' [*sic*] River: Summer of 1847, Return Journey," 92–93.

CHAPTER 19: A YEAR OF GREAT CHANGES, 1847–48

1. Anderson, "History of the Northwest Coast," 45.

2. Fort Yale, Bill of Lading for Summer Brigade, 1848, A/B/20/Y1, BCA.

3. Anderson, *Handbook and Map to the Gold Region of Frazer's and Thompson's River*, 5–6.

4. "Private Journal of Henry Peers from Fort Langley to Thompson's River, Summer 1848," E/A/P34, BCA.

5. Letter, A.C. Anderson to D. Manson, August 24, 1848, B.223/b/37, fol. 46b, HBCA.

CHAPTER 20: FORT COLVILE, 1849–50

1. Letter, A.C. Anderson to George Simpson, April 17, 1849, D.5/25, fol. 122, HBCA. The HBC fur traders considered New Caledonia part of the Columbia district.

2. Letter, A.C. Anderson to Governors & Chief Factors, September 21, 1849, D.5/25, fol.140, HBCA.

3. Letter, D. Manson to George Simpson, February 25, 1850, D.5.27, fol. 362, HBCA.

4. Letter, A.C. Anderson to George Simpson, April 17, 1850, D.5/28, fol. 104, HBCA.

5. Eden Colvile, *London Correspondence inward from Eden Colvile*, 1849–1852 (London: Hudson's Bay Record Society, 1956), Appendix, 234–35. Part of the reason for the shortage of horses was the high prices paid for the animals by American gold miners. Natives would no longer sell their horses to the fur traders at the old low prices.

6. Letter, P.S. Ogden to George Simpson, March 16, 1850, D.5/27, fol.456, HBCA.

7. Letter, J. Douglas to A.C. Anderson, March 18, 1850, A/C/20/Vi3D, BCA.

8. Letter, A.C. Anderson to Governor and Council, April 18, 1850, D.5/28, fol. 108, HBCA. David Finlay was probably a descendent of Jaco Finlay, who built the North West Company's Spokane House in 1810.

9. Anderson knew the Natives who surrounded Fort Colvile as the Skoielpoi, but today they are the Colvilles, part of the Confederated Tribes of the Colville Reservation. Today's tribal members sometimes refer to the Colvilles as Schulpi or Chulpay.

10. Letter, A.C. Anderson to George Simpson, April 21, 1851, D.5/30, fol. 635–6, HBCA.

CHAPTER 21: FORT COLVILE BRIGADES, 1850–51

1. Letter, J. Douglas to George Simpson, Oct. 15, 1850, D.5/29, fol. 57b, HBCA. Anderson would not have known that a horse-breeding operation was being set up at Kamloops, and it is probable that Fraser criticized him for bringing in the horses from Edmonton House.

2. Letter, J. Douglas to A.C. Anderson, October 28, 1850, A/C/20/Vi3D, BCA.

3. Letter, P.S. Ogden to George Simpson, July 28, 1850, B.223/b/39, fol. 71d–72, HBCA.

4. Chief Factor John Ballenden was apparently not related to employee Jacob Ballenden who committed suicide on the 1848 New Caledonia brigade. However, they both came from the Orkneys and so might have been from different branches of the same family. John Ballenden entered the fur trade in 1829 as a clerk, while Jacob entered in 1842 as a labourer.

5. Letter, P.S. Ogden to George Simpson, March 20, 1851, D.5/30, fol.442, HBCA.

CHAPTER 22: NO FUTURE IN HIS PAST, 1851–52

1. Letter, John Ballenden to George Simpson, April 24, 1852, fol. 459a, HBCA.

2. Letter, J. Douglas to J. Ballenden, December 15, 1851, B.226/b/4, fol. 23a, HBCA; James Douglas to A.C. Anderson, January 28, 1852, Fort Victoria Correspondence Outward, 1850–1859, part 2, A/C/20/V3D, BCA.

3. Letter, J. Douglas to A.C. Anderson, February 25, 1852, Fort Victoria Correspondence Outward, 1850–1859, A/B/20/Vi3D, BCA.

4. Alexander Caulfield Anderson, "A private memorandum for the gentlemen at Vancouver," MSS 559, vol. 1, folder 6, BCA.

5. Letter, A.C. Anderson to George Simpson, April 22, 1852, D.5/33, fol. 450, HBCA.

6. Letter, A.C. Anderson to George Simpson, Nov. 18, 1852, D.5/35, fol. 182, HBCA.

7. Letter, J. Ballenden to George Simpson, Nov. 10, 1852, D.5/35, fol. 160, HBCA.

8. Letter, George Simpson to P.S. Ogden, June 19, 1853, D.4/46, fol. 143–44, HBCA.

CHAPTER 23: LIFE AND DEATH IN NEW OREGON TERRITORY, 1853–57

1. Letter, A.C. Anderson to W.H. Tolmie, August 5, 1854, MSS 559, vol. 1, folder 5, BCA.

2. Letter, George Simpson to A.C. Anderson, May 2, 1855, D.4/83, fol. 490, HBCA.

3. Letter, A.C. Anderson to J. Birnie, August 20, 1855, Birnie Papers MSS, Oregon Historical Society Archives.

4. Anderson, "History of the Northwest Coast", 47.

5. Letter, A.C. Anderson to George Simpson, March 10, 1857, D.5/43, fol. 284, HBCA.

6. Letter, John Work to A.C. Anderson, April 7, 1858, MSS 599, vol. 1, file 1, 20a–20d, BCA.

CHAPTER 24: THE CURSE OF THE FUR TRADE, 1858–60

1. Alexander Seton was born at Tottenham, Middlesex, on October 4, 1814, and was the eldest surviving son of Anderson's uncle Alexander Seton. The same month A.C. Anderson arrived at Fort Vancouver to begin his fur trade career, Alexander Seton purchased a commission as second-lieutenant in the Royal North British Fusiliers. In 1847 he was transferred to the 74th Highlanders, and in 1852, Lieutenant-Colonel Seton took command of the raw recruits destined for the Cape of Good Hope where his own regiment was already involved in the Kaffir War. On the morning of February 26, the iron troopship *Birkenhead* struck a rock southeast of Cape Town and foundered. In spite of the urgency of the situation, Seton issued his orders with perfect calm—"Women and children first!" The crew prepared the ship's boats and loaded the soldiers' families into them, while the soldiers stood at attention on the *Birkenhead*'s sloping decks. The soldiers knew they were doomed; there were not enough boats to carry them ashore and the distance was too far to swim. In fact, Seton admitted to another officer that he could not swim. One of Seton's two horses made it to shore, but he did not. A survivor later reported that Seton had been killed by the fall of a mast.

CHAPTER 25: "AND I SAY YOU LIE, SIR!" 1859

1. "Confidential Report on Officers," James Douglas Papers, A/C/15/D75, BCA.

2. Letter, W.D. Gossett to R.C. Moody, June 1, 1859, Colonial Correspondence F485a 9p, BCA.

3. Letter, A.C. Anderson to H. Crease (barrister), June 8, 1859, Crease Collection, MSS 1879, box 6, folder 1, BCA.

4. Letter, A.C. Anderson to W.A.G. Young, July 18, 1859, Colonial Correspondence F14 12, BCA.

5. "The Alleged Customs House Fraud," *British Colonist*, June 6, 1859.

6. "Regina vs. Angelo," *British Colonist*, August 12, 1859.

7. "Regina vs. Angelo," *British Colonist*, August 12, 1859; Anderson, "Notes and Comments on early days and events in British Columbia, Washington and Oregon," 283.

8. This map is CM/B1094, BCA.

9. This map is CM/F9, BCA.

10. This map is CM/13665A, BCA.

11. This map is CM/13699A, BCA.

12. Draft copy of this map is CM/13666C, BCA.

13. Anderson's property was bounded by modern-day Rockland Avenue, Cook Street, Meares Street, and Linden Avenue.

14. Letter, Margaret Tappan to Arthur Anderson, December 8, 1862, Copy in Nancy Anderson Collection.

CHAPTER 26: THE UNSETTLED SETTLER, 1861–76

1. Letter, J. Douglas to Sir T. Maitland, September 9, 1861, B.A. McKelvie Collection, MSS 1, v. 41, BCA.

2. Anderson, "British Columbia," 3–4.

3. Benjamin Tappan Papers, MSS 127, Oregon Historical Society Archives.

4. Anderson, *The Dominion at the West*, 111.

5. The Anderson family Bible is in the possession of the author.

6. W.B. Anderson, "Chronicles of Old North Saanich," *Daily Colonist*, August 1, 1937, in the Brad Morrison Collection of North and South Saanich Material (hereafter Brad Morrison Collection); Brad Morrison, "An Eminent Figure Who Deserves More Recognition," *Beachcomber* [newspaper], March 4, 1998, Saanich Pioneers Society Museum and Archives.

7. *Victoria Daily Standard*, July 24, 1876, 3, Brad Morrison Collection.

CHAPTER 27: THE INDIAN RESERVE COMMISSION ON THE COAST, 1876–77

1. Alexander Caulfield Anderson, "Diary as Indian Reserves Commissioner," MSS 559, vol. 2, folder 5, BCA.

2. Archibald McKinlay, "Indian Reserve Commission, Diary," E/C/M21, fol. 96, BCA.

3. "Correspondence regarding the relations between the B.C. Reserve Commissioners and Superintendent James Lenihan, 1877," Canada, Department of Indian Affairs, Black (Western) Series, RG10, vol. 3653, file 8702, Library and Archives Canada (hereafter LAC).

CHAPTER 28: HAWKING ABOUT THE COUNTRY, 1877–83

1. "Correspondence regarding the relations between the B.C. Reserve Commissioners and Superintendent James Lenihan, 1877," Canada, Department of Indian Affairs, Black (Western) Series, RG10, vol. 3653, file 8702, LAC).

2. Selixt-asposem's name translated as "Five Hearts," according to Anderson's journal.

3. "Journal of proceedings of the Commission for the settlement of the Indian Reserves in the Province of British Columbia," entry for Tuesday, September 18, 1877. Canada, Department of Indian Affairs, Black (Western) Series, RG10, vol. 3659, file 9500, 57, LAC. It is possible that the Hudson's Bay Company medal was the same medal given to the principal chief of Thompson's River by Governor George Simpson in 1824; see Frederick Merk, *Fur Trade and Empire* (Cambridge, MA: Harvard University Press, 1931), 132.

4. "Journal of the Proceedings of the Commission for the settlement of the Indian Reserves in the Province of British Columbia," 63–64.

5. Ibid., 74–75.

6. Letter, G.M. Sproat to Minister of Interior, October 27, 1877, Canada, Department of Indian Affairs, Black (Western) Series, RG10, volume 3656, file 9063, 5, LAC.

7. "Extensive private memorandum from Sproat on reorganization of the management of Indian Affairs in British Columbia, 1877," Canada, Department of Indian Affairs, Black (Western) Series, RG10, volume 3656, file 9063, 4, LAC.

8. Letter, Father Grandidier to A.C. Anderson, April 19, 1878, MSS 1912, box 7, file 2, BCA.

9. Letter, A.C. Anderson to Hon. Minister of Dominion Indian Commission and Superintendent General of Indian Affairs, MSS 1912, box 7, file 2, BCA.

CHAPTER 29: INSPECTOR OF FISHERIES, 1876–83

1. H.H. Bancroft, *The Works of Hubert Howe Bancroft, vol. 32, History of British Columbia* (San Francisco: The History Company, 1887159.

2. Ibid., 158.

3. H.H. Bancroft, *The Works of Hubert Howe Bancroft, vol. 39, Literary Industries* (San Francisco: The History Company, 1890), 538.

4. Letter, Dr. I.W. Powell, November 22, 1881, in *Sessional Papers of the Dominion of Canada*, 6, no.6, 1882, vol. 15, "Indian Affairs Section," 139–156.

5. *Sessional Papers of the Dominion of Canada*, vol. 15, no. 4, 1882, Appendix: "Index to the Fisheries Statements for 1881," xiii–xxxix.

6. Letter, A.C. Anderson to William Anderson, June 13, 1883, MSS 559, vol. 1, folder 5, BCA.

CHAPTER 30: CROSS THE DARK RIVER

1. Newspaper clipping in Anderson Family Bible, from a newspaper other than the *Colonist*.

EPILOGUE

1. Derek Pethick, *Men of British Columbia* (Saanichton, B.C: Hancock House, 1975). The author devoted six pages to James Douglas, seven to Alexander Caulfield Anderson.

SELECTED BIBLIOGRAPHY

Most of my references are included in the many endnotes to this book. However, there are a few books and magazine articles from which I obtained important information that did not end up being included in the endnotes. These are the important resources I have listed here.

Information on the various incidents on the northwest coast, 1833–34, comes from:
Ships' Logs, *Dryad* (brig), C.1/281, fols. 81–191, Hudson's Bay Company Archives (hereafter HBCA); and Ships Logs, *Dryad* (brig), C.1/282, fols. 20–49, HBCA.
Ft. McLoughlin Post Journals, 1833—Extracts from the diary at Fort McLoughlin, Milbank Sound, in relation to an affair which occurred at that place, 10 October 1833, B.102/a/1, HBCA.
"P.S. Ogden's Report of Transactions at Stikine, 1834." In *The Letters of John McLoughlin from Fort Vancouver to the Governor and Committee, First Series, 1825–38*, edited by E.E. Rich, 317–18. Toronto: Champlain Society, 1941–44.
Fort Simpson (Nass) Post Journal, 1834–1838, B.201/a/3, fols. 2–10, HBCA.

Information on the Wreck of the *Hojunmaru* comes from:
Anderson, Alexander Caulfield. "Notes on the Indian Tribes of British North America." *Historical Magazine* VII, no. 3 (March 1863): 80–81.
Anderson, Alexander Caulfield. "Historical Notes on the Commerce of the Columbia River 1824 to 1848." (Item 6), WA Mss 5, Beinecke Rare Book and Manuscript Library, Yale University Library.
Igarashi, Yuzo, and Tei A. Gordon. "Otikichi; Adventures of the First Japanese in America." Unpublished manuscript, Otokichi Foundation, Tokyo, Japan.

Information on the Brigade Trails around British Columbia, 1835–1848, comes from:
Creech, E.P. "Brigade Trails of B. C." *The Beaver* (March 1953): 10–15.
Creech, E.P. "Similkameen Trails, 1846–61." *British Columbia Historical Quarterly* (October 1941) 255–67.
Favrholdt, Kenneth Cornaby. "The Cordilleran Communication: The Brigade System of the Far Western Fur Trade." MA Thesis, Department of Geography, University of British Columbia, 1998. AWF-B71, 1998-0334, Koerner Library.
Gibson, James R. *The Lifeline of the Oregon Country; the Fraser-Columbia Brigade System, 1811–47.* Vancouver: University of British Columbia Press, 1997.
Goodfellow, J.C. "Fur and Gold in Similkameen." *British Columbia Historical Quarterly* (April 1938): 67–88.
Gregory, David. "Priest Camp: A Typical Stopping Place on the Okanagan Brigade Trail." *Okanagan History, 61st Report of the Okanagan Historical Society* (1997): 45–49.
Harris, R.C. "A Good Mule Road to Semilkameen, Later Known as the Canyon, or Dewdney, Trail." *B.C. Historical News* 14, no. 3 (Spring 1981): 8–14.
Harris, R.C. "Old Trails and Routes in British Columbia; Blackeye's and 1849 HBC Trail." *B.C. Historical News* 12, no. 1 (November 1978): 15–17.
Harris, R.C. "The HBC 1849 Brigade Trail, Fort Hope to Kamloops—Collins Gulch Section." *B.C. Historical News* 12, no. 4 (Summer 1979): 22–26.
Harris, R.C. "The Hope-Nicola Trail, 1875–1913." *B.C. Historical News* 14, no. 1 (Fall 1980): 18–24.
Hatfield, Harley R. "Okanagan Brigade Trail." *39th Report of the Okanagan Historical Society* (1976) 97–103.
Hatfield, Harley R. "Brigade Trail, Fort Hope to Campement des Femmes." *36th Report of Okanagan Historical Society* (1972): 37–48.
Hatfield, Harley R. "On the Brigade Trail." *The Beaver* (Summer 1974): 38–43.

Hatfield, Harley R. "The Brigade Trail; Nicola Lake to Kamloops." *B.C. Historical News* 16, no. 3 (Winter 1983): 13–17.

Hatfield, Harley R. "Blackeye's Trail." *Okanagan History; 51st Report of the Okanagan Historical Society* (1987): 99–104.

Howay, Judge F.W. "The raison d'être of Forts Yale and Hope." *Proceedings and Transactions of the Royal Society Of Canada* XVI, 3d series, vol. (1922): 49–64.

Information on the incidents at Fort Alexandria and Fort St. James, 1842–1848, comes from:

Fort Alexandria Journal, 1842–1843, B.5/a/5, fol. 32a–end, HBCA.

Fort Alexandria Journal, 1843–1845, B.5/a/6, HBCA.

Fort Alexandria Journal, 1845–1848, B.5/a/7, HBCA.

Fort Alexandria Journal, 1848–1851, B.5/a/8, fol. 1–4a, HBCA.

Fort St. James Post Journal, 1840–1846, B.188/a/19, fols. 81a–88b, HBCA.

Information on Fort Colvile and district comes from:

British and American Joint Commission for the final settlement of the claims of the Hudson's Bay & Puget's Sound Agricultural Co. Montreal (1865–1869). Deposition of Alexander Caulfield Anderson, August 5, 1865, Vol. V, Section IV, 33–49.

Oliphant, J. Orin. "Old Fort Colvile." *Washington Historical Quarterly* 16 (April 1925): 29–101.

Partoll, Albert J. "Fort Connah; a Frontier Trading Post, 1847–1871." *Pacific Northwest Quarterly* 30 (October 1939): 399–415.

Webber, Jean "Fur Trading Posts in the Okanagan and Similkameen." *Okanagan History, 57th Report of Okanagan Historical Society* (1993): 6–33.

Information on Anderson's S'gatch poose name comes from:

Stanley, George F. *Mapping the Frontier.* Toronto: MacMillan, 1970.

Williams, Christina. "The Daughter of Angus McDonald." *Washington Historical Quarterly* 13 (1922): 115.

Additional help in tracking the name came from Steve Anderson, David Courchane, Jack Nisbet, Henry Zinc, Trina Fyant Felsman and Ann McRae.

Information on A.C. Anderson in Victoria comes from:

Anderson, Walter Birnie. "Chronicles of Old North Saanich." *Daily Colonist,* June 6, 1937 [Brad Morrison collection of North and South Saanich Material].

Anderson, Walter Birnie. "Chronicles of Old North Saanich," *Daily Colonist,* August 1, 1937 [Brad Morrison collection of North and South Saanich Material].

Careless, J.M.S. "The Lowe Brothers, 1852–70; A Study in Business Relations on the North Pacific Coast." *B.C. Studies* no. 2 (Summer 1969): 1–18.

Hacking, Norman. "Steamboating on the Fraser in the Sixties." *British Columbia Historical Quarterly* 10, no. 1 (January 1946): 1–41. The Victoria Steamship Company operated under various names: the Victoria Steam Navigation Company, the British Columbia Steam Navigation Company, and the Victoria & British Columbia Steam Navigation Company Ltd.

Information on Indian Reserve Commission, 1876–77, comes from:

"Report of the Proceedings of the Joint Commission, Report for the period 3 Nov. 1876 to 11 Mar. 1877." British Columbia, Provincial Secretary, Records relating to Indian affairs, 1876–1878, GR494, Box 1, File 22, p. 220-261, BC Archives (hereafter BCA).

"Report of the British Columbia Reserve Commission with Census reports, 1877." Canada, Department of Indian Affairs, Black Series, RG10, Volume 3645, File 3936, Library and Archives Canada (hereafter LAC).

"Summarized Report of the Indian Reserve Commissioners acting for the Government of British Columbia." March 27, 1877, British Columbia, Provincial Secretary, Records relating

ing to Indian affairs, 1876–1878, GR494, BCA.

General Correspondence to and from the British Columbia Reserve Commission regarding Reserves, 1877–8, Canada, Department of Indian Affairs, Black Series, RG10, Volume 3651, File 8540, LAC.

Anderson's reports as Inspector of Fisheries are found:

Anderson, Alexander C. Report of the Inspector of Fisheries for British Columbia for the year of 1876, *Sessional Papers of the Dominion of Canada, Volume X, No. 5, Session 1877*, Marine and Fisheries Section, 339–347.

Anderson, Alexander C. Report of the Inspector of Fisheries for British Columbia for the year 1877, *Sessional Papers of the Dominion of Canada, Volume XI, No. 3, Session 1878*, Marine and Fisheries Section, 287–305.

Anderson, Alexander C. Report of the Inspector of Fisheries for British Columbia for the year 1878, *Sessional Papers of the Dominion of Canada, Volume XII, No. 4, Session 1879*, Marine and Fisheries Section, 292–300.

Anderson, Alexander C. Report of the Inspector of Fisheries for British Columbia for the year 1879, *Sessional Papers of the Dominion of Canada, Volume XIII, No. 6, Session 1880*, Marine and Fisheries Section, 280–295.

Anderson, Alexander C. Report of the Inspector of Fisheries for British Columbia for the year 1880, *Sessional Papers of the Dominion of Canada, Volume XIV, No. 6, Session 1880–81*, Marine and Fisheries Section, 257–266.

Anderson, Alexander C. Report of the Inspector of Fisheries for British Columbia for the year 1881, *Sessional Papers of the Dominion of Canada, Volume XV, No. 4, Session 1882*, Marine and Fisheries Section, 202–221.

Anderson, Alexander C. Report of the Inspector of Fisheries for British Columbia for the year 1882, *Sessional Papers of the Dominion of Canada, Volume XVI, No. 5, Session 1883*, Marine and Fisheries Section, 188–193.

Anderson, Alexander C. Report of the Inspector of Fisheries for British Columbia for the year 1883, *Sessional Papers of the Dominion of Canada, Volume XVII, No. 5, Session 1884*, Marine and Fisheries Section, 190–199.

Additional Important Resources:

Innis, Harold A. *The Fur Trade in Canada: An Introduction to Canadian Economic History*. Toronto: University of Toronto Press, 1964.

Mackie, Richard Somerset. *Trading Beyond the Mountains: The British Fur Trade on the Pacific, 1793–1843*. Vancouver: University of British Columbia Press, 1997.

Palmer, Rod N. "Alexander Caulfield Anderson: An Ideal First Inspector of Fisheries." *British Columbia Historical News* 36 (Spring 2003): 28–30.

Philbrick, Nathaniel. *Sea of Glory: American's Voyage of Discovery, the U.S. Exploring Expedition, 1838–1842*. New York: Viking, 2003.

Podruchny, Carolyn. *Making the Voyageur World: Travelers and Traders in the North American Fur Trade*. Toronto: University of Toronto Press, 2006.

Van Kirk, Sylvia. *Many Tender Ties: Women in Fur-Trade Society, 1670–1870*. Winnipeg: Watson & Dwyer Pub., 1993.

INDEX

ACKNOWLEDGEMENTS

Alexander Caulfield Anderson lived through exciting times, and left behind a wealth of written material that has provided primary resources for historians and academics throughout the years. But much of this information would have been lost had it not been for the efforts of his son James Robert Anderson, who preserved Anderson's maps, essays and private writings in the fledgling British Columbia Archives. Anderson's letters to Hudson's Bay Company Governor George Simpson have been preserved in the Hudson's Bay Company Archives in Winnipeg, Manitoba. Correspondence between Anderson-Seton family members is kept in the Papers of the Seton Family of Mounie Collection at the University of Aberdeen, Scotland; in Georgina Pioneer Village Archives, Sutton, Ontario; and in the British Columbia Archives, Victoria, BC.

Many private individuals shared Anderson-Seton material with me. I especially thank the following persons: Virginia van der Lande for her Anderson-Seton family research in Great Britain, India and Australia; Brad Morrison for his collection of North and South Saanich material; Harry Burrows, retired fisheries officer, who led me to Anderson's Fishery Reports; Grant Keddie and Bob Griffin of the Royal British Columbia Museum; Yuzo Igarashi, Norie Akiyama, Professor Sachiko Tanaka and Tei Gordon, of the Otikichi Research Team in Tokyo, Japan, who shared the story of the wreck of the *Hojunmaru*; and Harley R. Hatfield and friends who tramped over the brigade trails and wrote their history.

I also thank other people who helped me: Steve Anderson, David "Chalk" Courchane, Pam Gaudio, David Gregory, David K. Hansen, Robert Harvey, Derek Hayes, Charles Hou, Sharon Keen, Michael Kennedy, Irene Martin, and Jack Nisbet and his circle of friends.

More than anyone else, I have to thank my editors, Audrey McClellan of West Coast Editorial Associates (www.westcoasteditors.com) and Liesbeth Leatherbarrow, whose work smoothed out the rough edges of my writing but kept my voice intact.

NANCY MARGUERITE ANDERSON studied art, sailed the west coast, worked for the government, managed and owned a delicatessen and sold products for a natural-health company before discovering her love for writing and researching. As a direct descendent of generations of fur traders who worked for the North West Company and the later Hudson's Bay Company, she is especially interested in discovering the stories of her heritage. Anderson has dedicated many years to writing this book about her great-grandfather. She is descended from A.C. Anderson through his youngest son, Arthur Beattie Anderson, born in 1864. Anderson lives in Victoria, BC. To learn more, go to furtradefamilyhistory.blogspot.com